KS3 HISTORY
FOURTH EDITION

Invasion, Plague and Murder

Britain 1066–1558

Aaron Wilkes

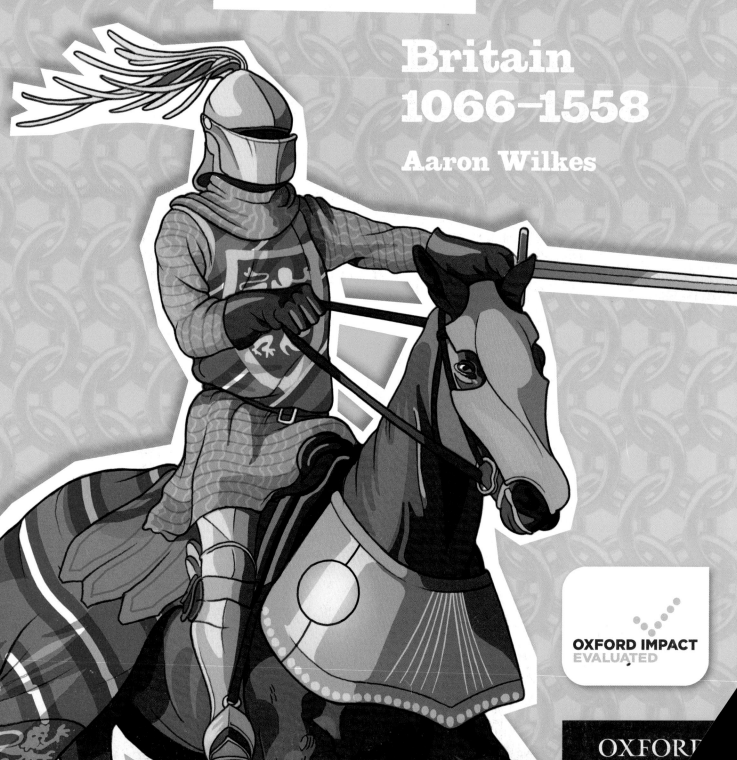

OXFORD IMPACT
EVALUATED

OXFORD

Contents

Contents

Introducing KS3 History Fourth Edition

So what is history?

History is about what happened in the past. It's about people in the past, what they did and why they did it, and what they felt. To enjoy history you need to be able to imagine what life was like long ago, or what it may have been like to be involved in past events.

How does this book fit in?

This book will get you thinking. You will be asked to look at different pieces of evidence and to try to work things out for yourself. Sometimes, two pieces of evidence about the same event won't agree with each other. You might be asked to think of reasons why that is. Your answers might not be the same as your friend's or even your teacher's. This is OK. The important thing is to give *reasons* for your thoughts and ideas.

How to use this book

Features of the Student Book are explained here and on the opposite page.

Kerboodle support

Kerboodle provides digital Lessons, Resources and Assessment for the classroom and at home. This book contains icons that highlight some of the digital resources available:

 Animation

 Film clip

 Assessment presentation

 Knowledge organiser

Key to features

Objectives All lessons in this book start by setting you objectives. These are your key aims that set out your learning targets for the work ahead.

History Skills These activities test a range of history skills, so each box has its own title. The tasks will challenge you to think a little deeper about what you have been studying. These are also important skills to develop if you are going to study GCSE History.

Over to You This is your opportunity to demonstrate your knowledge, and your understanding, of history skills. In each box the tasks become progressively more challenging.

Meanwhile... 1066 This gives you an idea of what else is going on in the world (perhaps in another country on a different continent) at the same sort of time as the period you are studying in the lesson.

Earlier on... and Later on... 1300 You will be challenged to think how the topic you are studying relates to events, people, ideas or developments that may have happened many years before... or might connect to things in the future.

Key Words These are important words and terms that are vital to help you understand the topics. You can spot them easily because they are in bold red type. Look up their meanings in the glossary at the back of the book.

Fact ✓ These are funny, fascinating and amazing little bits of history that you don't usually get to hear about! They're important because they give you insights into topics that you'll easily remember.

 History Mystery These sections give you an opportunity to pull all your skills together and investigate a controversial, challenging or intriguing aspect of history, such as how King Harold *really* died at the Battle of Hastings or what happened to the Princes in the Tower.

 Depth Study In each book, there is a depth study that focuses on an important event, person or development. This gives you the chance to extend and deepen your understanding of key moments in history.

Literacy and Numeracy Throughout the book you will see icons like these when a task is particularly focused on your literacy or numeracy skills.

Have you been learning?

There are different types of assessments at the end of every chapter.
These are opportunities for you to showcase what you have learned and to
put your ability to recall key information and history skills to the test.

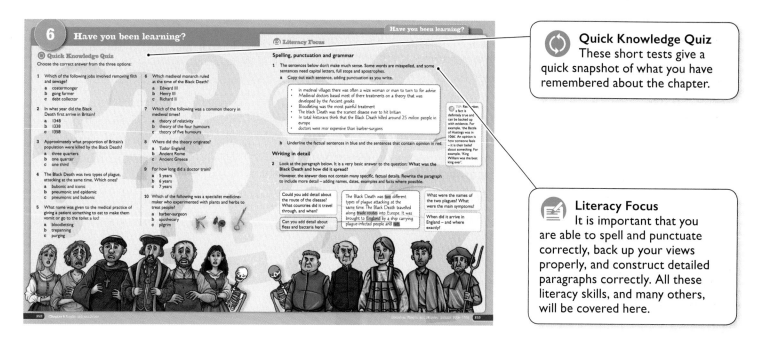

Quick Knowledge Quiz
These short tests give a quick snapshot of what you have remembered about the chapter.

Literacy Focus
It is important that you are able to spell and punctuate correctly, back up your views properly, and construct detailed paragraphs correctly. All these literacy skills, and many others, will be covered here.

History skills assessments

The assessments at the end of each chapter are designed to help you
improve the way you think about history, write about history and apply
your historical knowledge when you are being assessed. These step-by-
step guides will help you write clear, focused answers to some challenging
history questions. These concepts and skills are essential if you wish to go
on to study History at a higher level, so by tackling these you are giving
yourself a good foundation in history.

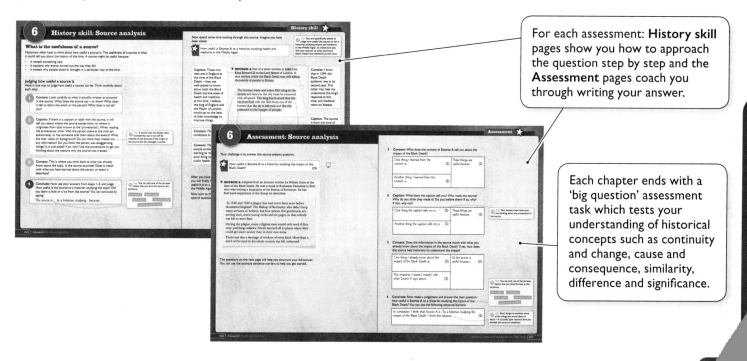

For each assessment: **History skill** pages show you how to approach the question step by step and the **Assessment** pages coach you through writing your answer.

Each chapter ends with a 'big question' assessment task which tests your understanding of historical concepts such as continuity and change, cause and consequence, similarity, difference and significance.

Invasion, Plague and Murder: Britain 1066–1558

What is chronology?

One of the most basic ideas that any good History student must understand is something called **chronology**. Simply speaking, chronology is the study of when things happened. And, as you know, it's vitally important when studying history to know *when* things happened – knowing this means you can begin trying to work out *how* and *why* things happened!

When historians (people who study history) put events in the correct time order, starting with the thing that happened earliest, the events are said to be in **chronological order**. One of the best ways to show chronological order is on a timeline. For example, the timeline below could be used to put your school day in chronological order:

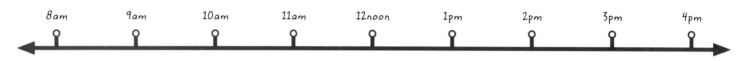

8am   9am   10am   11am   12noon   1pm   2pm   3pm   4pm

And by changing the scale of the line, events covering a whole year can be added to the timeline:

January   February   March   April   May   June   July   August   September   October   November   December

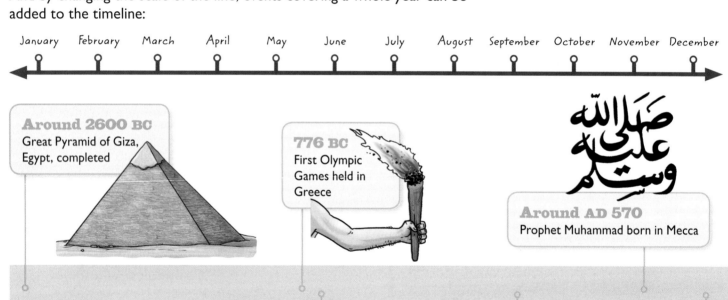

Around 2600 BC
Great Pyramid of Giza, Egypt, completed

776 BC
First Olympic Games held in Greece

صَلَّى الله عَلَيْهِ وَسَلَّم

Around AD 570
Prophet Muhammad born in Mecca

221 BC
First complete Great Wall of China linked together

Around 4 BC
Birth of Jesus

AD 793
Large-scale Viking raids on Britain begin

Over to You

1 a What does 'chronological order' mean?
  b Why is it important for historians to get events in the right order?

2 Make a timeline to show either:
  a your school day
  b your life.

  Try to divide your timeline into sections or chunks. Hint: Why not label your sections? Words like 'period', 'age', 'era' and 'times' are all common terms most often used by historians. For example, if you are making a timeline of your life, your time before primary school could be the 'Baby Period' and the 'Toddler Era'.

3 Think of different periods in history you have studied, perhaps at primary school. Make a list. Where would you put each period in the large timeline on this page?

Key Words chronology

Fact ✓

Years with the initials BC or BCE after them refer to the time before the birth of Jesus Christ. Years with the initials AD before them – or CE after them – refer to the period after his birth.

AD 1939
Second World War begins

AD 1837
Queen Victoria becomes queen

Any length of time can be shown on a timeline. For example, the large timeline on these pages goes back to over 4500 years ago, when the Ancient Egyptians were building pyramids. The period in history covered by this book, known as the 'Middle Ages' and the 'Early Tudor period', is highlighted in the timeline.

Around AD 1300
Gunpowder first used in cannons in Europe

AD 1415
English win the Battle of Agincourt during the Hundred Years War

AD 1666
Great Fire of London

AD 1066
Battle of Hastings

AD 1348
The Black Death, a killer plague, reaches Britain

AD 1485
First Tudor King of England, Henry VII

AD 1509
Henry VIII becomes the second Tudor king

AD 1969
Neil Armstrong becomes the first person to walk on the moon

Invasion, Plague and Murder: Britain 1066–1558

Timeline from 1066 to 1558

What's it called?

This book covers the years 1066 to 1558. It is a remarkable period, famous for invasion, war, mystery, murder, revolt, plague… and more war!

Historians love to give names to different periods of time – and this book features two periods in British history:

The Middle Ages: This is what historians in Britain call the time from about 1066 (around 950 years ago) to around 1485. Another name for this part of history is the 'medieval period'. In fact, the word 'medieval' comes from the Latin language and means 'middle'. This period of history is called the Middle Ages in Europe because it comes between the end of the Roman Empire (seen as a golden age of learning and civilisation) and more modern times, when there was another great age of learning and discovery.

The early Tudor period: This comes directly after the Middle Ages. The Tudors were a royal family of important monarchs, including Henry VIII and 'Bloody' Queen Mary! This book will examine who the Tudors were, how they came to be Britain's royal family, and what impact some of the Tudor monarchs made.

During these periods in British history, new discoveries and inventions changed the way people thought and behaved. New laws meant that more people had a say in how decisions were made, rather than the monarch ruling everything. The landscape of Britain changed too. Villages grew into towns, and towns grew into large and bustling cities. The landscape became dotted with magnificent cathedrals, huge stone castles, monasteries and churches, many of which can still be seen today. This was also a time of great, and lasting, changes to both religion and knowledge of the world. Many people's view of the world changed dramatically as explorers and traders discovered new routes to previously unknown lands.

Look at the timeline on these pages carefully – it shows some of the big events, ideas and discoveries of this time.

1381
The Peasants' Revolt

1348
The Black Death arrives in Britain

1337
The Hundred Years War begins

1095
Crusades begin

1066
Battle of Hastings: William, Duke of Normandy becomes King of England

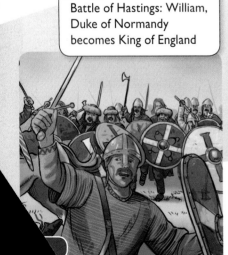

1070s
Work begins on the Tower of London

KEY

- ⊕ Warfare
- ⊕ Political
- ◐ Trade/exploration
- ⊖ Religious
- ⊗ Disease

1558
Elizabeth I begins her 44-year reign

1455
The Wars of the Roses begin

1492
Christopher Columbus (an Italian) lands in the Americas

1509
Henry VII dies and his son becomes Henry VIII

1485
Henry Tudor becomes King of England after beating Richard III at the Battle of Bosworth Field

1453
The Hundred Years War ends, after 116 years

1314
Scots defeat the English invaders

1283
Final conquest of Wales by the English

1265
The first parliament meets

1215
Magna Carta is signed

Magna Carta

1170
Thomas Becket, Archbishop of Canterbury, is murdered

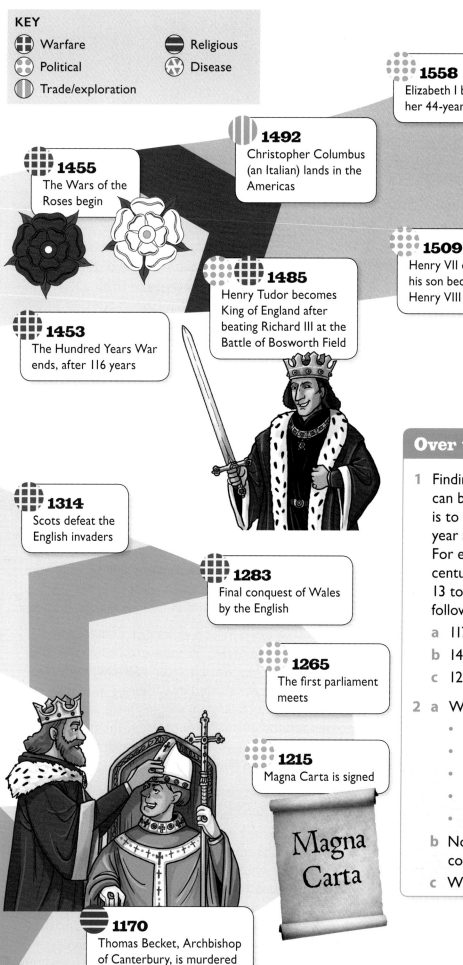

Over to You

1. Finding out which year is in which century can be difficult. The easiest way to find out is to cover up the last two numbers in a year and add one to the first two numbers. For example, 1348 is in the fourteenth century (cover up the '48' and add one to 13 to make 14). Which century are the following years in?

   a 1170
   b 1492
   c 1265
   d 1095
   e 1509

2. a Which century were the following events in?
   - The Peasants' Revolt
   - The Battle of Hastings
   - Henry Tudor becomes King of England
   - The meeting of the first parliament
   - Henry VIII becomes King of England

   b Now put the five events above in the correct chronological order.

   c Which century were you born in?

Invasion, Plague and Murder: Britain 1066–1558

.1A The story of Britain up to 1066

The British Isles (the correct term for the islands that make up most of what people call 'Britain') lie off the north-west corner of mainland Europe (see **A**). Incredibly, there are over 5000 islands that make up the British Isles, but fewer than 200 of these are **inhabited**. The two largest islands – Great Britain and Ireland – have the most people living there, but other smaller islands – such as the Isle of Wight, Anglesey, Jersey, Shetland, Orkney and the Isle of Man – have lots of people living there too.

Objectives

- Describe Britain's early history before 1066.
- Organise early British history into different periods of time.
- Evaluate the contribution of different groups of invaders and settlers to Britain.

▼ **MAP A** Some islands in the British Isles have very few people living on them – in 2011, the island of Rùm (to the west of mainland Scotland) had a population of 22!

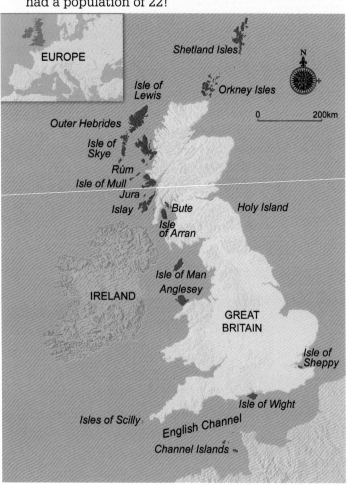

Early settlers

We don't know much about the first people who lived in Britain. People didn't write things down at that time, so most of our information comes from **evidence** such as fragments of bone, bits of stone, fossils, pottery and other **artefacts**. From these simple clues, experts have built up a basic picture of life in Britain thousands of years ago.

The latest thinking is that for hundreds of thousands of years, there were probably no humans in Britain at all, but there were animals. The sea level was a lot lower at that time, so these animals were able to walk across the floor of what is now the English Channel – a 'land bridge' that linked the British Isles to mainland Europe.

Then, about half a million years ago, people from Europe began to arrive. These were Britain's earliest **immigrants**. They were **hunter-gatherers** who (as their name suggests) lived by gathering food (like nuts and fruit) and by killing animals for meat and furs. They moved around in small groups, took shelter in caves or built basic huts. They learned skills such as lighting fires and making sharp flint tools (see **B**).

Fact ✓

In this book, the word 'Britain' will generally be used instead of the term 'British Isles' when describing the nation as a whole. However, the main island is now divided into different countries (England, Scotland and Wales), and the second largest island is made up of Northern Ireland (a part of the **UK**) and the Republic of Ireland (an independent country).

▼ **SOURCE B** A collection of stone and flint tools, dating from around 2700–1800 BC. They were found in Essex, in the east of England, and would have been used for hunting, building and fighting.

The British Isles are born

For many thousands of years, Ice Age hunter-gatherers could easily cross to Britain from Europe and back again across the land bridge where the English Channel now is. Then, around 8500 BC, the climate started to warm up and the ice began to melt. Over the next few thousand years, the land bridge gradually disappeared under water as the sea level rose, and Britain became an island.

More settlers

Life in Britain remained largely unchanged for thousands more years. More hunter-gatherers arrived from Europe by boat, and others left. Some fought with other groups while others stayed isolated. Then, around 7000 years ago, an important change happened. People learned how to farm and produce their own food rather than having to hunt it and gather it. New settlers coming to Britain from Europe brought wheat and barley seeds to grow crops. They also brought animals for meat, including pigs, sheep and goats, and they owned tame dogs too. They built more permanent homes and cleared large areas of woodland for farming (see **C**).

▼ **INTERPRETATION C** This is an artist's idea of what historians think an early settlement from between 5000 BC and 4500 BC would look like. Most of the tools people used were made from wood and stone rather than iron or other metals – which is why this period is usually known as the Stone Age.

The Bronze Age and Iron Age

In about 2500 BC, a new wave of settlers began arriving in Britain from central Europe. They were known as the Beaker people because of the decorated pottery they used. They knew how to make things out of metals like copper and gold. When tin was added to copper it made bronze, so the time of the Beaker people is often known as the Bronze Age. Soon, tools and weapons made from metal replaced the ones made from stone and wood. Around 800 BC, people learned how to make weapons and tools from iron. As a result, this period in British history is sometimes called the Iron Age.

Over to You

1   a   Why don't we know much about the people who first lived in Britain?

   b   How have historians tried to build up a picture of life back then?

2   a   Put the following periods in history in the correct chronological order:

     Bronze Age   Iron Age

         Stone Age

   b   How did each of these periods get its name?

3   Describe what happened to Britain's 'land bridge'.

4   Look at **Interpretation C**. Work with a partner and discuss how the artist managed to create this picture. What evidence do you think they would have needed to make the image as accurate as possible?

After the Bronze Age

Over the next few thousand years, different tribes arrived in Britain. Some came peacefully, while others were hostile. Some came for only a short time, but others settled for good. Study each group carefully, thinking about how each one helped to shape the nation.

Fact ✓

The Romans used the name 'Britannia' for Britain. This was based on 'Pretannia', which is what the Ancient Greeks called the British Isles because they thought a Celtic tribe called the 'Pretani' lived there. In fact, the Pretani tribe lived mainly in Ireland – but the name 'Pretannia' stuck, and later became Britannia, and then Britain.

The Celts

Around 500 BC, Celtic tribes from central Europe arrived. The tribes fought brutally with each other, and with the people already settled in Britain.

The Celts were proud of their appearance and kept themselves clean using special soaps and perfumes.

Priests (druids) led religious rituals. Some traditions survive today – Halloween and May Day, for example.

Tribal business was done at yearly assemblies – land disputes were settled, criminals were tried, and people were voted into important positions.

They farmed the land and built forts.

The Romans

The Romans, from Italy, invaded Britain in AD 43 and soon conquered most of the British tribes. They stayed for around 400 years.

Many of our roads are based on old Roman roads.

Many Roman towns are still important today – for example, Chester, York, Bath, Lincoln, Colchester and St Albans.

Romans were the first in Britain to use calendars, coins and bricks, and they introduced peas, wine, grapes, carrots and cats.

Many English words (such as 'peace' and 'street') and laws can be traced back to the Romans.

The Romans who stayed in Britain were made up of diverse, multi-ethnic people including Gauls (from France), Germans, Hungarians and North Africans.

The Anglo-Saxons

In about AD 410, the Romans returned to Italy to defend their homeland from invasion. The British people (now known as Britons) were left to fend for themselves, and it didn't take long for new tribes to invade. These tribes, from modern-day Denmark and northern Germany, were called Angles, Saxons and Jutes. Collectively, the invaders became known as **Anglo-Saxons**.

Anglo-Saxon is one of the key 'base' languages of English – 'bed', 'cat', 'dog', 'tree', 'lick', 'game', 'hunt' and 'fox' are all words of Anglo-Saxon origin.

The Anglo-Saxons drove many of the British tribes into Wales, Cornwall, Cumbria and Scotland.

Before converting to Christianity, they worshipped many gods.

They gave England its name – 'Angle-land', meaning 'land of the Angles'; this later became 'England'.

Lots of counties are named after the Anglo-Saxons. East Anglia is an obvious one. Another is 'Essex', the land of the East Saxons.

Many towns were created and named by Anglo-Saxons – if the name ends in '-ton', '-wich', '-worth', '-burn', '-hurst' or '-ham', Anglo-Saxons probably lived there.

They were excellent farmers.

The Vikings

In the late eighth **century** the Anglo-Saxons faced invasion from across the North Sea by **Vikings**. At first, the Vikings raided the coast: they stole valuable treasures, like gold, jewels and books. They also took food, cattle, clothes and tools. In 865, the Vikings began to settle in Britain, rather than just raid it and return to their homelands. They knew that Britain had treasures that could make them rich, and fertile land for farming.

1 There were many battles between the Anglo-Saxons and the Vikings. Gradually, the Vikings took control of most of the large Anglo-Saxon kingdoms.

2 By AD 874, only the Anglo-Saxon kingdom of Wessex in south-west England was not controlled by the Vikings. This area was ruled by King Alfred the Great. He beat the Vikings in battle, but couldn't drive them out of the country completely.

3 Eventually, after many more years of fighting, Alfred and the Vikings made a peace agreement. It was decided that the country should be split into two – Anglo-Saxon lands in the south and west and the Viking lands in the north and east (see **D**).

4 Gradually, despite many more years of fighting and arguments between the two sides, the Anglo-Saxons and Vikings became neighbours and there were many years of peace.

5 By the mid-1000s, the country was united under one king, Edward. His father had been an Anglo-Saxon king and his mother had once been married to a Viking king.

▼ **MAP D** A map showing where the Vikings settled around AD 900. The area that the Vikings controlled was called the Danelaw.

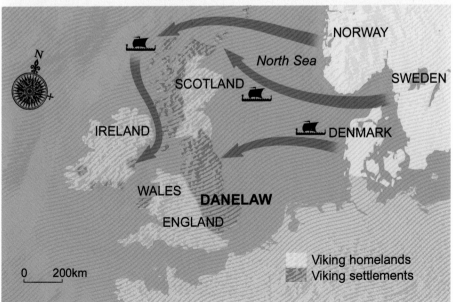

Meanwhile...

At this time, a variety of tribes (called Picts, Scotti, Britons and Angles) lived in what we now call 'Scotland'. The Picts were the largest tribe – but it was the Scotti that the country was named after!

Over to You

1 a Explain how Britain got its name.

   b Explain how England and Scotland got their names.

2 Create a mind-map titled 'What did the foreign invaders and settlers bring to Britain?' Each branch should outline the contribution and impact of the different groups of invaders and settlers – Celts, Romans, Anglo-Saxons and Vikings.

Cause and Consequence

It is important for historians to understand how Britain has been shaped and influenced by the wider world, right from the earliest times. This is useful because if you go on to study history in future, you may be asked to consider the consequences of Britain's contact with the wider world – or how other nations have made an impact on countries that they have come into contact with.

1 Explain how invaders and settlers from other countries made an impact on Britain up to 1066.

Before 1066: Anglo-Saxon England

1066 is one of the most famous dates in English history. It is a year when two vast armies, one from Norway and another from France, invaded the country and fought great, bloody battles with the English king. But before we go on to study what exactly happened in that very famous year, it is important that we explore what England was like at this time. How was it ruled? How did the people live? Was England a rich prize for an invader?

Objectives ✓

- Identify how England was governed in the years up to 1066.
- Examine the impact and achievements of the Anglo-Saxons in the years up to 1066.

Who ruled?

England contained quite a mixture of different groups whose ancestors came from all sorts of different places. Historians call it Anglo-Saxon England because many of the people who lived there were descendants of tribes of Angles and Saxons who had settled there from the fifth century onwards.

In 1042, Anglo-Saxon England was peacefully united under one king – Edward the Confessor (see **A**). He was helped in his role by a group of advisers, called the **Witan**. Most of these advisers were from rich, important families who looked after an area of England on behalf of the king. The heads of these families were known as **earls** – and the area of land they looked after was known as an **earldom** (see **B**). The king might also invite **thegns** (local landowners; pronounced 'thane'), bishops and other religious leaders to the Witan. But King Edward also took advice from some friends he had in an area of northern France called Normandy. Edward's mother was from Normandy and Edward had spent lots of time there after Vikings had invaded England when he was young.

Fact ✓

Some women had different roles from men in Anglo-Saxon society. A woman married to a king, earl or thegn stayed at home, weaving thread, sewing and looking after the children. However, poorer women not only cooked, cared for children and made clothes, they also worked just as hard on the farms with the men.

▶ **INTERPRETATION A** Edward the Confessor, King of England from 1042 to 1066. This image is from the thirteenth century, after the **Pope** had made Edward a saint in 1161 as a result of his holy work.

How many people lived in Anglo-Saxon England?

The population of the whole of England was about 1.5 million people. Nearly everybody worked on the land and lived in small villages where they spent most of their lives. There were few towns – only about 15 – with more than 1000 people living there. And only eight towns had a population of more than 3000 (see **B**).

The ordinary villagers were known as **ceorls** (pronounced 'churl') and they owned enough land to grow their own food and keep some animals. Some ceorls were skilled craftsmen, such as cloth-weavers, pottery-makers or metal-workers. There were also slaves, known as **thralls**. Thralls were either prisoners captured during wars, lawbreakers or people who were unable to pay off debts.

▼ **MAP B** A map showing the eight largest towns in England in 1066. The key shows the names of King Edward's earls and the areas they helped him run.

Scotland was a completely separate country from England, ruled by its own king.

■	Morcer
□	Edwin
■	Waltheof
□	Gryth
■	Harold
□	Leofwine

SCOTLAND

York•

WALES Stamford• •Lincoln

Cardiff• ENGLAND •Norwich •Thetford

Winchester• •London

N

0   200km

Wales, at this time, was divided into a number of kingdoms, each ruled by a powerful local leader or king. Like England, Wales had been invaded by Romans and Vikings.

Key Words

ceorl earl earldom
Pope thegn thrall Witan

▼ **INTERPRETATION C** An image from a thirteenth-century medieval manuscript showing Anglo-Saxons preparing a field for crops.

Over to You

1 a What was the Witan?

   b Explain why you think the king invited the most powerful men in the country to help him rule.

2 Explain the role played by each of the following:
   • king
   • earl
   • thegn
   • ceorl
   • thrall

3 Look at the two men in **Interpretation C**. Which social group (earls, thegns, ceorls or thralls) do you think each of these people come from? Explain your answer.

What were the achievements of the Anglo-Saxons?

Anglo-Saxon society and culture had become very advanced by the eleventh century. Look carefully at the spider diagram below and **Map H**.

Coins

When the Anglo-Saxons first came to Britain, they didn't use coins. Most people exchanged their goods for other goods – this was called bartering. During the 700s, coins were being used widely in Europe. Soon, Anglo-Saxons began to produce their own coins to make trading easier. Coins also allowed Anglo-Saxon **monarchs** to show their importance and wealth.

▶ **SOURCE D** An Anglo-Saxon coin from the time of Coenwulf, an Anglo-Saxon king (ruled 796–821). When this was sold in 2006 it was the most expensive coin ever purchased.

Poetry and storytelling

The Anglo-Saxons loved to create poems, songs and stories. They would gather together to sing songs and hear poems such as *Beowulf*, the story of a heroic warrior who fights to save his people.

Anglo-Saxon achievements

Crafts

The Anglo-Saxons were highly skilled craft workers. **Archaeologists** have found dice and board games made from bone, pottery, glass and stone. They have also found a musical instrument called a lyre (like a small harp). Metalworkers made iron tools, pots and swords. Woodworkers made wooden bowls, furniture, farming equipment and wheels. Jewellers made beautiful belt buckles, brooches, necklaces, purses and ornaments. These were made from gold, silver, glass and precious stones that were traded when Anglo-Saxon traders visited other countries.

▶ **SOURCE E**
This Anglo-Saxon artefact is called the Alfred Jewel and is made of gold and crystal. Around the edge it reads 'Alfred had me made'. A long stick fitted into the bottom. The artefact then became a pointer for following words in a book.

Writing

Some educated Anglo-Saxons communicated with people in other European countries. For example, letters survive that were sent between important Anglo-Saxon King Offa and people who ruled over parts of France, Italy and Germany. Books were written about the history of Britain that included beautifully and expertly decorated pages.

▶ **SOURCE F** A page from an Anglo-Saxon book, written by the Bishop of Lindisfarne around 710. In monasteries (large buildings where **monks** lived) monks kept huge official diaries called **chronicles**. They wrote about religion, politics, history, towns, kings, gossip and even the weather.

Buildings

At first the Anglo-Saxons avoided the old, abandoned Roman stone-built towns and built their own villages instead, using wood. Over time, the Anglo-Saxons began to re-use the stone from Roman towns, villas and roads. **G** shows an Anglo-Saxon church from the 700s. Several villages became important trading centres and began to grow. On the south and east coasts of England, several ports were founded. These quickly grew into busy centres of trade as local people and merchants bought and sold goods from all over Europe.

▼ **SOURCE G** The Anglo-Saxon church of St Laurence in Bradford on Avon, Wiltshire. The stone walls made the building strong and it may have been used as a fortress in times of trouble. Anglo-Saxon England was a Christian country.

▼ **MAP H** This map shows the goods produced in medieval Britain and where they came from.

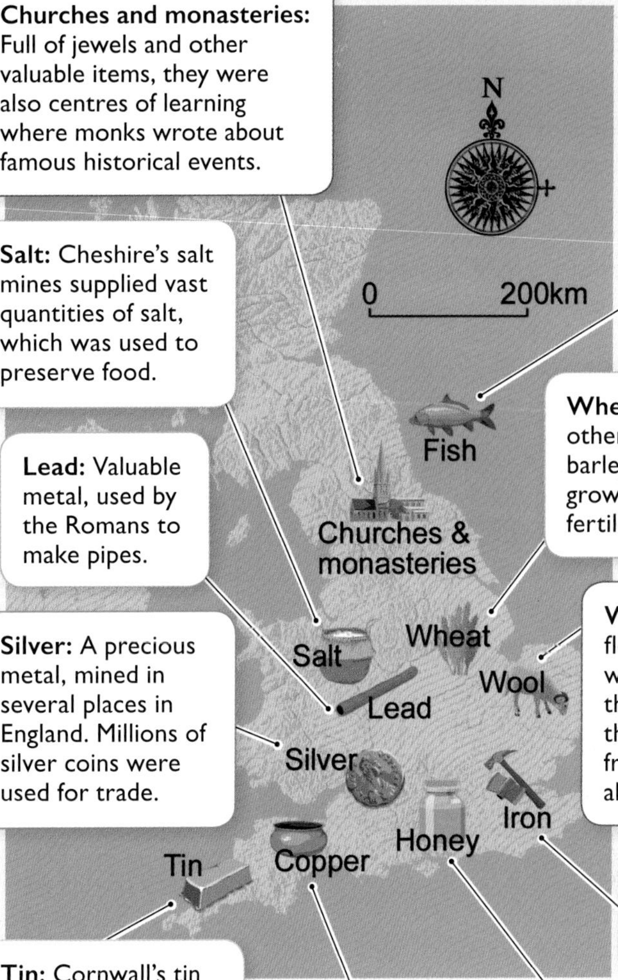

Churches and monasteries: Full of jewels and other valuable items, they were also centres of learning where monks wrote about famous historical events.

Salt: Cheshire's salt mines supplied vast quantities of salt, which was used to preserve food.

Lead: Valuable metal, used by the Romans to make pipes.

Silver: A precious metal, mined in several places in England. Millions of silver coins were used for trade.

Fish: Lots of fish stocked the seas around England.

Wheat: Wheat and other crops such as barley and oats were grown on England's fertile land.

Wool: Large flocks of sheep were kept and their wool and the cloth made from it were sold all over Europe.

Iron: Used to make tools and weapons.

Tin: Cornwall's tin mines are said to be one of the main reasons why the Romans invaded Britain. By 1066, England supplied most of Europe's tin.

Copper: Combined with tin to make bronze and then used to make tools and jewellery.

Honey: Produced all over the country, it was used as a medicine, an ingredient in beer and as a sweetener.

Map labels: N · 0 — 200km · Fish · Churches & monasteries · Wheat · Salt · Wool · Lead · Silver · Iron · Tin · Copper · Honey

Over to You

1 Use pages 14–17 to write your own fact file about England in the years before 1066. You should use ten sentences to write ten different facts.

2 a Look at **Sources D** to **G**. What do these sources tell us about Anglo-Saxon society? Make a list of everything you can think of.

  b Share your list with a partner – then make a class list of everything the sources tell you.

Cause and Consequence

1 With a partner or in a small group, discuss why people might want to invade England.

2 Explain why Anglo-Saxon England might be attractive to invaders. You may use the following in your answer:
  • England's natural resources
  • England's highly-skilled craftsmen

Who will be the next King of England?

1066 is one of the most famous years in British history – it was the last time England was invaded and taken over by a foreign power. The English king and many of his key followers were killed and the country was divided up between the new invaders. England's language, rulers and way of life changed forever!

Objectives

- Investigate the three different men who wanted to be King of England in 1066.
- Assess the claims of the three contenders and judge who you think had the best claim.

The old king dies...

In January 1066, Edward the Confessor, King of England, died. He was 62 years old and left no children behind. At this time, there were no strict rules as to who should become the new ruler after a monarch's death. Instead, there were a few traditions that most people accepted as the best way to decide:

- The monarch's son always had the strongest claim (reason to be king) – but Edward had no children.
- Another male relative might have a good claim.
- The dying king could say who he wanted.
- The king's close advisors (the Witan) could nominate someone.

Fact ✓

Most people in medieval times believed that a monarch should be male.

When King Edward died, he had very few close male relatives. His great-nephew, Edgar, was only a teenager and lacked the experience or military skill to become king. Instead, three other men each believed that they had the best claim to be the next king – and they were ready to use their armies. Read the fact files on each contender.

The Norman

Name: William of Normandy

Position: Duke of Normandy – the most powerful part of France, with a strong army.

Family history: William came from a fighting family. He had been in control of Normandy since he was a young boy and was used to having to fight to keep his lands.

Links to King Edward: Edward had lived in Normandy from 1016 to 1041. When Edward returned to England to be king, William sent soldiers to help him. As a result, William claimed that Edward had promised him the throne in 1051.

Was he tough enough? His nickname was 'William the Bastard' because his father wasn't married to his mother. In 1047, people from the town of Alençon made fun of his mother's family. William captured the town and ordered that 30 of the townsmen be skinned alive.

Support for his claim: According to William of Poitiers, a Norman writer, 'Edward, king of the English, loved William like a brother or son… so he decided that William should be the next king.' Harold Godwinson had visited William in 1064, and may have promised to support William's claim to the English crown.

The Englishman

Name: Harold Godwinson

Position: Earl of Wessex, one of the most powerful men in England.

Family history: His father, Godwin, argued a lot with King Edward. At one time Harold and his father were banished from England, but they returned a year later.

Links to King Edward: Harold's sister was married to King Edward.

Was he tough enough? Harold was a brave, respected and tough soldier. In 1063, King Edward sent Harold to crush a Welsh uprising. The Welsh leader was beheaded on Harold's orders.

Support for his claim: He was the only Englishman claiming the throne. The Witan wanted Harold as king. English monks wrote: 'Harold and his brothers were the king's favourites… on his deathbed that wise king promised the kingdom to Harold.'

The Viking

Name: Harald Hardrada

Position: King of Norway

Family history: He had fought alongside several Norwegian and foreign kings and had taken part in raids on the English coast. When he became King of Norway, he began to plan a full-scale invasion of England.

Links to King Edward: None – but a Viking called Canute had ruled Norway and England from 1016 to 1035.

Was he tough enough? He was the most feared warrior in Europe – tough, bloodthirsty and he enjoyed watching his enemies suffer. 'Hardrada' means 'hard ruler' and his nickname was 'the Ruthless'.

Support for his claim: Harald's claim was supported by Tostig, Harold Godwinson's brother. The two brothers had fallen out and Tostig wanted revenge.

The Englishman's advantage

When King Edward died on 5 January 1066, Harold had one big advantage over his two rivals. William and Hardrada were miles away across the sea while Harold was already in England. He wasted no time and was crowned king the very next day. But he knew the other two would soon hear the news and come looking for him… and they'd both want him dead.

▼ **MAP A** The locations of the contenders for the throne.

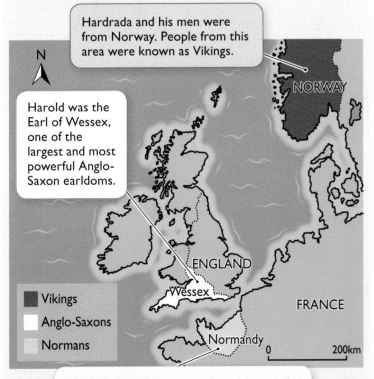

Hardrada and his men were from Norway. People from this area were known as Vikings.

Harold was the Earl of Wessex, one of the largest and most powerful Anglo-Saxon earldoms.

Vikings
Anglo-Saxons
Normans

William and his men came from Normandy. They were known as Normans.

Over to You

Now you have read about the three contenders for the throne, you must decide who you think had the best claim.

1   Copy and complete the following table. Try to include as many reasons as possible.

Contender	Reasons why he should be king	Reasons why he shouldn't be king
Harold Godwinson		
Harald Hardrada		
William of Normandy		

2   a   List the three contenders in order of who you think had the strongest claim. Label your first choice 'strongest' and your last choice 'weakest'.

   b   Explain why you placed the three contenders in the order you have chosen.

3   Divide into groups. Each group should choose a contender (perhaps pull a name out of a hat) for the English crown. Design a poster that will convince people that your contender should be king… and that the other two shouldn't!

Cause and Consequence

Historians often have to weigh up different evidence and opinions about the past. In your further studies you could be asked to respond to statements such as:

1   'Harald Hardrada had the strongest claim to the English throne.' How far do you agree with this statement?

There are many ways to answer this kind of question, but you will need to be able to identify the reasons why the three men believed they could be king, and decide who had the strongest claim. This is exactly what you've done in the Over to You questions.

Round 1: the Battle of Stamford Bridge

After becoming king, Harold of England sat nervously on his throne, waiting for his rivals to attack. For months Harold waited… and waited… but nothing happened. Then, finally, at the end of summer 1066, Harold's wait finally came to an end. In mid-September, Hardrada, King of Norway, landed near York in the north of England – and he wasn't leaving until the crown was his!

Objectives

- Identify the contenders for the English throne who fought at the Battle of Stamford Bridge.
- Evaluate the physical and mental condition of the winning side at the end of the battle.

▼ **MAP A** This map shows what happened in the week after Hardrada's invasion. He was joined by King Harold's younger brother, Tostig, and about 10,000 bloodthirsty Vikings!

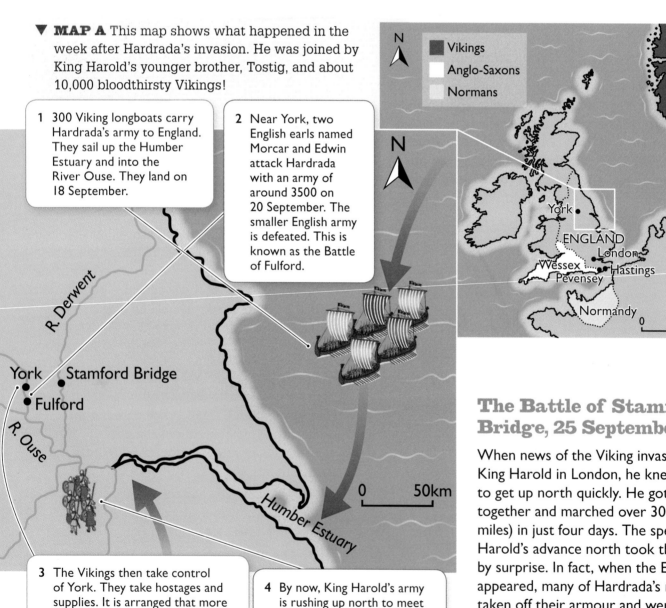

1 300 Viking longboats carry Hardrada's army to England. They sail up the Humber Estuary and into the River Ouse. They land on 18 September.

2 Near York, two English earls named Morcar and Edwin attack Hardrada with an army of around 3500 on 20 September. The smaller English army is defeated. This is known as the Battle of Fulford.

3 The Vikings then take control of York. They take hostages and supplies. It is arranged that more hostages and supplies will be delivered to them a few days later at a place called Stamford Bridge.

4 By now, King Harold's army is rushing up north to meet Hardrada's army. More soldiers are collected on the way to help fight the Vikings.

Vikings
Anglo-Saxons
Normans

NORWAY

York
ENGLAND
London
Wessex   Hastings
Pevensey
FRANCE
Normandy
0   200km

R. Derwent
York   Stamford Bridge
Fulford
R. Ouse
Humber Estuary
0   50km

The Battle of Stamford Bridge, 25 September 1066

When news of the Viking invasion reached King Harold in London, he knew he had to get up north quickly. He got his army together and marched over 300km (190 miles) in just four days. The speed of King Harold's advance north took the Vikings by surprise. In fact, when the English appeared, many of Hardrada's men had taken off their armour and were relaxing in the sun. Read through the story on the following page to find out what might have happened at Stamford Bridge.

1 It is early morning…

Wake up, wake up! King Harold is here!

STAMFORD BRIDGE

2 The battle starts badly for Hardrada's men. Some have left their armour several miles away.

Where did you leave your chain mail?

Near the boats… sorry!

3 However, Hardrada's men soon gain control. One brave Viking blocks the bridge so the English can't reach the Vikings.

I've killed 40 Englishmen with my mighty axe.

4 With no way over the bridge, Hardrada's army fight Harold's men to a standstill. But some of Harold's men come up with a plan.

5 After an hour, King Harold's men try to stop the warrior on the bridge.

Float under the bridge and stab him from below.

I'll try!

6 The Viking is killed and the English can get across the bridge.

Quick! Let's attack the Vikings while we have the chance!

Arghhh!

Hurry — some have no armour.

7 By midday King Harold's army is in control. Hardrada is killed, but the Vikings fight on.

Our great King of Norway is dead!

8 Later on, Tostig is found and cut into pieces.

Kill him!

Cut him up!

9 King Harold is the winner.

They only need 24 ships to take their battered army home to Norway.

10 Harold buries his dead brother in York. But bad news arrives…

You'll have to fight again soon, my Lord. William of Normandy has landed near Hastings.

Earl Tostig

Over to You

1 Put the following events in chronological order:
- The Vikings leave England in 24 ships and sail back to Norway.
- King Harold and Hardrada begin fighting at Stamford Bridge.
- Edwin and Morcar are defeated at the Battle of Fulford.
- King Harold hears that William of Normandy has landed near Hastings.
- The Vikings sail up the Humber Estuary and into the River Ouse.
- The Vikings leave Norway in over 300 ships.
- Hardrada and Tostig are killed. King Harold wins.

Knowledge and Understanding

An 'account' is a story about the past, written in chronological order and full of factual details and dates. It should be written in the third person and in the past tense.

1 Make a list of ten key words, terms or phrases that you think should be included in an account of the Battle of Stamford Bridge. For example: 'Hardrada', 'Vikings', 'Harold, 'armour'…

2 Write an account of the Battle of Stamford Bridge – and make sure you include all the ten words, terms or phrases.

Match of the day: weapons and battle tactics

King Harold of England defeated Hardrada and the Vikings on 25 September 1066. Three days later, William of Normandy landed on the south coast of England at Pevensey, near Hastings. This must have been devastating news for Harold – after fighting (and winning) a fierce battle in the north, he knew that he now had to travel back down south and fight another huge invading army. What weapons and tactics would King Harold use? How would William try to defeat the English? What were the strengths and weaknesses of each army?

Objectives

- Compare the weapons and tactics that were used by William's and Harold's men at the Battle of Hastings.
- Identify strengths and weaknesses of each army.

William lands

William's invasion force was huge. It had taken over 300 ships to transport around 10,000 men and 2000 horses from France. William fully expected to have to fight Harold as soon as he landed, but the English king was still in the north of England. So, William quickly moved his army along the coast to Hastings, burning villages along the way. The soldiers arrived in Hastings and spent several days resting. William brought plenty of supplies for his men and horses so that they could refuel before the battle.

How did the two armies compare?

Harold's army consisted of two groups of fighters – the housecarls and the fyrd (pronounced 'fird').

William's army was very different from Harold's. For a start, it was made up of three units – foot soldiers, archers and knights.

HOUSECARLS

KILLING POWER: 9/10	
DEFENCE: 9/10	
SPEED: 1/10	
RANGE OF ATTACK: 1/10	

The housecarls were the backbone of King Harold's army. There were usually around 2500 of them, but up to half had been killed at Stamford Bridge. They were well paid, fully trained and armed with the finest weapons. Their favourite weapon was a huge battleaxe. The handle of the axe was over a metre long and its heavy blade was made of razor-sharp iron – a very precious material in 1066. A housecarl with a battleaxe could cut a man in half with a single blow. Their helmets, chain mail, large round shields and discipline made them excellent in defence too. The housecarls would stand together when attacked and lock their shields together to form a shield wall.

THE FYRD

KILLING POWER: 3/10	
DEFENCE: 5/10	
SPEED: 3/10	
RANGE OF ATTACK: 3/10	

The housecarls were supported by the fyrd. This mobile army wasn't as experienced or well equipped as the housecarls but it was still a fierce fighting force. The leaders of the fyrd were armed with swords and javelins but most of their men used farming tools such as pitchforks and scythes. They may not have been pretty, but they numbered over 6000 and they were fighting on their home turf.

NORMAN FOOT SOLDIERS

KILLING POWER: 7/10

DEFENCE: 8/10

SPEED: 2/10

RANGE OF ATTACK: 2/10

These formed the main part of William's army and were armed with metre-long swords and kite-shaped shields. They attacked after the enemy's strength had been weakened by the archers' arrows and charges by the knights.

THE ARCHERS

KILLING POWER: 4/10

DEFENCE: 1/10

SPEED: 4/10

RANGE OF ATTACK: 9/10

William's 1500 archers were armed with small wooden bows that could fire six or seven arrows a minute. A skilled archer could kill a man from about 180 metres away. Archers had very little, if any, armour and were not much use when the fighting got up close and personal.

Similarity and Difference ⭐

1 Explain two ways in which Harold's army and William's army were different.

THE KNIGHTS

KILLING POWER: 8/10

DEFENCE: 8/10

SPEED: 10/10

RANGE OF ATTACK: 8/10

William's best warriors were his 2000 knights: highly trained and fiercely loyal professional soldiers. They rode into battle on big, strong warhorses and were protected by a suit of small metal rings sewn together (called a chain mail suit or hauberk) and kite-shaped shields. Knights carried spears (which could be thrown or used to stab the enemy), a sword or a **mace** (a heavy metal club covered in spikes). Knights charged at full speed towards their opponents, hacking and slashing at the much slower soldiers fighting on foot beneath them.

Over to You ..ıl

1 Match the words on the left with the correct description on the right:

- housecarl
- fyrd
- archer
- knight
- chain mail
- mace
- battleaxe

- rides a horse into battle
- a suit of small metal rings sewn together
- carries a battleaxe
- a housecarl's main weapon
- there are 6000 of them in Harold's army
- can fire six to seven arrows per minute
- a spiked club used by knights

2 a Describe two ways that you think William's army was better than Harold's.

  b Describe two ways that you think Harold's army was better than William's.

3 Which army do you think is more likely to win the battle? Give reasons and answer in full sentences.

Invasion, Plague and Murder: Britain 1066–1558   **23**

Round 2: the Battle of Hastings

The showdown between King Harold of England and William of Normandy took place on Saturday 14 October 1066. Harold had already defeated Hardrada and his Viking army, and now, just a few weeks later, he and his army were going to have to fight all over again. Unfortunately for Harold and his men, there had been no time to rest after winning the Battle of Stamford Bridge – they had to march 400km (250 miles) to meet William's men. Where did the two armies finally face each other? What tactics were used by each side? And who won?

Objectives

- Analyse the tactics used by Harold and William in the Battle of Hastings.
- Evaluate how the battle was won.

The build-up to the battle

Harold reached the area around Hastings on 13 October. He then positioned his army on top of a steep hill (Senlac Hill), hoping that William's army would wear themselves out fighting uphill. There were streams and boggy areas on both sides of the hill, which would make it difficult for William's men to attack from the sides – they would have to face Harold's men by directly charging up the hill. At dawn on 14 October, William and his men set off from their camp. They carried a flag given to them by the Pope – they believed this meant God was on their side. After they had travelled around 8km (5 miles), they saw Harold's soldiers waiting on the high ground in front of them, blocking their path.

The battle begins

The battle began around 9am. At first, William ordered his archers to fire at Harold's men, but the English had formed a solid shield wall and the arrows either bounced off the shields or flew harmlessly over their heads. William then sent his foot soldiers up the hill – but they were unable to break the shield wall. Next, William sent in his knights, but their charges again proved useless against the English line.

At one point, a rumour began among the Normans that William had been killed. To stop his men panicking, William quickly galloped among them, lifted his helmet and shouted, 'Look at me! Look at me! I am alive and, with God's help, will be the victor!'

A new tactic

After a short break in the fighting, to allow both sides to recover their dead and wounded, the battle started again in the early afternoon. At around 3pm, William came up with an idea. Read through the cartoons to discover how the battle was finally won.

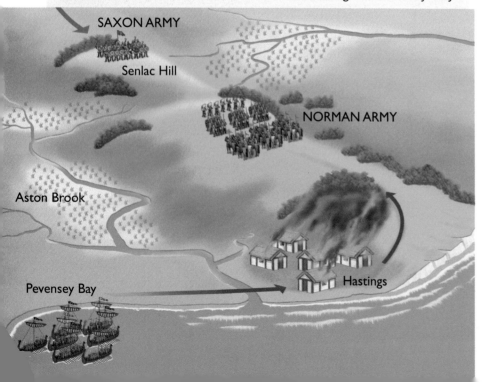

▼ **MAP A** The route William took after landing at Pevensey Bay

SAXON ARMY

Senlac Hill

NORMAN ARMY

Aston Brook

Pevensey Bay

Hastings

Cause and Consequence

1 'William's archers were the main reason why he won the Battle of Hastings.' How far does your study of the Battle of Hastings show this? Explain your answer, referring to the Battle of Hastings and your own knowledge.

1 William had to get the English off the top of the hill. He ordered some of his soldiers to run away down the hill as if they were retreating. The English, thinking they were winning, charged down the hill after the Normans.

2 Without the safety of the shield wall, Harold's men who had run down the hill were quickly cut to pieces by William's knights on horseback.

3 William saw this was his chance to win the battle – and the crown. He hoped that if he kept repeating the trick, the English would keep falling for it. And they did! The English shield wall grew weaker and weaker. William then turned to his archers once more and arrows rained down on Harold's men.

4 As the sun set, Harold was killed and the battle was lost. Some said he had been shot in the eye by an arrow before being cut to pieces by some of William's men. William had the body buried at a secret location despite Harold's mother offering her son's weight in gold in exchange for the body.

Over to You

1 **a** Which factors (or reasons) below would help Harold win the battle? Which factors might help William?
- William's army had been blessed by the Pope
- Harold's men had just come from a battle with Hardrada
- The housecarls protected Harold's army with a strong shield wall
- William had a large army of 10,000 men
- There were streams and boggy areas on both sides of Senlac Hill
- Harold had positioned his soldiers on top of a steep hill

b Who do you think had the best chance of winning *before* the battle began? Explain your decision.

2 It's time to make up your mind about William's victory. Why did William win the battle? Was it because:
- he was a brilliant and skilful leader?
- Harold was a poor soldier who made mistakes?
- the Normans were better equipped and prepared?
- Harold was unlucky?
- of a combination of all or some of these reasons?

3 Work in a group to discuss your answers to question 2. As a group, write a paragraph to explain why you think William won the Battle of Hastings.

Historians know a lot about the events of 14 October 1066. But historians have got a problem with the death of King Harold. We just don't know *how* he died. The problem is that the sources (pieces of evidence written at the time) don't all say the same thing about his death. Since then, people have tried to come to their own conclusions (known as interpretations). However, neither the sources nor the interpretations paint a clear picture of Harold's death. So, your task as a 'History Mystery Detective' is to look through all the evidence and try to piece together how he actually died.

Objectives

- Examine sources and interpretations relating to the death of King Harold.
- Summarise the cause of Harold's death.

Source and Interpretation Analysis

There is an important difference between sources and interpretations:

- A **source** is created from the period you are studying. A source may record the experiences (like a letter) of someone who was directly involved with the event, or it might be a cartoon, newspaper or painting from the time. The person who created these might not have witnessed the events, but they might have spoken to people involved or had insight into the events because they were around at the time. Sources then help people make an interpretation.
- An **interpretation** is made much later, perhaps decades or centuries after the event. The person creating the interpretation (a book, news article, film or cartoon for example) has had time to reflect on the events and review the sources, and tries to show a particular opinion about what happened.

As a historian, you will analyse sources and interpretations so you can judge their usefulness and assess how they can be used to answer questions about the past.

▼ **SOURCE A** The earliest written record of Harold's death was written sometime before 1068 by Guy of Amiens, a Norman churchman who spent a lot of time with the new King William's wife, Matilda.

'With the point of his lance the first knight pierced Harold's chest, drenching the ground with blood. With his sword the second knight cut off his head. The third cut him open with his javelin. The fourth hacked off his leg.'

▼ **SOURCE B** This account of the battle was written in 1070 by William of Jumièges, a Norman monk. He wrote a history book for King William called *Deeds of the Norman Dukes*, which glorifies the Norman Conquest.

'Duke William engaged the enemy at the third hour [about 9am] and continued until nightfall. Harold fell in the first shock of battle, pierced with lethal wounds.'

▼ **SOURCE C** William of Poitiers wrote the most detailed account of the battle around 1070. He was a Norman priest and a trained soldier who knew William well. However, he does not write much about Harold's death.

'The king [Harold] himself, his brothers, and the leading men of the kingdom had been killed.'

▼ **INTERPRETATION D** One of the 72 pictures from the 70-metre-long, embroidered cloth called the Bayeux Tapestry created in the 1070s.

Key Words interpretation
lance   source

This English soldier has an arrow in his eye.

Probably made in England on the orders of Bishop Odo, King William's half-brother. Odo was at the Battle of Hastings.

'Hic Harold Rex Interfectus Est' means 'Here King Harold has been killed'.

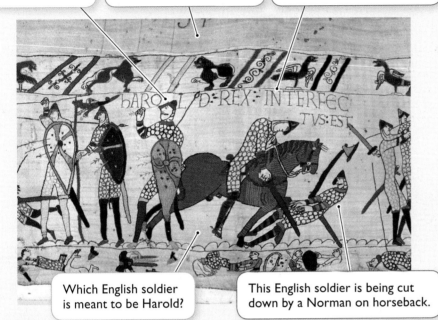

Which English soldier is meant to be Harold?

This English soldier is being cut down by a Norman on horseback.

▼ **INTERPRETATION G** Historian Simon Schama, speaking on a TV documentary called *A History of Britain: Conquest!* in 2000.

'In recent years some people have thought that Harold might be the figure on the floor being attacked by knights, rather than the man with the arrow in his eye. But it seems obvious that the words 'Harold Rex' are written directly above the arrow-struck man. This is significant.

▼ **INTERPRETATION E** The first written record of Harold being shot in the eye by an arrow was recorded in 1080, 14 years after the battle, by Amatus of Montecassino, a monk from Italy. He wrotewthat William achieved victory after he had:

'gouged out his [Harold's] eye with an arrow'

▼ **INTERPRETATION F** William of Malmesbury was a monk who spent his whole life in England. His father was a Norman and his mother was English. Around 1125 he wrote *The History of the Kings of England* which includes this adapted account of King Harold's death. Some historians think he may have written this after seeing the Bayeux Tapestry.

'His brain was pierced by an arrow and he fell, the English fled without respite [rest] till the night... One of the knights hacked at his thigh with a sword as he lay on the ground; for which he was branded with disgrace by William for a dastardly [cruel] and shameful act.'

Over to You

To try to solve the mystery of how King Harold died, look closely at all the evidence on these pages.

1 List the different ways Harold may have died. What weapons were used? At what stage of the battle did he die?

2 a Do any pieces of evidence agree on how Harold was killed? Explain how they agree.

b Judge whether or not you trust the evidence. If you don't trust it, explain why.

c You may believe all the evidence is useful or perhaps just some of it. Is there any Anglo-Saxon evidence? If not, suggest why.

3 Now decide how Harold died. Like a detective, use evidence to back up your theory. If you're not sure, say why. In History it's OK to say you're uncertain, as long as you can explain why.

Have you been learning?

⟳ Quick Knowledge Quiz

Choose the correct answer from the three options:

1 After the Romans left Britain, which of the following tribes began to invade?

  a Celts and Picts
  b Angles, Saxons and Jutes
  c Hunter-gatherers

2 The population of Anglo-Saxon England in the eleventh century was approximately how much?

  a 1.5 million
  b 15 million
  c 150 million

3 Anglo-Saxon kings were helped by a group of advisors known as what?

  a the Triumph
  b the Whitlock
  c the Witan

4 Harold Godwinson was the earl of which of these Anglo-Saxon earldoms?

  a Mercia
  b Wessex
  c Kent

5 Harald Hardrada was king of which of these countries?

  a Norway
  b France
  c Hungary

6 Hardrada and Tostig died at which battle on 25 September 1066?

  a Battle of Fulford
  b Battle of Stamford Bridge
  c Battle of Hastings

7 Who were the best-trained and equipped soldiers in King Harold's army?

  a the knights
  b the fyrd
  c the housecarls

8 Duke William was from which part of France?

  a Normandy
  b Norway
  c Wessex

9 Which of the following types of soldier would go into battle on a horse?

  a the knights
  b the fyrd
  c the housecarls

10 On what date was the Battle of Hastings?

  a 14 September 1066
  b 14 October 1066
  c 16 October 1066

 **Literacy Focus**

Note-taking

Note-taking is a vital skill. To do it successfully, you must pick out all the important (key) words in a sentence. The important words are the words that are vital to the meaning (and your understanding) of the sentence. For example, in the sentence:

> 'The Battle of Hastings began at 9 o'clock on the morning of 14 October 1066. Harold, the Anglo-Saxon king of England, was killed during the battle, possibly by an arrow to the eye. However, some historians debate this version of events and think that he was killed in another way.'

… the important words are: Battle, Hastings, 9am, 14 Oct. 1066, A-S, king, Harold, killed, arrow, eye, historians, debate.

The original sentence was 50 words long – but the shortened version is fewer than 15 words long and contains abbreviations. Note-taking like this will help your understanding of events – and provides you with a great revision exercise.

1   Write down the important words in the following sentences. These important words are your notes.

    a   In about 2500 BC, a new wave of settlers began arriving in Britain from central Europe. They were known as the Beaker people because of the decorated pottery they used. They knew how to make things out of metals like copper and gold.

    b   Around 500 BC, Celtic tribes from central Europe arrived. The tribes fought brutally with each other, and with the people already settled in Britain.

    c   The Romans, from Italy, invaded Britain in AD 43 and soon conquered most of the British tribes. They stayed for around 400 years.

    d   In about AD 410, the Romans returned to Italy to defend their homeland from invasion. Soon, new tribes from abroad to invade Britain. The British people (now known as Britons) were left to fend for themselves, and it didn't take long for new tribes to invade. These tribes, from modern-day Denmark and northern Germany, were called Angles, Saxons and Jutes.

    e   In the late eighth century the Anglo-Saxons faced invasion from across the North Sea by Vikings.

1 History skill: Write a narrative account (causation)

When something happens (historians usually call them 'events'), that event will have **causes**. Historians use the term 'causes' to describe the things that made it happen. Most events have a number of causes. Also, events have **consequences**. A consequence is a result or effect of something. Like causes, there can often be several consequences.

Writing about the causes and the consequences of an event can help historians create a well-explained story. A good story, or a narrative account, should:

- show off your knowledge of a period in history

- show that you can get a story in the right chronological order (so it makes sense)

- explain why things happened (cause) and what they led to (consequence).

> ⌖ **TIP:** For example, the Battle of Stamford Bridge had a number of causes, such as King Harold's determination to drive the Vikings out of England, and Hardrada's attempt to take the English throne.

> ⌖ **TIP:** Using the Battle of Stamford Bridge as our example again, two of the consequences of this battle could be the death of Hardrada and Tostig, and the weakening of King Harold's army in the build up to the Battle of Hastings.

How to write a narrative account

Here is one way to write a story, or narrative account:

1 **Plan:** What story are you asked to tell? Firstly, it is important to make sure you know the key events. What should you include? What should you leave out? Make a plan of the main events.

2 **Check order and add detail:** To tell the story in a logical way, organise the key events in your plan in the right order. Don't forget to add some dates to the events.

3 **Write your story:** When you are sure of the order of events, it's time to start writing the story down. Try to add details to the events.

4 **Make links:** To improve your narrative, you need to make sure that your story is not just a detailed description. Try to link events together, to show the causes and consequences of why and how things happened. This helps you to show that you know how the different parts of the story are connected and moves you beyond a collection of detailed facts. Sometimes these 'linking' words and phrases are called 'connectives'.

> ⌖ **TIP:** You can use words and phrases like:
>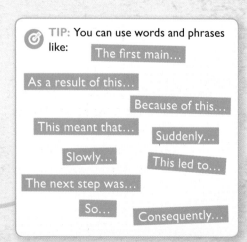
> The first main...
> As a result of this...
> Because of this...
> This meant that...
> Suddenly...
> Slowly...
> This led to...
> The next step was...
> So...
> Consequently...

Let's go through an example of a narrative account (story) question:

> Write a narrative account of the events in January to October 1066 that led to the start of the Battle of Hastings.
>
> You may use the following in your answer:
>
> • the death of Edward the Confessor
>
> • the Battle of Stamford Bridge.
>
> You must also use information of your own.

1 **Plan:** You are asked to write about what happened in 1066 that led to the Battle of Hastings. The list below shows a plan of the main events.

- Battle of Stamford Bridge
- Duke William of Normandy invades
- Battle of Fulford
- Hardrada and Tostig invade
- Edward the Confessor dies
- Battle of Hastings
- King Harold marches south to fight Duke William

2 **Check order and add detail:** Write down the statements in step 1 in the correct chronological order. If possible, try to add some dates to the events. For example: Edward the Confessor died on 5 January 1066. Look back through pages 18–25 to help you with some of the dates. While looking, are there any other important events or details missing from the story?

> **TIP:** For example, you can add what happened on 6 January 1066 (the crowning of King Harold as King of England) – this was the event that probably led to Hardrada's and Duke William's decision to invade.

3 **Write your story:** A simple version of the story might start like this:

Edward the Confessor died. Harold was crowned King of England. Hardrada and Tostig invaded. At the Battle of Fulford...

At the moment, this answer is a collection of short facts. It could be improved by including more detail. For example:

Edward the Confessor died on 5 January 1066. Harold, the powerful Anglo-Saxon Earl of Wessex, was crowned king. On 18 September, 300 Viking longboats carrying Hardrada's army of 10,000 Viking warriors landed in England near York. Anglo-Saxon earls Edwin and Morcar attacked Hardrada and Tostig on 20 September at the Battle of Fulford...

> **TIP:** The Battle of Fulford was not mentioned in the question – it is important that you go beyond the two events mentioned in the question, and provide 'extra' information.

> **TIP:** It is always useful to add in more key dates.

> **TIP:** An important aspect of writing a good narrative account, or story, is to demonstrate your own knowledge.

4 **Make links:** Add 'linking' words, known as 'connectives', to show how the events are connected. For example, you could write:

The first major event of 1066 was the death of King Edward the Confessor on 5 January 1066. Immediately, Harold Godwinson, the powerful Anglo-Saxon Earl of Wessex, was crowned King of England. As a result of this, Hardrada, the King of Norway, gathered an invasion force and on 18 September, 300 Viking longboats carrying...

> **TIP:** The use of connectives makes the account flow, and demonstrates you can link the chronological events together.

Now turn to the next page to have a go at answering this type of question.

1 Assessment: Write a narrative account (causation)

Your challenge is to answer this narrative account question:

⭐ Write a narrative account of events in October 1066 that led to William winning the Battle of Hastings.

You may use the following in your answer:

- the positions of Harold's and William's soldiers on the morning of 14 October

- the fake retreats used by William during the battle.

You must also use information of your own. (20)

The questions on the next page will help you structure your answer. Use the tips and sentence starters to help you get started.

1 **Plan:** Study the statements below which show events linked to what happened in October 1066. What key facts are missing? Can you add any?

For example:
- King Harold makes his way south from Stamford Bridge
- Harold arrives near Hastings
- Duke William sets off from his camp near Hastings towards London at dawn
- Harold arranges troops behind a wall of shields on top of Senlac Hill
- William sends his knights up the hill to attack the shield wall
- There is a rumour that William has been killed, but William quickly gallops among his men to stop them panicking and show that he is still alive
- The shield wall gradually gets weaker after repeated Norman attacks
- Harold is killed, William is the winner

2 **Check order and add detail:** Organise the events, including any new ones you added, in chronological order. Can you add any dates to the events?

3 **Write your story:** Write about the events in the right order by using the events in step 2. (15)

> In October 1066, William, Duke of Normandy defeated...
>
> In early October 1066, King Harold of England, having heard of the Norman invasion, began to make his way south to...

TIP: To begin, introduce what you are going to write about.

TIP: This is where you start to tell the story.

4 **Make links:** Try to connect the events together. It's important that your account *flows*. (5)

TIP: When linking events, you can use words or phrases like:

At first   Secondly   Then

Next   After   Finally

Meanwhile   At the same time

Suddenly   Slowly

Because of this   So

TIP: For example, when describing the moments surrounding the series of Norman retreats on the afternoon of the battle, you might write: 'Then, in the afternoon, some of William's soldiers began to run away down the hill as if they were retreating. In response, some of Harold's men, thinking they were winning, charged down the hill after them. While this was happening, William's knights...'

On the evening of 14 October 1066 (the night of the Battle of Hastings), William must have realised he was in a very dangerous position. As a foreign invader, he knew the English would want to get rid of him – soon! His army had killed the English King Harold after all, and William knew that if he gave the English time to recover they might gather another army and fight for another king. So how did William deal with these problems?

Objectives

- Examine William's key problems after his victory at the Battle of Hastings.
- Analyse how William dealt with the problems.

William's problems

William had several problems to deal with, as shown on **Map A**.

▼ **MAP A** Some of the problems William had to deal with.

1 Viking threat
There is still a possibility that Vikings will invade from Norway and Denmark. If they join up with angry Englishmen in the north, they will be a very serious threat.

2 Getting to London
Anyone wishing to control England must control London. Some of Harold's army did not go with him to the Battle of Hastings; instead they stayed in London to guard it. Two powerful Anglo-Saxon earls, Edwin and Morcar, had not fought at the Battle of Hastings and were also in London.

Stamford Bridge
York
N
Worcester
Berkhamsted
Oxford • London
Wallingford •
Canterbury •
Arundel
Dover
Exeter • Corfe Hastings
Pevensey
0   135km

3 Defeating Dover
There is a fort at Dover full of tough and angry English soldiers. William must defeat these men before he marches to London or else they may attack him from behind.

4 A tired army
William's army is very tired. The Battle of Hastings was fierce. Some supplies are running low.

William secures the ports

William dealt with some of his problems very swiftly. Firstly, he marched eastwards along the coast to make sure he controlled the ports there. This made it easier to get supplies from Normandy delivered by boat. William of Poitiers, a Norman priest and former soldier who knew William well, wrote about William's takeover of the port of Dover (see **B**).

▼ **SOURCE B** Adapted from a book written by William of Poitiers, a friend of William's, around 1070.

'William marched to Dover where the English, stricken with fear, prepared to surrender. But our men, greedy for loot, set fire to the town. William, unwilling that those who had offered to give up, should suffer loss, gave them money for the damage his men had caused. Having captured Dover, William spent eight days making it stronger.'

The march to London

After securing the ports, William marched to Canterbury (where many expensive treasures and religious artefacts were kept) and the town quickly surrendered. William then began his march towards London. Florence of Worcester, a monk, describes William's movements (see **C**).

▼ **SOURCE C** Adapted from the chronicle of the English monk Florence of Worcester, written at the time.

'Meanwhile, William was laying waste to Sussex, Kent, Hampshire, Surrey, Middlesex, and Herefordshire. He was burning villages and slaughtering the people. Then he was met at Berkhampstead by religious leaders, the English earls Edwin and Morcar, Prince Edgar [the young nephew of Edward the Confessor] and some powerful Londoners. They all accepted William as their king, but he still allowed his troops to burn the villages.'

▼ **INTERPRETATION D** A section of the Bayeux Tapestry, completed in the 1070s, that shows the Normans burning an English house.

William is crowned

In total, William took two months to reach London. On the way, his army burned buildings and stole many items as they passed through villages and towns. He was crowned King of England in Westminster Abbey on Christmas Day, 25 December 1066 (see **E**). William now had to conquer the rest of England.

▼ **INTERPRETATION E** William is crowned King of England, as shown in a medieval manuscript from around 1250.

Over to You

1 Describe two problems William faced immediately after the Battle of Hastings.

2 Explain why you think William took control of the following places on his way to being crowned King of England on Christmas Day 1066:
   • ports on the south coast, including Dover
   • Canterbury
   • London.

Source Analysis

Look at **Sources B** and **C**.

1 Suggest a reason why you think William was kind to the English in Dover but so cruel as he marched towards London.

2 Is there anything in **Source C** that suggests the writer did not like what William was doing? Give a reason for your answer.

3 Study **Sources B** and **C**. How similar are they?

Rebellions against the new king

By the end of 1066, King William controlled much of the south of England. However, in the rest of the country there were some major **rebellions** against his rule:

- In Shropshire, a rebellion led by an Anglo-Saxon named Edric the Wild was defeated by a large Norman army.

- In the south-west there was strong resistance to Norman rule. The city of Exeter held out against the Normans in a **siege** that lasted for 18 days – before they eventually surrendered. There were further rebellions in Gloucester and Bristol.

- In the Fens (a marshy area of East Anglia), Anglo-Saxon rebels led by Hereward the Wake also refused to accept Norman rule. It took the Normans over a year to beat the rebels.

The Harrying of the North

Perhaps the most famous rebellion against the Normans was in the north of England in 1069. It was led by two Anglo-Saxon earls, Edwin and Morcar, and 18-year-old Edgar the Aetheling, the great-nephew of Edward the Confessor. Their army was joined by Viking and Scottish armies.

When William's trusted friend, Earl Robert, and 900 of William's soldiers were murdered by the English rebels, William acted quickly – and brutally – to deal with the situation.

Firstly, he paid the Vikings to abandon the rebels and return home. At this, the rebel army panicked and scattered. Determined to teach the people of the north a lesson, William ordered villages to be destroyed and people killed. Crops were burnt and animals were slaughtered. Many of those who survived then starved to death – it is estimated that the population was reduced by 75 per cent. William even ordered the land to be poisoned to prevent people growing crops in the future. William's actions were called the 'Harrying of the North'. 'Harrying' means attacking an enemy or an enemy's territory again and again.

William shows his power

By 1071, five years after he had won the Battle of Hastings, King William was master of England – William the Conqueror. He had dealt with his immediate problems but knew that his next challenge was to stay in control for the long term.

> **Fact** ✓
>
> King William introduced **Murdrum Fines**. It meant that if a Norman was killed, the entire area around where the crime took place was heavily fined.

▼ **INTERPRETATION F** Written by Simeon, a monk who lived in the north of England, in Durham Priory. Adapted from a book called *A History of the Kings*, written in the early 1100s.

'King William quickly gathered an army, and hurried to Northumberland in great anger, and did not stop destroying the country and killing the men...

Because of this, there was so great a **famine** that people, forced by hunger, ate human flesh, that of horses, dogs and cats, and everything that is horrible. It was horrific to see human bodies decaying in the houses, the streets and the roads, swarming with worms, while they rotted with a terrible stench. No one was left to bury them, for everyone had either been killed by the sword, or by the famine, or had left the country because of the famine.

Meanwhile, the land was deserted. The villages between Durham and York were empty. They became hiding places for wild animals and robbers.'

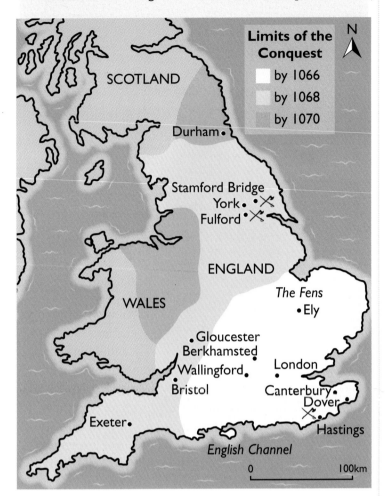

▼ **MAP G** The stages of the Norman Conquest.

SCOTLAND

Limits of the Conquest

by 1066
by 1068
by 1070

N

Durham

Stamford Bridge
York
Fulford

ENGLAND

WALES

The Fens
Ely

Gloucester
Berkhamsted
Wallingford
Bristol

London

Canterbury
Dover

Exeter

Hastings

English Channel

0   100km

Key Words

famine   Murdrum Fine
rebellion   siege

▼ **INTERPRETATION H** King William's deathbed confession, written by an English monk called Orderic Vitalis, in about 1130 – about 43 years after William's death in 1087. Orderic wasn't there when William died and wrote his own version of what William said.

> 'I fell on the North like a hungry lion. I ordered their houses and corn with all their tools and goods to be burned, and great herds of cattle to be butchered. By doing so, I became the cruel murderer of many thousands, both young and old, of those fine people.'

Interpretation Analysis

1 Read **Interpretation F**. In no more than 30 words, briefly summarise what the monk writes in this interpretation.

2 Before a historian uses this as evidence of the Harrying of the North, what questions would they need to ask?

3 Suggest one reason why the author of **Interpretation F** might have this view about the Harrying of the North.

Over to You

1 Match the heads with the tails.

Heads	Tails
• Edric the Wild	• led a rebellion in the north of England in 1069
• Exeter	• leader of a rebellion in Shropshire
• Hereward the Wake	• William's response to the rebellion in the north
• Edwin, Morcar and Edgar	• held out against the Normans for 18 days
• Harrying of the North	• led a rebellion in East Anglia

2 a In your own words, write down what is meant by the word 'famine'.

   b How did William use famine as a weapon?

   c What were the advantages and disadvantages of doing this?

3 a Some historians have said that William punished the people in the north to teach the whole country a lesson. What do you think this means?

   b Explain why you think William was so brutal in some of his actions.

4 a What can we learn from **Interpretation H** about the character of King William?

   b Why do we need to be careful about using this interpretation as evidence about William?

William the castle builder

The defeated English did not want King William as their ruler. The new king had managed to defeat several rebellions against him, but he knew he needed a long-term solution to help him stay in control. One of William's most famous strategies to help him control the English was the building of castles. In fact, between 1066 and 1086, the Norman invaders built over 500 castles! How and where were they built? What did they look like? How did they help William control the English?

Objectives

- Define what is meant by a 'motte and bailey' castle.
- Explain the features and functions of Norman castles.

William builds castles

William brought his rich and powerful friends over from Normandy to help control the English. In return for their support he gave them large areas of English land. These friends became powerful landowners known as **barons**. They soon realised that they needed protection from attacks by unhappy Englishmen. So, they decided to build castles. The diagram below shows the sort of castles that William's barons built.

▼ **A** A drawing of a **motte and bailey** castle. These were built all over England within a few years after the Norman invasion. Each one took about seven to fourteen days to build.

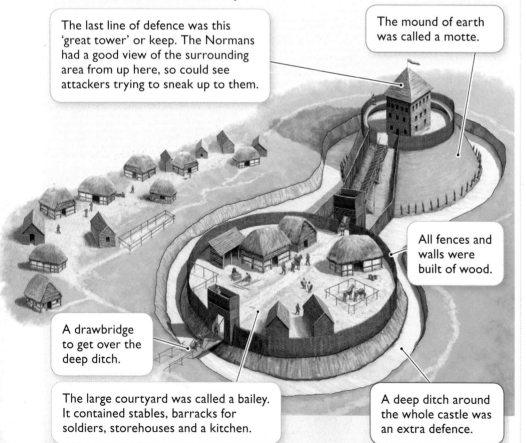

The last line of defence was this 'great tower' or keep. The Normans had a good view of the surrounding area from up here, so could see attackers trying to sneak up to them.

The mound of earth was called a motte.

All fences and walls were built of wood.

A drawbridge to get over the deep ditch.

The large courtyard was called a bailey. It contained stables, barracks for soldiers, storehouses and a kitchen.

A deep ditch around the whole castle was an extra defence.

Reduced to rubble

These new buildings were known as motte and bailey castles. They had to be built quickly and wherever the Normans wanted them. If some houses or a village stood where the baron wanted a castle, he simply destroyed them and built on top of them. In Lincoln, the Normans pulled down over 100 houses to make space for the castle.

The purpose of castles

Norman barons and their soldiers used their castles as bases and controlled the local area from them. The castles were built at key points – to guard important roads, ports, river crossings, and towns. They became the focus for local trade in the area, which the baron could then **tax**. Castles were also built to intimidate the local English population and show power. Building castles involved moving large amounts of earth and wood, which demonstrated to the English just how strong and powerful the Norman invaders were. **Map B** shows some of the larger castles built by the Normans.

Meanwhile...

Castles weren't the only large new structures that appeared during the Norman Conquest. Religious buildings such as cathedrals and monasteries – often very large and grand – were built. They were built to show devotion to God, and were also used to impress the locals. Like castles, they reminded the locals that the Normans were powerful – and in charge.

▼ **MAP B** Some of the main Norman castles built during the reign of William the Conqueror (1066–1087).

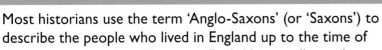

However, the problem with castles that go up quickly is that they can be brought down just as fast. Wooden buildings can burn, be smashed down, or rot. So, by as early as 1070, any barons with a bit of time and money began to build their castles in stone instead.

Fact ✓

Most historians use the term 'Anglo-Saxons' (or 'Saxons') to describe the people who lived in England up to the time of the Norman invasion. The term 'English' is usually used to describe them in the years after 1066.

Key Words baron   motte and bailey   tax

▼ **SOURCE C** One of the world's most famous castles, the Tower of London was once the home of King William. It was originally built out of wood and later replaced with stone. The Tower of London was the first stone keep in England.

Over to You

1 Why do you think the keep was built on a high mound of earth? What advantages would the height give to those in the keep?

2 How were the sites of castles chosen?

3 Imagine you are an angry Englishman who has just led a failed attack on a wooden motte and bailey castle. Describe the obstacles you faced on the way to the keep before you were finally defeated. Remember to include what you think were the weaknesses of the wooden castle.

Knowledge and Understanding ⭐

1 Describe two ways in which Norman castles were used.

The Domesday Book

Most of us know how much money we've got. We know what we own and are usually interested in what other people own too. William the Conqueror was exactly the same – he was keen to know all about the country he had conquered, how much it was worth, and the people who lived there. In 1085 he decided to find out.

Objectives

- Examine the purpose of the Domesday Survey and the Domesday Book.

The survey

Around Christmas 1085, William sent officials to visit towns and villages all over England and ask a series of detailed questions. In each village, they interviewed the priest, the steward (the man who organised the farm work in the village) and six elderly villagers.

The officials (and the soldiers who travelled with them) visited over 13,000 villages in less than a year – this was very quick by medieval standards. A second group of officials visited the villages later to check the people had been honest!

Fact ✓

The change in land ownership made very little difference for many ordinary English **peasants**. Before the Normans arrived, Anglo-Saxon earls controlled the land – and now it was a Norman lord or baron. Life changed very little – peasants still had crops to grow and taxes to pay! It was only in places where there had been rebellions, and where the Normans had been harsh, that life changed dramatically.

How much is the land worth?	How many people live here?	Who owned this land before William was king?
How much farmland is there?	How many mills are there?	How much woodland is there?
How many fishponds?	How many pigs are there?	How many cows?

▼ **SOURCE A** Adapted from the *Anglo-Saxon Chronicle*, a collection of historical records, mainly written by English monks between the ninth and twelfth centuries. This is part of the entry for 1085.

'The king held a large meeting with his council about this land, how it was occupied and by what sort of people. Then he sent his men over all England to find out how much land there was, what and how much each person owned, how much livestock there was, and how much he should have from each place… So very closely was it searched that there was not one single yard of land, not even (and it is shameful to tell, though he had no shame to do it) an ox, nor a cow, nor a pig was left out. And all the documents were to be brought to him afterwards.'

The books

All the records from the surveys were sent to Winchester where one man wrote it all down in Latin. The surveys filled two huge books (which are together called the Domesday Book) and contained approximately two million words.

The book gave William knowledge. It meant:

- he could work out how much each person in England could afford to pay him in taxes

- he knew exactly how many people he could get to fight for him

- he could settle any quarrels over who owned which bit of land.

However, William never got to see the finished book in use. He was in Normandy in 1087 and, while riding his horse, he slipped forward in his saddle and burst open his bladder. He died in agony. He wouldn't have been able to read it himself anyway – he couldn't read!

What does the Domesday Book tell us?

The Domesday Books tells us a lot about who had control in Norman England.

Key Words   peasant

▼ **SOURCE B** Adapted from the Domesday Book. Birmingham is now the second largest city in Britain! Note: Villeins and bordars lived on, and farmed, the lord's land. A plough team was made up of eight men and two oxen. A league was a unit of distance, about 5km (3 miles) in length.

'Richard holds Birmingham from William, son of Ansculf. There are nine households – five villeins and four bordars. There is enough land for six ploughs. There is one lord's plough team and two men's plough teams. There is a wood, half a league in length. Wulwin was the lord in the time of King Edward. The value to him was £1. It is still worth £1.'

Norman England

- In the years before 1066, England was controlled by Anglo-Saxons – now it was mainly controlled by foreigners.
- There were around 10,000 Norman settlers.
- Around ten of King William's important followers controlled 25 per cent of England between them.
- King William and his family directly controlled around 20 per cent of the land.
- Christianity was a very important part of medieval life, and the Church held about 25 per cent of the land.
- 170 other Normans controlled the rest – this meant all the land in England was held by just 250 people!

Over to You

1 Create a diagram, fact file or mind-map that shows:
- what the Domesday Book is
- why the survey was carried out
- what the survey investigated
- what the Domesday Book revealed

2 a Read **Source A**. Write a list of what it tells us about how the Domesday Survey was carried out.

b Do you think the writer of this source was happy about King William's survey or not? Explain your answer. Include any clues that might tell us how the writer felt.

Significance

To decide if an event is historically significant or not, you have to assess whether a) it was important at the time it happened *and* b) whether it's also important over a long time, perhaps even until now.

Let's practise just part a) for now.

1 Was the Domesday Book important for ordinary peasants? Why or why not?

2 Was it important for Norman barons? Why or why not?

3 Look at your answers for 1 and 2. Overall, do you think the book was important to people *at the time* it happened? You can use words like very, somewhat, a little, not very, etc.

4 Explain the significance of the Domesday Book in the 1080s.

The feudal system: who's the boss?

Wherever we go, wherever we've been, there's usually someone in charge – at home, in the classroom, at work or at a sports club. The person in charge might be a parent, a teacher or a manager. None of us lives in a world where we can do what we want, when we want to. Knowing this makes the next two pages very straightforward. By the end you'll understand exactly how King William controlled England.

Objectives

- Examine how the feudal system worked.
- Explain how the feudal system helped William control England.

Clever King William

King William said that all the land in England belonged to him. But England was too large for him to manage by himself, so how did he stay in charge? His answer was to use a system of sharing out the land. He gave large areas of land to people in return for their **loyalty**.

William kept around 20 per cent of the land for himself and his family to use. He gave another 25 per cent to the Church. The rest of the land was lent to people who had helped him in the Battle of Hastings or who were his loyal supporters from Normandy. William didn't give his barons single large areas of land – he carefully gave them several pieces dotted around England. He did this to make it difficult for the barons to build up large armies in the same area. If they became too powerful, he feared they might rebel against him.

This new system of land control became known as the **feudal system**.

Fact ✓

King William loved hunting – so he converted some of the vast forest areas that covered England into 'Royal Forests'. New Forest Laws protected these areas. These laws meant that anyone caught hunting in a 'Royal Forest' could be fined, blinded or even executed.

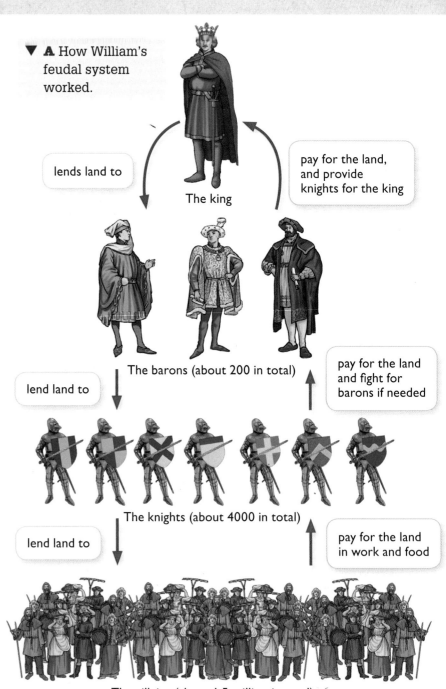

▼ **A** How William's feudal system worked.

lends land to

pay for the land, and provide knights for the king

The king

The barons (about 200 in total)

lend land to

pay for the land and fight for barons if needed

The knights (about 4000 in total)

lend land to

pay for the land in work and food

The villeins (about 1.5 million in total)

How did William control his kingdom?

King William's idea was very clever. He knew he needed help running England, so he used all the land he owned as a way of getting assistance. He also knew that religion was very important in people's lives at this time – so he made sure the Church had plenty of land… but put his fellow Normans in all the senior Church positions. By giving lots of land to his friends (the barons), he got their support and help, and some money when he taxed them.

▼ **SOURCE B** An oath, from the early twelfth century, which a baron made to the king when he was given land.

> 'I become your man from this day forward, for life and limb and loyalty. I shall be true and faithful to you for the lands I hold from you.'

But how did the barons get their money? Simple – by giving away some of their land to knights (very well-trained soldiers) who then paid taxes to the barons. The knights were very loyal to the barons because if they weren't, the barons could take their land away!

In turn, the knights shared much of their land with the peasants (known as **villeins**) who then farmed the land, and gave a portion of their crops and paid taxes to the knights. In this way, nearly every man in the country got some land – but he had to promise to be loyal to the man who gave it to him. If he broke his promise, he lost his land.

So this very clever system meant that William had a constant supply of money rolling in from his barons (who got it from the knights, who got it from the peasants)… and he still managed to own all the land! Even though most of the land was being used by other people, nearly everyone was loyal to him.

▼ **SOURCE C** The feudal system established by William stayed in place for many years. Here, Jean Froissart, a medieval poet and historian, describes the feudal system in 1395. 'Nobility' refers to the rich landowners (**nobles**) and 'serfs' were the peasants.

> 'It is the custom in England, as with other countries, for the nobility to have great power over the common people, who are serfs. This means that they are bound by law to plough the field of their masters, harvest the corn, gather it into barns, and prepare the grain; they must also cut and carry home the hay, cut and collect wood, and perform all manner of tasks of this kind.'

Key Words   feudal system   loyalty   noble   villein

Over to You

1 Complete the sentences below with an accurate term:

   a The _____ gave land to the knights, who paid taxes and fought for him when required.

   b The peasants were loyal to the _____, but he was loyal to the baron and the king.

   c The _____ was at the bottom of the system – everyone was his or her lord.

   d In the feudal system, the owner of all the land was the _____.

2 a Explain why King William introduced the feudal system.

   b Why do you think William was careful not to give his barons pieces of land that were close together?

3 Read **Source B**. Write a sentence to summarise what the baron is promising the king.

4 Read **Source C**. This source is written in 1395, over 200 years after William was king. What does that tell you about the impact of the feudal system?

Change and Continuity

Historians compare different periods in order to understand what has changed and what stayed the same.

1 Look back to pages 14–15 to remind yourself how the Anglo-Saxons controlled England. Write down some notes.

2 Explain two ways in which Anglo-Saxon and Norman methods of control were different.

2.5 How did life change under the Normans?

When the Normans began to rule England in the years after 1066, things certainly changed. For a start, a foreign army had invaded England, and had killed the English king and many of his most loyal followers. The leader of the foreign invaders had then made himself King of England. He brought over lots of his French-speaking friends to help him run the country and many of them built big, new castles. But to what extent did everyday life change? Was life dramatically different in the first few decades of the Norman Conquest? Were the changes greater for different groups?

Objectives

- Outline the ways in which the Normans changed life in England.
- Assess how much the Normans changed everyday life.

Meet Edmund, Mildred and Edith. It is 1086 – 20 years since the Norman invasion. Edmund, Mildred and Edith are just like most people in England at this time. They are ordinary villagers who grow their own food, and they keep animals on land owned by the local Norman lord. Their lord is Henry de Ferrers.

They each remember what life was like before the Norman invasion. Over the last 20 years they have seen the changes that have taken place in England. Some changes were huge and affected lots of people, while others affected only a few. Read what they have to say carefully and think about how some of the other information on these pages will have made an impact on their lives.

My life has gone on much the same as it did before. The person who used to own the land I work on was killed at the Battle of Hastings, and now a Norman lord named Henry de Ferrers owns the land. I still don't own my own land! I work as hard now as I ever did – and still pay taxes in the same way as always. It's true that when the Normans came to this area they forced us all to help build the castle – but now I feel that the castle provides protection and security for the area.

They are foreigners – they are not my people. If the lord demands more corn, we must give him more corn. And they rule us from up high, in their castles. The old rulers used to live among us, but the Normans rule from behind thick stone walls. And it's not like we can go into the forests and take what we used to – strict laws stop us hunting rabbits in the 'Royal Forests'.

The Normans were rude and cruel when they came. There were stories of how brutal they could be if you did not obey them. But things have settled now. They certainly still like to show their power and wealth though – the castles they first built are now larger and made from stone, and the new cathedrals they are building are the largest I have ever seen.

Edmund

Edith

Mildred

Ways in which Normans changed everyday life in England

Land ownership

Before the Norman invasion, a few Anglo-Saxon earls owned *huge* areas of land. William split these earldoms up into smaller pieces of land and gave them to French-speaking Normans. For ordinary peasants, this had little impact. They just had a new lord to work for.

The landscape

Normans built large, stone castles and cathedrals, which could be seen for miles around. Over time, as well as being important for defence, castles also became centres for trade, and towns grew around them. Many northern towns and villages had been destroyed in the 'Harrying of the North'. Vast forests were also set aside for King William to go hunting in (known as 'Royal Forests')

New laws

New Forest Laws meant that anyone caught hunting in a Royal Forest could be fined, blinded or even executed! New 'Murdrum Fines' meant that if a Norman was killed, the people living in the area where the crime took place were heavily fined. However, King William kept much of the old Anglo-Saxon legal system – but it was run by Normans.

Language

The Normans spoke French while ordinary peasants continued to speak the English they were used to. Over time, French words crept into everyday use – for example, armour, baron, judge and market.

armour
baron
market

The Church

The Normans set about gradually replacing the wooden Anglo-Saxon churches with stone ones. Most of the important church roles were held by Normans.

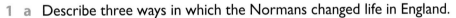

Over to You

1 a Describe three ways in which the Normans changed life in England.

   b Describe three ways in which life in England stayed the same after the Normans arrived.

2 The Norman Conquest affected people in different ways. Explain how you think the following people were affected:

   a an Anglo-Saxon landowner (known as a thegn) who owned a large area of land in the north of England

   b an ordinary Anglo-Saxon peasant (known as a ceorl) such as Edmund, Mildred or Edith

   c a Norman baron who fought with King William at the Battle of Hastings.

3 In a group, create a role play between Edmund, Mildred or Edith. Imagine they are discussing how life has (or hasn't) changed. You could ask a fourth person to play the part of an Anglo-Saxon landowner.

Fact ✓

In the Middle Ages, a 'lord' was anyone above you in the feudal system. So, a peasant had several lords, while a baron had just one – the king!

Change and Continuity

1 'The Norman Conquest completely changed England'. Do you agree with this statement? Explain your answer.

◔ Quick Knowledge Quiz

Choose the correct answer from the three options:

1 On which day was William crowned King of England?

   a 14 October 1066
   b 25 October 1066
   c 25 December 1066

2 What was the name of the Anglo-Saxon who led a rebellion against Norman rule in the Fens of East Anglia?

   a Edric the Wild
   b Hereward the Wake
   c Edgar the Aetheling

3 When a rebellion against William took place in the north of England, the king responded by ordering villages there to be burned and crops destroyed. This is known as what?

   a The Slaughter of the North
   b King William's Revenge
   c The Harrying of the North

4 What is a 'motte'?

   a a high mound of earth upon which a castle's keep was built
   b a large courtyard containing stables and storehouses
   c a deep ditch that surrounds a castle

5 The earliest wooden motte and bailey castles took approximately how long to build?

   a 7 to 14 days
   b 2 to 3 hours
   c 3 to 6 months

6 By 1086, approximately how many Normans had settled in England?

   a 1000
   b 10,000
   c 100,000

7 As well as castles, what other large stone structures did the Normans famously build?

   a cathedrals
   b hospitals
   c motorways

8 Approximately how many villages were visited during the Domesday Survey?

   a 1300
   b 130
   c 13,000

9 What is the name given to the Norman system where each group of people owed loyalty to the group above, starting with villeins, knights, barons and ending with the king?

   a the fearless system
   b the Domesday system
   c the feudal system

10 What was the name of a fine that a whole area was forced to pay if a Norman was killed there?

   a Forest Law
   b Murdrum Fine
   c Norman Fine

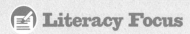 **Literacy Focus**

Writing in detail

1   Look at the paragraph below. It is a very basic answer to the question:
    What was the feudal system and why was it introduced?

    However, the answer does not contain many specific, factual details.
    Rewrite the paragraph to include more detail – adding names, dates,
    examples and facts where possible.

> Saying it was a 'new way of controlling the land'
> is too simplistic. Could you add detail about
> when it was introduced, and *how* it worked?

> Which king introduced it?

> The feudal system was a new way of controlling
> the land. It was introduced because the king
> needed help running the country so he gave
> land away to people so they would help him.

> Could you add more detail about the reasons
> why William needed help running the country?
> Think about the fact that England was a large
> country, full of Anglo-Saxons who might not
> want him as their king!

> Is this the only reason the system was
> introduced? The question asks why it
> was introduced. There were several
> reasons. Look back over pages 42–43
> to help you recall some more reasons.

Vocabulary check

2   In each group of historical words, phrases or names below, there is an odd one
    out. When you think you have identified it, write a sentence or two to explain
    why you think it doesn't fit in with the other words in its group. The first one
    has been done for you:

a   Duke William   Harald Hardrada   (King Edward)   Harold Godwinson

*I have chosen King Edward because he was the Anglo-Saxon king at the start
of 1066, whilst the others were the three main contenders who wanted his
throne after his death.*

b housecarl	fyrdsman	knight	archer
c baron	motte	bailey	keep
d axe	shield	sword	cannon
e Normandy	Spain	Norway	England
f Edwin	Hereward	William	Edric

History skill: Interpretation analysis

Historians study all sorts of different evidence to help them understand the past. Historical evidence can generally be divided into two main groups:

Source: This is evidence from the period you are studying. It can be created by someone who was directly involved with an event or an eyewitness to an event. A source can also be created by someone who didn't have direct involvement with an event, but created a cartoon or newspaper article (for example) at the time. Sources provide information historians need to create 'interpretations'.

Interpretation: This is evidence that is created much later than the period you are studying. Interpretations are produced by people with a particular opinion about an event in the past. For example, a historian or an artist could write or create an interpretation to share their view about a particular moment in history.

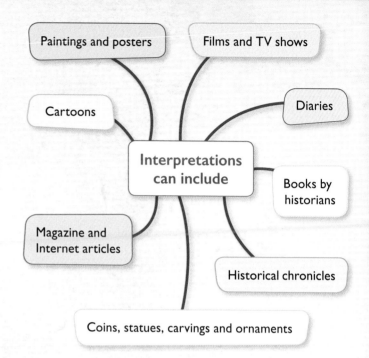

Paintings and posters

Films and TV shows

Cartoons

Diaries

Interpretations can include

Books by historians

Magazine and Internet articles

Historical chronicles

Coins, statues, carvings and ornaments

Comparing interpretations

When analysing different interpretations, a good historian should firstly work out what is being said, or what message the person who created the interpretation is trying to get across, before comparing the different interpretations.

Here is one way to compare two interpretations.

1 **Think about the content:** First you need to understand what the person is saying and/or showing in each interpretation. What is the content of **Interpretation A** saying? What is the content of **Interpretation B** saying?

2 **What are the main differences?** Now that you understand what each interpretation is saying, compare them. Find the ways in which the content of the interpretations is different. In other words, spot the difference!

3 **Think about the author or artist:** Look at the captions. What can they tell you about why the two interpretations might show different opinions about the topic?

4 **Why are there differences?** Look at the captions. Can you suggest reasons *why* the two people who made the interpretations might have different opinions about the topic?

Now, imagine you have been asked:

> **Interpretation A** and **Interpretation B** both provide views on William the Conqueror's actions and behaviours. How do they differ, and what might explain the differences?

▼ **INTERPRETATION A** William of Malmesbury was born in c1095 in England to a Norman father and an English mother. He was a monk who wrote *Deeds of the Kings of England*, first published in 1125. William often shows his feelings when he writes.

'William was of normal height, extraordinary, fat, fierce; his forehead was bare of hair; of such great strength of arm that no one else was able to use his bow and arrow. He could use this when his horse was in full gallop; he was majestic whether sitting or standing, but his belly was large. He was of excellent health and never ill. His desire for money was his only bad point. He looked for every opportunity to scrape money together, he cared not how; he would say and do some things and indeed almost anything in the hope of getting money. I have here no excuse whatever to offer.'

▼ **INTERPRETATION B** From *Look and Learn*, a popular 1960s children's magazine. The magazine was designed to appeal to teenagers and was packed with facts and colour stories that covered all sorts of topics, including history. This image was painted by Cecil Doughty, one of the magazine's best-known artists. The artwork title is 'The Conqueror Comes to London'.

TIP: It is always important to read about the author. Think about why he might say positive or negative things about William the Conqueror. Might his parents' background influence what he writes? How?

TIP: How does he describe William? Is he being mainly complimentary – or not?

TIP: This was a time before the Internet. Even colour TV was new – and still rare in some places. So, these vivid, full-colour illustrations would be a sharp contrast to other images children might see at the time.

TIP: This is William. What impression do you get of him?

TIP: How has the artist interpreted the event? What impression do you get from the image?

TIP: What do you already know about William's actions after the Battle of Hastings up to the time he was crowned in London on Christmas Day, 1066? Does this interpretation 'fit' with it?

TIP: Why do you think the artist has included the woman and child?

2 Assessment: Interpretation analysis

Your challenge now is to answer this question about analysing interpretations:

> **Interpretation C** and **Interpretation D** both provide views on William the Conqueror's actions and behaviours. How do they differ and what might explain the differences? (20)

▼ INTERPRETATION C Written by a monk, Simeon of Durham, in *A History of the Kings*, in the early 1100s. Simeon lived in the north of England. He describes what William the Conqueror did in the northern part of England in 1069–1070.

'King William quickly gathered an army, and hurried to Northumberland in great anger, and did not stop for the whole winter from destroying the country and killing the men...

Because of this, there was so great a famine that men, forced by hunger, ate human flesh, that of horses, dogs and cats. It was horrific to see human corpses decaying, swarming with worms, while they rotted with a terrible stench. For no one was left to bury them, for everyone had either been killed by the sword, or by the famine, or had left the country because of the famine.

Meanwhile, the land was deserted. The villages between Durham and York were empty. They became hiding places for wild animals and robbers.'

▼ INTERPRETATION D Adapted from a book written by a monk and historian called Ordericus Vitalis (1075–1142). Born near Shrewsbury, his father was a Norman and his mother was English. At the age of ten he left England to live in Normandy. The book is a history of the Normans, written from a Norman viewpoint, but Ordericus sometimes criticises the Normans. However, he often attacks the English for being immoral or corrupt, and benefiting from Norman rule.

'After his coronation at London, King William ran the country carefully, with justice and mercy. He thought about the profit and honour of London, advantages of the whole nation, and the benefit of the church. His laws were honourable and everyone who demanded justice obtained it. He made his nobles act respectfully and with good judgement. He banned the poor treatment of the conquered Anglo-Saxons, reminding his nobles that everyone was equal under the eyes of God. He said that they must be careful not to cause a revolt among the people they had defeated. He did not set harsh taxes.'

TIP: Is there any reason you can think of why Simeon might have strong opinions about what happened in the north?

TIP: What impression of William do you get from what Simeon has written here?

TIP: How does this sentence make you feel about what has happened? Remember, Simeon has chosen to write it like this, so he is intending for you to feel this.

TIP: It's also important to work out what is actually being said. The author is describing William's actions during the 'Harrying of the North' in 1069–1070.

TIP: Simeon is talking about the area in which he lives. Might a person who lives in the area have a different opinion to someone who has never been to the area? What do you think?

TIP: What impression of William do you get from what Ordericus has written here? Does this differ from **Interpretation C**?

TIP: Does this differ from what you read in **Interpretation C**? In what ways?

TIP: Do you feel this account is supportive or critical of William?

The questions below will help you structure your answer. Use the tips and sentence starters to help you get started.

1   **Think about the content:** What is the content of **Interpretation C** saying? What is the content of **Interpretation D** saying? Make a list of the ways they are different.

Answer the question: What is the main difference between the two interpretations? Can you find any other differences?   (8)

One way that Interpretation C is different from Interpretation D is that C writes... **(You can quote the interpretation if you like.)**	(2)
On the other hand, D writes...	(2)
This means they are different because C focuses more on...	(2)
However, D focuses more on...	(2)

TIP: You can add more than one difference.

2   **Think about the author or artist:** Look at the captions. What can they tell you about *why* the two interpretations might show different opinions about William the Conqueror's actions and behaviours?

Answer the question: Why might there be differences between the opinions of the two writers?   (12)

TIP: People tend to say what they say and think what they think because of their beliefs, background, upbringing and influences. What about the two people here? Can you think of reasons why they might have written what they have written?

One reason the authors have different views is...	(2)
The writer of C is...	(2)
This means...	(3)
However, the writer of D is...	(2)
This means...	(3)

Religious beliefs

Today, there are many different religions in Britain, including Christianity. Although many people consider themselves **Christian**, only around three people in every 100 go to church on a Sunday. Things were very different in medieval Britain, when religion was a much more important part of daily life. So what role did religion play at this time? What did people think about heaven and hell? How important was the role of the local church leader?

Objectives

- Analyse the importance of religion in the Middle Ages.
- Evaluate the role of religion in everyday life.

Medieval religious beliefs

In the Middle Ages almost everyone in Britain believed in God. They believed that heaven and hell were real places – as real as France or Denmark – and where you ended up when you died depended on how you had lived your life. People in medieval Britain followed **Roman Catholic** Christianity. They believed that the Pope, who lived in Rome, had been given authority by God to be the supreme head of the Church on earth. The Pope led all the people who worked for the Church – including bishops, priests and monks.

God's will

People used religion to explain things. At a time when there was limited scientific knowledge about how the world worked, people looked to God for answers. Bad harvests, nasty illnesses and unfortunate accidents were viewed as punishments from God for sins that had been committed. But if you tried to lead a good life and went to church regularly, heaven was the reward that made up for the suffering on earth.

The heart of the community

The biggest building in a village or town would probably be the church, unless there was a castle or cathedral. Churches were very noisy because they were used as meeting spaces. People didn't want to spend too much time in their tiny homes, with smoky fires and smelly animals! Children's games, plays and summer fairs were sometimes held in the churchyard. A church would have been a lively place, full of laughter, conversation and activity.

▼ **A** This diagram shows the functions of a village church and its priest.

Performing games, plays and fairs

Bible teaching

A meeting place

Marriage

Praying

Giving local news

Baptising a child

Burying the dead

The priest

Most churches were run by the local priest, a man specially trained to perform religious duties. The priest would be able to speak and read Latin because the Bible was written, and church services were held, in this language. He played a very important role in medieval society, and was part of most people's lives from their birth to their death. He was an adviser and a local leader. During confession the priest would listen while villagers told him of the sinful things they had done. At services he would tell villagers that they would go to heaven if they were good but to hell if they were bad. There were pictures, statues, stained glass and paintings to remind people of this. Huge **doom paintings** showed angels welcoming good people into heaven and devils pulling murderers into pots of boiling oil in hell.

Pay up!

The Church was a major landowner in England (see page 42) and peasants had to work on Church lands for free. Also, villagers had to give the local church one tenth (or a **tithe**) of all the food they grew. As you can imagine, the villagers were often unhappy about this, especially if the harvest was bad. In addition, when someone died, the priest received their second-best working animal! For the peasants, worshipping God could be an expensive business.

> ### Fact ✓
>
> When 'church' is written with a lower case 'c', it refers to the religious building in the town or village. When written with an upper case 'C' (as in 'Church'), it refers to the whole religious organisation, including the belief system, the traditions and the Church leaders.

▼ **SOURCE B** A doom painting (c1200) from a medieval church in Chaldon, Surrey, thought to have been painted by a travelling monk. Bottom left: murderers are boiled in a large pot, demons pull people from a ladder and a woman who fed her pets well and ignored starving people is bitten by a wolf. Bottom right: tradesmen are forced to cross a bridge of spikes and a money lender is sitting in flames.

Key Words

Christian
doom painting
Roman Catholic
tithe

Over to You .ıll

1 a What was a tithe?

   b Villagers had to give the local church one tenth of their harvest. What is this as a percentage?

2 Look at **Source B**.

   a In your own words, explain what is happening in the painting.

   b Why was it important to have paintings like this on church walls in the Middle Ages? Hint: Think about the language used by the priest in his services.

   c What was the purpose of a doom painting? How do you think these kinds of paintings might affect the way someone behaved after leaving church?

   d Draw your own doom painting. Remember, it has to show people what will happen to them in heaven and hell, and must not include any words.

Consequence

1 List three different roles of a medieval priest.

2 Explain the following:
   • the importance of religion in the Middle Ages
   • the importance of a priest in a medieval town or village.

3.2A A day in the lives of monks and nuns

Some medieval men and women devoted their whole lives to the service and worship of God. They left their families and largely cut themselves off from the outside world. The men who chose to do this were called **monks**, and the women were called **nuns**. Monks usually lived in monasteries (also known as abbeys). Nuns lived in nunneries (convents). Why did these men and women do this? What was their life like? What role did monasteries and nunneries play in the medieval world?

Objectives

- Explain why some men and women became monks and nuns.
- Examine daily life for a monk.
- Assess the importance of monasteries and nunneries in medieval society.

Why become a monk or nun?

There many different reasons why someone might choose to become a monk or a nun. However, the most important were:

- **They wanted to get to heaven** – remember, people were convinced that heaven and hell were real places and the best way to get to heaven was to lead a religious life and obey Christian teachings.

- **They wanted to lead peaceful, safe lives** – monasteries and convents were usually built away from towns and villages. This allowed monks and nuns to live a quiet life, away from a noisy and sometimes dangerous world.

- **They wanted an education within a fine building with a well-stocked library** – some monasteries and nunneries could afford this because they owned land nearby and sold wool from their sheep and wood from their forests. Also, rich people often paid monks and nuns to pray for them. This also allowed them to eat good food – in fact, some monasteries and nunneries employed people to cook their food, wash their clothes and clean the buildings. Some paid actors and musicians to entertain them.

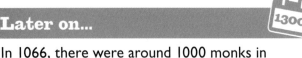

Later on...

In 1066, there were around 1000 monks in England – but this number quickly rose after William's invasion. By 1300, there were over 12,000 monks in England.

When someone decided to become a monk or a nun they made three promises or vows:

- **Poverty** – individual monks and nuns did not own personal property.

- **Chastity** – they could not marry.

- **Obedience** – they had to obey the person in charge (an **abbot** or an abbess) and follow strict rules.

Different types of monks and nuns

There were different groups of monks and nuns, known as **orders**. Each order had its own rules, usually made by the person who founded it. In England, the largest order were the Benedictines, who followed the rules of St Benedict, an Italian monk who lived in the sixth century. Benedictine monks were known for their long, black gowns (or 'habits') with wide sleeves and a black hood. Often monks would shave the top part of their head as a sign of their religious devotion (known as a 'tonsure'). The Carthusian Order was very strict. Carthusian monks lived alone in basic rooms and were rarely allowed to speak.

Nuns and monks – daily life

No matter which order a monk or nun belonged to, their life was not easy. They had to pray often – day and night. The rest of their day was spent studying, helping the sick, teaching in the community, growing crops, writing religious or historical books – and sleeping.

Boys and girls could enter a monastery or nunnery from the age of seven. The story opposite describes a typical day in the life of a young monk, known as a 'novice'.

The diary of Novice Arthur aged 13 ¾

Brother Gerald woke me up at 2am for an hour of prayers. It was so cold.

I was up again at 6 for more prayers. We then ate our breakfast of bread and ale in the refectory. Sometimes we have porridge. No talking when we're eating... you're beaten or whipped if you do!

At 8am we met in the chapter house to sort out our work for the day. There's no choice, we are just told what to do. After a walk in the cloisters I went off to the scriptorium. I cut and smooth animal skins to make vellum. Sometimes I copy out books and decorate the letters at the start of paragraphs. We prayed again at 11am and at midday ate our lunch of soup, bread and ale.

After more prayers I tended the fields. We help the locals by occasionally giving them food or medical care. Some monks know how to make medicines from herbs. When we are ill we go to the infirmary and are looked after by these clever monks. We also teach local children to read and collect clothing and money for the very poor.

We prayed again at 6 before supper... and again afterwards. I've just polished my tonsure with a piece of stone to keep it free of hair. It's 9pm now and I'm off to bed in my dormitory. I have to be awake again at 2am...

▼ **SOURCE A** A photograph of Fountains Abbey today.

Key Words   abbot   chapter house   cloister   dormitory   infirmary   monk   nun   order   refectory   scriptorium   vellum

▼ **SOURCE B** A picture of nuns looking after the sick in their nunnery. The word 'hospital' comes from the Latin word 'hospitalis', which means 'a place for guests'.

Over to You

1 Explain why so many men and women chose to lead the hard life of a monk or nun in the Middle Ages.

2 Read Novice Arthur's diary. Answer these questions.

   a When did Arthur get up for prayer?

   b When did he go to sleep at night?

3 a In what ways did monks in monasteries try to help local people?

   b Why do you think they did this?

4 Look at **Source B** and read the caption. Describe what is going on in the image. Think about:
   * what the older nuns are showing the younger nuns
   * what the nun on the right is doing to the sick man
   * how the sick are treated.

The importance of monasteries and nunneries

Monasteries and nunneries not only provided a place where monks and nuns could dedicate themselves to God. They also played an important role in medieval life.

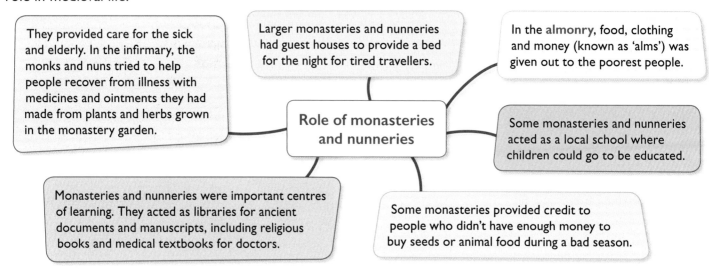

They provided care for the sick and elderly. In the infirmary, the monks and nuns tried to help people recover from illness with medicines and ointments they had made from plants and herbs grown in the monastery garden.

Larger monasteries and nunneries had guest houses to provide a bed for the night for tired travellers.

In the almonry, food, clothing and money (known as 'alms') was given out to the poorest people.

Role of monasteries and nunneries

Some monasteries and nunneries acted as a local school where children could go to be educated.

Monasteries and nunneries were important centres of learning. They acted as libraries for ancient documents and manuscripts, including religious books and medical textbooks for doctors.

Some monasteries provided credit to people who didn't have enough money to buy seeds or animal food during a bad season.

▼ **C** A plan of Fountains Abbey in Yorkshire, built in 1132. The river flows from west to east and took the dirty water away from the toilets. Monasteries and nunneries were noted for their cleanliness.

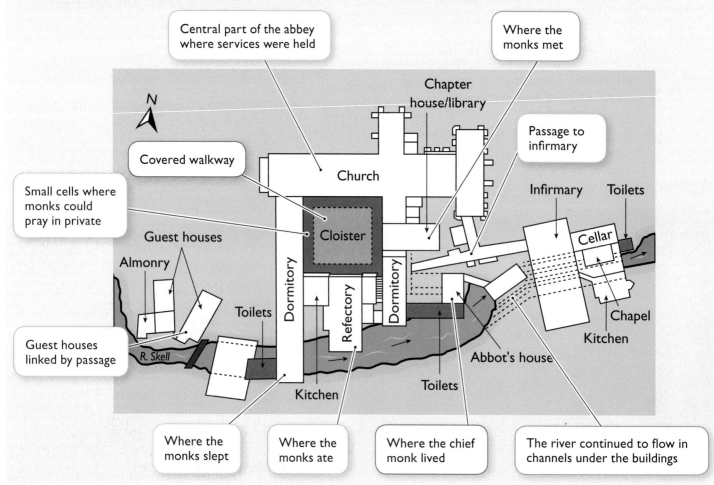

Central part of the abbey where services were held

Where the monks met

Covered walkway

Small cells where monks could pray in private

Guest houses

Almonry

Guest houses linked by passage

Where the monks slept

Where the monks ate

Where the chief monk lived

The river continued to flow in channels under the buildings

Illuminating work

Monks and nuns made sure that knowledge was preserved for future generations by making copies of books by hand. Sometimes monks wrote their own books called chronicles. Also, both monks and nuns often **illuminated** books with tiny, beautiful paintings around the edges of the page and on capital letters.

▼ **SOURCE D** This page is from an illuminated Bible from 1407, on display at Malmesbury Abbey, Wiltshire.

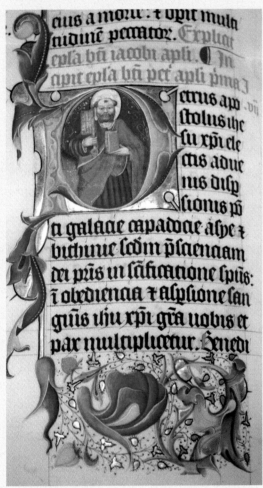

▼ **SOURCE E** Adapted from the rules of St Benedict, who lived from c480 to 547.

'Care for the sick stands before everything. You must help them as Christ would... Also, you must be patient with them and you will gain greater merit with God. The sick should not be neglected at any single point.'

Key Words almonry   illuminated

▼ **SOURCE F** Written by William of Malmesbury in his book *Deeds of the Kings of England* (c1140). He is describing the Cistercian Order. Fountains Abbey (see **Source A** on page 55) was a Cistercian abbey.

'To be a member of the Cistercian order... is now believed to be the surest way to heaven... Certainly many of their regulations seem severe... they wear nothing made with furs or linen... They have two tunics with hoods, but no other clothes... they do not take more than one meal a day, except on Sunday. They never leave the cloister except for work, nor do they ever speak, except to the abbot or prior while they look after the stranger and the sick.'

Over to You

1 Outline three ways in which monasteries and nunneries played a role in the local community.

2 Look at **C**, the diagram of Fountains Abbey. Name the place where a monk:
   a slept
   b looked after the sick
   c prayed in private
   d ate
   e gave out alms
   f met with other monks
   g went with other monks to take part in large services.

Source Analysis

1 Read **Source E** and the caption.
   a What does St Benedict say about caring for the sick?
   b Does **Source B** (on page 55) show that these nuns are following St Benedict's instructions?

2 Read **Source F** and the caption.
   a Describe how these monks live their lives.
   b What part of the source tells us why the monks followed such strict rules?

3 What can be learned from **Sources E** and **F** about life in a medieval monastery or nunnery?

What were the Wars of the Cross?

Most people in medieval Europe had one thing in common – their religion. They were Christians (specifically Roman Catholics) and their religious leader on earth was the Pope. For Christians, Jerusalem was the most important city in the world. Jesus often visited there, and was buried there. But Jerusalem was important to other religions too. What happened to make Christians go to this place to fight the 'Wars of the Cross'?

Objectives

- Explain why Jerusalem was an important city for Christians, Muslims and Jews.
- Recall why the Pope ordered the Crusades.

In the Middle Ages, the whole area around Jerusalem was known as the Holy Land – a term used to refer to the area where important events in Jesus' life occurred (see **A**). Religious travellers – called **pilgrims** – made the long journey there from all parts of Europe.

Fact ✓

A journey of religious importance (a **pilgrimage**) is common in many religions. While many Christians visit Jerusalem and Bethlehem – cities linked to the life of Jesus – many Hindus gather to bathe in the sacred River Ganges which flows through India and Bangladesh. Sikhs visit the Golden Temple in the city of Amritsar in India, and Muslims try to travel to the holy city of Mecca at least once in their lifetime.

▼ **MAP A** Europe, North Africa, the Middle East and the Holy Land.

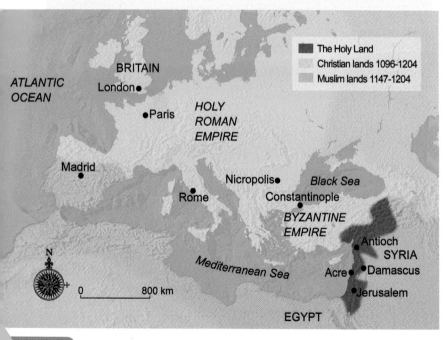

Not just Christians

The Holy Land (in the Middle East) was, and still is, important for many religions. According to Jewish tradition, all of creation began in Jerusalem. Other key events in Jewish history happened there too. Jerusalem is also a holy site for Muslims because their leader, the Prophet Muhammad, is said to have visited the city and ascended from there to heaven. So, for Christians, Jews and Muslims, Jerusalem was and still is a sacred place, with important shrines and buildings that relate to these religions (see **B**).

As Jerusalem is a very important city to many cultures and religions, it has been conquered and controlled by many different **empires** throughout its history. By the early Middle Ages, the Arab Muslims controlled Jerusalem. They were tolerant of other religions and allowed Jews and Christians to visit and live in the Holy Land, but in 1071, all that began to change.

All change

In 1071, a warrior tribe called the Seljuk Turks took over Jerusalem and the Holy Land. They conquered Syria and other parts of the Middle East too. The Seljuk Turks were Muslims, but believed that only Muslims should set foot in the Holy Land. Christians who returned home from the Holy Land told stories about how they had been treated badly by the Seljuk Turks. Some pilgrims were even killed. Christians in nearby lands, such as those living in the Christian city of Constantinople, felt threatened by the Seljuk Turks.

▼ **MAP B** Jerusalem is a sacred city for three different religions. People still struggle for control of Jerusalem to this day. In the Middle Ages it was very important for members of all three religions to secure safe access to their sacred sites.

The Church of the Holy Sepulchre is built on the site where Christians believe that Jesus was buried.

The Wailing or Western Wall is the last remaining part of King Herod's temple and is a site of pilgrimage for Jews.

The Dome of the Rock mosque is built on the site where Muslims believe the Prophet Muhammad rose up and visited heaven.

Key Words

Crusades empire
infidel pilgrim
pilgrimage Saracen

A religious war

In 1095, the Emperor Alexius I of Byzantium (a Christian empire with Constantinople as its capital) wrote to the Pope asking for help. He feared the Seljuk Turks would attack him and wanted Christians from Western Europe to come and defend him. The Pope, Urban II, decided to help. He urged all Christian monarchs, lords, soldiers and ordinary people to go and fight the Seljuk Turks. Thousands of people decided to go. They sewed crosses, the Christian sign, onto their clothes and flags. These journeys became known as the **Crusades**, which means 'Wars of the Cross'. Between 1096 and 1250 there were many Crusades to the Holy Lands.

Over to You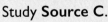

1 Explain why Jerusalem is an important city for:
  a Muslims
  b Christians
  c Jews

▼ **SOURCE C** Part of the speech made by Pope Urban II in 1095 to Church leaders and nobles in France. **Saracen** is a word for Muslims in the Middle Ages. **Infidel** was a word used to describe non-Christians.

'Brothers, I speak as a messenger from God... Your fellow Christians in the east desperately need help. The Saracens have attacked them and have pushed deep into Christian land. They are killing great numbers of Christians. They are destroying churches and land. In the name of God, I beg you all to drive out these foul creatures.

Your own land has too many people. There is not much wealth here. The soil hardly grows enough to support you. Set out for Jerusalem. Take that land from the wicked infidel and make it your own.

If you die on the journey or if you are killed in a battle against these Saracens all your sins will be forgiven at once. God Himself has given me the power to tell you this.'

Source Analysis

Study **Source C**.

1 Read the caption. Who said this? Describe where he was and who he was speaking to.

2 Why was this man important to Christians?

3 Why do you think he mentioned God so often?

4 Read the content. How does the author try to encourage people to go on the Crusades? Make a list of ways.

5 How useful is this source to a historian studying the reasons why people decided to go on the Crusades?

Meet Cuthbert, the second oldest son of a rich and powerful English landowner. Cuthbert is a knight who is about to leave England and travel to the Holy Land with his fellow Crusaders. On his journey through Europe he'll be joined by thousands of people including fellow knights, lords, peasants, kings, women and even children. But what are their reasons for going? Which route would they take? How long would it take to get there?

Objectives

- Categorise reasons why people went on Crusades.
- Evaluate several different routes to the Holy Land.

a The Crusades were a chance for a knight to become a hero. One French knight wrote to his wife: 'It breaks my heart to leave you but in the Holy Land I will win praise and your true love.'

b Many people went because they felt it was their duty to obey the Pope, who had urged people to go.

c Some felt it was their Christian duty to make sure that fellow Christian pilgrims could travel to the Holy Land in peace, without being attacked by Seljuk Turks.

d Some people went to travel around the world and thought of it as a great adventure.

e The Holy Land was rich with luxuries such as gold, spices and perfumes. One knight wrote in 1098: 'My dear wife, I now have twice as much silver and gold as when I set off.'

f The Pope promised to forgive all a person's sins if they went on a Crusade.

g Some kings promised to reward fellow Crusaders with lands and titles when they returned.

h Some younger knights went to try to get land overseas. This was tempting for people who, like Cuthbert, were not an eldest son, and so wouldn't **inherit** land.

i Some kings encouraged violent and aggressive knights to go on Crusades to get them out of the country.

j Crusaders paid no taxes while they were away and any money they owed didn't have to be paid until they returned.

Tunic, usually white with a red cross sewn on it

Heavy metal helmet (weighing up to 4kg)

Crusader's horse

Wooden shield covered with leather

Chain mail suit covering the whole body

Sword, up to 1.2 metres long

Meanwhile...
From 1095

During the time of the Crusades, there was religious hatred in some parts of Europe. People were often intolerant of others, especially if they didn't share religious beliefs. In 1095 and 1096, there were attacks on Jews in France and Germany. And in 1290, all Jews were expelled from England by King Edward I.

So how would Cuthbert and his Crusaders get there?

Key Words   inherit

The journey to the Holy Land was long and difficult. Travelling across land took a long time, and there were bandits and robbers to contend with. Travelling by boat was quicker, but there was the danger of shipwreck or pirates. **A** shows some possible choices for Cuthbert and his Crusaders – but which one should he choose?

▼ **MAP A** This map shows four possible routes (A–D) to the Holy Land. Land routes were long and dangerous – Crusaders could travel about 16km (10 miles) a day. Sea routes were faster, but also dangerous – Crusaders could travel about 160km (100 miles) per day.

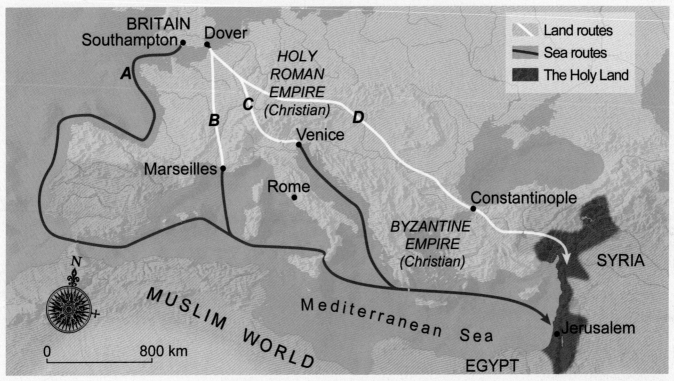

Over to You .ıl

1 Look at **Map A**. What are the advantages and disadvantages of:

   a sea routes   b land routes?

2 Imagine you are Cuthbert. You have four possible routes to the Holy Land (routes A to D). Work out how long each journey will take using the scale on the map (this will be an approximate time).

   a Which route would take the longest?

   b Which route would take the least time?

   c So which route should you choose? Give your reasons.

3 Explain why people went on Crusades.

Cause and Consequence ⭐

In history, there are often lots of different reasons why people do things. As you have seen, people had different reasons for taking part in the Crusades. You could put the reasons into categories, such as religious or financial reasons, for example.

1 Look at the ten different reasons (labelled **a** to **j** on page 60) why people decided to go on a Crusade. Try to sum up each of the reasons in only *three* words.

2 Place each of the ten reasons (which should now be summarised in three words or fewer) in one of the following categories:

    Religion   Money   Power   Other

3 Has money been the main reason for people joining the Crusades? Explain your answer with reference to money and to other reasons.

The age of the Crusades lasted for 300 years. Time and again, Christian armies set off from Europe to fight for control of Jerusalem and the Holy Land. There were victories and defeats on both sides. Who had gained control of the Holy Land by the end of the Crusades?

Objectives

- Define the period in history known as 'the Crusades'.
- Construct a timeline of key events.

1. First Crusade, 1096–1099

An army of peasants, led by French priest Peter the Hermit, was the first group to set off for the Holy Land. Almost all were killed by Turkish forces. Then, an army of knights followed, led by a group of nobles including Robert of Normandy (eldest son of William the Conqueror). It has been estimated that around 50,000 people went on this Crusade. After many bloody and brutal battles (the Crusaders tortured and killed up to 10,000 civilians, including children), they captured Jerusalem in 1099. It remained in Christian hands for the next 88 years. The Crusaders then swept through the Holy Land creating Christian kingdoms and building castles.

3. Third Crusade, 1189–1192

In 1174, one man became leader of all the Muslims from Egypt to Syria. His name was Salah ad-Din (known to the Crusaders as 'Saladin'). In 1187, his army recaptured Jerusalem and took other Christian-controlled land. In 1189, the Crusaders captured the town of Acre, but quarrelled among themselves and failed to capture Jerusalem. Richard and Saladin respected each other greatly, despite being on different sides of the conflict. Eventually, in September 1192, they made a deal – Jerusalem remained in Muslim hands, but Christians were allowed to visit without harm.

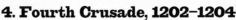

1096–1099   **1145–1149**   **1189–1192**   **1202–1204**

2. Second Crusade, 1145–1149

Till now, Muslim armies had not fought as a united force, which made it easier for the Crusaders to beat them. But in 1144, the Muslims began to unite – and they soon started to take back land. In response, King Louis VII of France set off to regain the land, but was heavily defeated. However, the Crusaders still held onto Jerusalem and large areas of the Holy Land.

4. Fourth Crusade, 1202–1204

Pope Innocent III asked all Christians to capture Jerusalem once again. But the Crusaders never reached the Holy Land because different groups fell out with each other on the way. In the end, Christians fought other Christians.

▼ **SOURCE A** Adapted from a chronicle of Richard I, written by an English monk in London in the early 1200s. A 'persecutor' is a person who treats others cruelly and unfairly.

'I will tell you about Saladin, this great persecutor of Christianity... He devoted much of his time to taverns [drinking] and gaming. When he became ruler he took over surrounding countries either by force or trickery. This greedy, cruel leader, not satisfied with these possessions, concentrated all of his efforts on seizing the Holy Land.'

▼ **INTERPRETATION B** Painting (1400s) of Crusaders in Jerusalem in 1099, created by a Christian French lord who had not been on the Crusades.

Key Words   civilian

1 a Put these dates in chronological order and explain what happened in each year.

1202   1099   1096   1145   1192   1396
1144   1212   1174   1189   1187

2 Look at **Interpretation B**.

a What are the attackers doing?

b What impression does this give of Crusaders and their reasons for going on a Crusade?

c This interpretation wasn't painted until the 1400s, but it shows an attack in 1099. Does this mean it may not be useful to a historian?

3 Read **Sources A** and **C**.

a Write a sentence each to describe what the writers of **Source A** and **Source C** thought about Saladin.

b Suggest reasons why they give different opinions.

c Why do different opinions sometimes make the study of history so challenging?

5. Children's Crusade, 1212

Thousands of young people set off to recapture Jerusalem. Many died from hunger and exhaustion on the way. Others returned home, but thousands were kidnapped and sold as slaves.

6. Fifth, Sixth and Seventh Crusades, 1217–1250

None of these Crusades repeated the success of the First Crusade and recaptured Jerusalem.

1212   **1217–1250**   **1396**

7. Crusade of Nicopolis, 1396

At the Battle of Nicopolis (in modern-day Bulgaria), an army of French, Hungarian and German knights was defeated. This is sometimes called 'the Last Crusade'.

▼ **SOURCE C** Adapted from a description of Saladin, written at the beginning of the thirteenth century by Baha ad-Din ibn Shaddad, a Muslim historian who knew him.

'Saladin was so determined to fight the Holy War that he thought of nothing else... He also made sure that his men were fed and cared for properly when they were ill. So pure was his character that he would not allow a bad word to be said about anyone, preferring to only hear the good points.'

Cause and Consequence

1 What is meant by the term 'turning point'?

2 Do you think any of the important dates you have looked at could be called 'turning points'? Explain your choices.

3 'The recapture of Jerusalem by Saladin's army in 1187 was a turning point in the Crusades.' How far do you agree? Explain your answer.

What was the impact of the Crusades?

Muslims had been in contact with Christians from Europe long before the Crusades began. They had conquered Spain in the seventh century and had traded with some of their European neighbours for centuries. However, Christians from some northern European countries such as France and England had not had much contact with the Islamic world. They had very little respect for Muslims at first and thought they were uncivilised. They were in for a surprise. In times of peace, in between the fighting, the two sides mixed. Which side seemed to learn the most?

Objectives

- Examine how life in Europe changed after contact with the Muslim world.

- Assess which change was most important and why.

Look carefully at the diagram below and think about which side gained the most knowledge.

New products

Crusaders brought back lots of things from the Holy Land. These included foods such as lemons, melons, apricots, sugar, syrup and spices like nutmeg and cinnamon. Cotton, silk and slippers changed the way people dressed. Muslims used pigeons to carry messages too – something that was copied by Europeans.

Technology

Muslims thought that study and education were very important. As a result, they had made advances in science and technology that amazed the Christians. These included mirrors, the magnifying glass, and a tool that could measure the distance between stars. They had also made advances in sailing and had improved surgical tools. Muslims had better maps and used compasses to help them navigate – which meant that European sailors could use these ideas to explore the world and find new opportunities to trade.

Knowledge

Muslims used the numbers 1, 2, 3, 4 and so on. When Europeans saw this, and learned how these numbers worked, they realised it was more straightforward than their system of Roman numerals (I, II, III, IV...). Arabic numbers made complicated mathematics far easier and the Crusaders brought the system back to Europe. The Crusaders learned the game of chess from the Muslims. Also, books from Ancient Greeks, which had been lost in Europe, had been translated by the Muslims. This meant that the ideas of Plato and Socrates could be rediscovered by Europeans – this would have a major impact on European arts and culture for centuries after. Many Muslims also had greater knowledge of diseases and medical treatment. In many Muslim countries there were famous medical schools and highly skilled doctors and surgeons.

Warfare

Muslims used archers in their armies. European armies, especially the English, started to use archers much more. They also copied Muslim castle designs and a weapon used to attack castles called a **trebuchet**, which was like a huge catapult.

▼ **SOURCE A** Usamah ibn Munqidh writing in 1175 about an encounter with Christians while he went to pray. 'Franks' refers to the Crusaders.

'When I used to enter the Aqsa Mosque, which was occupied by the Christian Crusaders who were my friends, they would leave so that I might pray in it. One day as I began to pray one of the Franks rushed on me, and turned my face eastward. "This is the way thou should pray!" he said. A group of Christians seized him. They apologised to me saying: "This is a stranger who has only recently arrived from the land of the Franks. He has never before seen anyone praying except eastward."'

▼ **SOURCE B** Written by a French priest, Fulcher of Chartres, in c1120. He went on the First Crusade with a Norman lord. Fulcher lived in the Holy Land.

'We who were Westerners find ourselves transformed into inhabitants of the East. The Italian or Frenchman of yesterday has become a citizen of the Holy Land. We have already forgotten our native land. Some men have already taken Syrian women as wives. Races utterly unlike each other live together in trust.'

▼ **SOURCE C** A Muslim medieval poet, writing in his autobiography in 1175 about the cruel way some Christians held trials to find out if someone was guilty or not.

'A man was accused of a crime, so they dropped him in water. Their idea was that if he was innocent he would sink, but if he was guilty he would float. This man did his best to sink but he could not do it. He was found guilty and they pierced his eyes with red hot metal – may Allah's curse be upon them.'

Views on the Crusades

At the time, the Crusaders were viewed as Christian heroes. However, some modern historians and writers in the Western world view the Crusades as an attempt by Christians to replace Islam with Christianity.

Muslim writers in the Middle Ages were obviously critical of the Crusades and saw them as an attempt to build a Christian empire in the Middle East. Many even saw the Crusades as unimportant, because the Holy Land stayed under Muslim rule.

Even today, some people have strong feelings about the Crusades. Some think that they have affected how many Muslims view Europeans.

▼ **INTERPRETATION D** Adapted from a speech made in 2015 by US President Barack Obama. His speech was about politics and faith.

'Remember that during the Crusades, people committed terrible deeds in the name of Christ.'

▼ **INTERPRETATION E** Akbar S. Ahmed, a Pakistani author and writer for the BBC, wrote about the Crusades in 1995.

'The memory of the Crusades lingers in the Middle East and colours Muslim perceptions of Europe. It is the memory of an aggressive, backward and fanatical Europe.'

Over to You

1 Look at the diagram on page 64.
   a List all the things that the Crusaders learned from fighting Muslims.
   b Now list all the things the Crusaders learned from living peacefully and talking to the Muslims.
   c Which list is longer – fighting or talking? Explain why you think this is.

2 Explain two consequences of the Crusades.

Source Analysis

Read **Sources A**, **B** and **C**.

1 For each source, explain in your own words the point that the writer is trying to make.

2 What can be learned from **Sources B** and **C** about the impact of the Crusades?

⟳ Quick Knowledge Quiz

Choose the correct answer from the three options:

1   Who is the supreme head of the Christian Roman Catholic Church on earth?
    a   the King of England
    b   the Pope
    c   the Archbishop of Canterbury

2   Villagers had to give the local church one tenth of all the food they grew. What was the payment called?
    a   tithe
    b   feudal system
    c   Murdrum fine

3   All medieval priests would be able to speak and read which language?
    a   Norwegian
    b   Latin
    c   German

4   What name was given to the large images in churches that showed angels welcoming good people into heaven and devils punishing sinners?
    a   order images
    b   doom paintings
    c   illuminated scenes

5   When someone decided to become a monk or a nun, they made three promises (or vows). They were poverty, chastity and…?
    a   obedience
    b   gluttony
    c   envy

6   In England, which of the following was the largest order of monks?
    a   Carthusians
    b   Saints
    c   Benedictines

7   A journey of religious importance, often to a sacred place, is known as what?
    a   a pilgrimage
    b   a sacrilege
    c   a privilege

8   The 1095 speech by which pope urged Christians to go to the Holy Land and fight the Seljuk Turks?
    a   Pope Clement VII
    b   Pope Benedict IX
    c   Pope Urban II

9   Who became leader of a large Muslim army in 1174?
    a   Richard I
    b   Saladin
    c   Jerusalem

10 What word did most Muslims use to describe Christian crusaders?
    a   Franks
    b   Edwards
    c   Germans

Literacy Focus

Writing in detail

When writing answers, it is very important that you structure your paragraphs properly and support what you write with evidence. One way of doing this is to use the PEEL paragraph writing approach:

> Your point should include:
>
> **P**oint: Make your point.
>
> **E**vidence: Back your point up with supporting evidence and examples.
>
> **E**xplanation: Explain and elaborate how the evidence supports your point.
>
> **L**ink: Link it to the following point in the next paragraph or link it back to the question.

1 The paragraph below is the beginning of an answer to the question:
Explain two reasons why people went on Crusades.

The PEEL paragraph writing approach is used to explain one of the reasons – religious reasons. Use the approach to explain the other reason – to make money for themselves.

Point: Here, the two reasons are *pointed* out in the first sentence.

Evidence: Religion has been identified as one of the reasons – now the answer is going on to back up the point with evidence.

> Two of the main reasons why people went on Crusades were for religious reasons and to make money for themselves. Firstly, many people went because they felt it was their duty to obey the Pope, Urban II, who had urged people to go. In 1095, Pope Urban II urged all Christian monarchs, lords, soldiers, and ordinary people to go and fight the Muslim Seljuk Turks in the Holy Land, whom he had heard were threatening Christians there. He promised that anyone who died fighting would go straight to heaven. Thousands of people decided to go. They sewed crosses, the sign of Christianity, onto their clothes and flags. These journeys became known as the Crusades, which means 'Wars of the Cross'. Between 1096 and 1250 there were many Crusades to the Holy Lands and the defence of Christianity was one of the main reasons for going.
>
> Secondly, some people went on Crusades....

Explanation: Detail is added here, which supports the point that people went on Crusades for religious reasons.

Link: This sentence links back to the question.

Now it's time for you to complete the answer about the second reason – that people went on Crusades to make money for themselves. Use pages 60 to 61 to help you.

History skill: Significance

How to analyse whether something is significant in History

In History, you will study all sorts of events and people from different periods. Sometimes you will be asked whether an event, a development or a person is **significant**. When you see this word, don't think that this simply means 'important' – it is more than that!

The spider diagram shows you how to judge how significant something is.

SIG

Special at the time
- Was the event/person/ development important at the time?
- What was its impact? How did it affect people?

Important changes
- Was the event/person/ development important in the long term? Were there long-lasting effects?
- Did it cause important changes?

Going on today
- Is the event/person/ development still important? Is it making an impact today?
- Are they still relevant in today's world?

For this assessment, we are going to think about the significance of the Crusades.

1 **What do you know?** Make a list of facts that you know about the event/person/development.

> **TIP:** What impact did the Crusades have on the Holy Land? (Look at page 62 of this book to help you.)
>
> You might also think about the impact on the people who went on the Crusades – how did life change for them?
>
> Remember to think about the people back home in Europe. Did the Crusades make any impact on them? (Look at pages 64–65.)

2 **Impact at the time:** Consider the impact of the event/person/ development at the time it happened. Make notes on how it changed things.

3 **Long-term impact:** Now think about how the event/person/ development might have had an impact in the longer term. Did some of the changes last for much longer than the time of the event/person/development?

> **TIP:** There are lots of good examples of new products that were brought back from the Crusades and became part of everyday life long after. See pages 64–65 for some of these.

4 **Still significant today?** You should also think about our world today. Does the event/person/development still make an impact in the modern world? Remember that the significance of a person, event or development can *change* over time. So, sometimes a lot of time might pass before it is seen as significant. Equally, something that was significant at the time may lose its significance as a result of later developments or new knowledge. As a result it may no longer influence our thinking or our world today.

> **TIP:** The 'Views on the Crusades' paragraph and **Interpretation E** on page 65 will help you consider this.

5 **Conclude:** It is also important to conclude your answer. In other words, you will need to sum up your thoughts on the significance of the topic you have been asked to consider – in this case, the Crusades.

Assessment: Significance

Now, after considering all the points on the previous page, try putting them into practice with this question:

 Explain the significance of the Crusades for Britain. (20)

The steps below will help you structure your answer. Use the example sentence starters to help you begin each point.

1 **What do you know?** Start with a brief explanation of what the Crusades were when they took place, and what happened at the time.

The Crusades were a time when...	(3)
During the Crusades...	(3)

2 **Impact at the time:** Next, focus on what impact the Crusades had on the Holy Land at the time? How was Jerusalem affected? How did life change for those on the Crusades? And how did life change for those back home in Europe?

At the time...	(3)

3 **Long-term impact:** Did some of the new products, knowledge and technology last for longer than the time of the Crusades? In other words, did it make a *long-term impact*?

In the longer term...	(3)

4 **Still significant today?** Are the Crusades still relevant in the modern world?

Today, the Crusades...	(3)

5 **Conclude:** It's important to write a concluding paragraph that sums up what you think. Here, you are being asked to judge the significance of the Crusades and offer an opinion. Are they very significant? Did they make a major impact at the time – and do they still play a part in society today?

In conclusion...	(5)

The earliest castles were built of wood – and built quickly. They were intended to keep out enemies and to keep people, horses and treasures safe. They dominated river crossings, roadways and towns and were used as a base from which the Normans could control the local population. So how and why did castle-building change?

Objectives

- Define key terms in the development of castles.
- Examine how and why castles changed after 1066.

The early wooden castles were built by the Normans after their victory at the Battle of Hastings. They were good for reminding the English people that they had been beaten – but they were weak against attacks. The wooden walls could easily be chopped or burnt down, or just climbed over with ladders. So by 1070, a few lords with the time, money and a suitable location began to build their castles in stone (see **A**).

▼ **A** An early stone castle. The massive square keep towered over the countryside, striking fear or respect into the hearts of those who saw it.

A wide, deep ditch called a moat made it difficult for attackers to get close to the castle walls.

Stone **keeps** replaced wooden ones. They were usually much larger than wooden ones and contained most of the important rooms – the lord's personal rooms, the kitchen, chapel, main hall, guardroom and dungeon.

The curtain wall was often wide enough for soldiers to walk along.

A well-guarded drawbridge.

Battlements provided a barrier for soldiers to hide behind when they fired arrows.

The bailey contained storerooms, stables and rooms for soldiers.

Thick, tall, stone walls (called **curtain walls**) replaced the weaker wooden ones.

Don't keep the keep!

If a castle's outer walls were strong, sometimes the lord didn't even bother with a keep. They were dark, noisy, smoky places, and lacked privacy, so sometimes a lord built all the rooms and buildings he needed within the bailey itself. He would then strengthen the curtain wall with extra towers and build an especially tough entrance or gatehouse called a **barbican** (see **B**).

▼ **B** In this castle there is no great tower or keep. Instead, the main rooms are built up against the thick, strong outer walls.

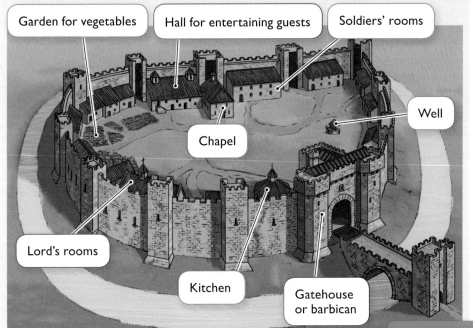

Garden for vegetables

Hall for entertaining guests

Soldiers' rooms

Chapel

Well

Lord's rooms

Kitchen

Gatehouse or barbican

Key Words

barbican   battlements
curtain wall   keep   portcullis

Later on...   TODAY

In 1070, William the Conqueror started building Windsor Castle, which today is an official residence of Britain's kings and queens. It is the oldest and largest inhabited castle in the world.

▼ **C** A gatehouse or barbican.

Defending soldiers

Defending soldiers would sometimes pour boiling water, tar or lead down holes in the roof of the barbican known as 'murder holes'. Heavy stones could also be dropped onto attackers, while archers shot arrows at intruders through slits in the wall.

Hot water

Portcullis (gate) made from iron

Attackers

Two wall towers, containing guardrooms for the soldiers

Over to You

1 Look at the five statements below. Three are correct, while two have mistakes in them. Copy out all five sentences, making sure you correct the two that are wrong.
   - The first Norman castles were built on King William's orders.
   - The earliest castles were built of stone.
   - A motte was a deep ditch that surrounded a castle.
   - The stone wall built around a castle was called a curtain wall.
   - After 1070, some wooden castles were replaced with stone ones.

2 Match up the features on the left with the correct definitions on the right.

   - motte
   - bailey
   - keep
   - moat
   - barbican
   - portcullis
   - battlement

   - a wall with gaps along the top for firing through
   - the strongest and tallest place in the castle
   - a deep ditch around the castle
   - an extra-strong gatehouse
   - a courtyard in which the buildings stood
   - a mound of earth upon which the keep was built
   - a tough iron gate

Mission impossible

By the early 1200s, it was incredibly difficult for an attacker to break into a stone castle with thick walls. However, it didn't take long before attackers came up with new ideas. It was discovered that the square corners of towers and keeps could be undermined. This meant they collapsed if attackers dug tunnels underneath them. Also, new machines (such as massive catapults called trebuchets) could throw huge boulders that could break down the walls. As a result, the defenders had to come up with new ideas to protect themselves. Before long, concentric castles began to appear.

Clever castles

The concentric castle was an idea brought back by the Crusaders fighting abroad in the Holy Land. They were more regular in shape than earlier castles and used water defences wherever possible. This made it harder for attackers to get their catapults near the walls. The towers were round, so they were harder to undermine, and each set of walls decreased in height so that archers on the upper walls could shoot over the heads of the soldiers below (see **D**).

▼ **D** A concentric castle. This drawing is based on the design of Beaumaris Castle in Wales, built between 1295 and 1330. King Edward I employed the greatest medieval castle architect – James of St George – to design it. James was involved with 12 of the 17 Welsh castles that Edward I had either built, rebuilt or strengthened.

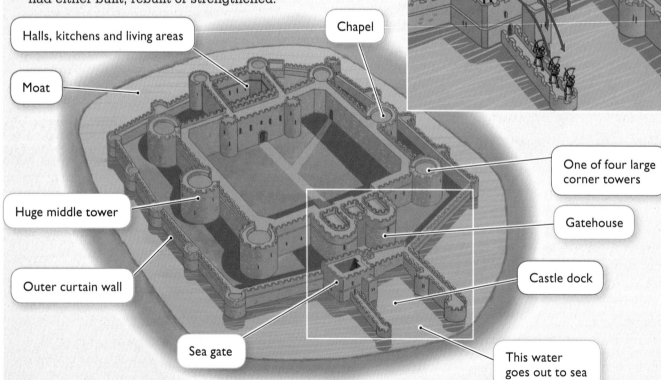

Walls of different heights helped defenders. The enemy can be fired upon from several different levels

Halls, kitchens and living areas

Chapel

Moat

One of four large corner towers

Huge middle tower

Gatehouse

Outer curtain wall

Castle dock

Sea gate

This water goes out to sea

Comfier castles

The age of castle-building began to decline in the early 1400s. The country became more peaceful and there was no need for such strong, expensive castles. Instead, they were modified to become lavish homes, and new ones were built for comfort first and defence second (see **E**).

Key Words

concentric castle   undermine

▶ **SOURCE E**
A picture of Herstmonceux Castle in East Sussex, built in the 1440s. It was built of brick and had large windows, rather than narrow arrow slits.

Castles today

There are still hundreds of castles dotted all over Britain. While lots are now ruins, some have undergone dramatic restoration and have been converted into hotels and conference centres. Others are still privately owned and are used as homes. Many, though, are looked after by groups and organisations such as English Heritage, Cadw and the National Trust. You can go and visit some of our finest castles, wander around the grounds, look through the display areas and gaze at medieval artefacts, models and old suits of armour. Sometimes there are even demonstrations by knights on horseback or archers shooting arrows! Every year thousands of people visit Britain's castles – clearly there is still a huge interest in the way people lived in them.

Later on... TODAY

The Tower of London, situated on the north bank of the River Thames, in London, is the UK's most visited castle. It was completed during the reign of William the Conqueror – and two of Henry VIII's wives (Anne Boleyn in 1536 and Catherine Howard in 1542) were beheaded there. Over 2 million people visit the Tower of London every year.

Over to You .ıl

1 Work with a partner to come up with a series of questions to ask one of the medieval world's most famous concentric castle designers – James of St George. This person really existed and designed several of Britain's most famous castles, including Conwy, Harlech and Beaumaris (see **D**). You want to impress him with your interview skills and historical knowledge, so come up with some really interesting questions. Then, write down the answers he might have given.

Change and Continuity ⭐

During the period you are studying there will be things that changed and things that continued (stayed the same). In History, we call this 'change and continuity'.
Look back at the early motte and bailey castle built around 1066 on page 38. Compare it to the concentric castle on page 72.

1 Make two lists: one of the similarities and one of the differences between the two types of castle.

2 Outline how castles changed between 1066 and the 1400s.

4.2A Who's who in a castle?

A castle was very busy because it was a lord or baron's home – and it was full of people who looked after him, such as servants, cooks and entertainers. But it was also a local centre of government and used as a base from which the lord or baron ruled the local area. On behalf of the king, a lord or baron would be expected to collect taxes, arrest criminals, prevent rebellion and guard against invasion. Lots of different people were needed to do this.

A castle was rather like a town hall and a police station combined, and was always full of people busily going about their business. So, who were the castle's most important and interesting inhabitants?

Objectives

- Identify some of the key roles in a medieval castle.

- Analyse what daily life in a castle was like.

I am the baron. I own the castle and all the land around it. I even control the peasants working on my land. I have other castles in different parts of the country. I spend my money on fantastic food, beautiful wall hangings, gold and silver jewellery, and entertaining my friends. The king sometimes asks my advice, or asks me for taxes, or gets me to provide men to guard the royal castles.

I am the baron's wife, one of the few women who live in the castle. I look after our children, with help from my personal servants known as ladies-in-waiting. I can sew, sing and play musical instruments, so I can impress my husband's important friends when they come and visit. When the baron is away I help run the castle and his lands – I might visit local farms or organise supplies or repairs.

As the steward, I am responsible for all the servants — the cooks, butlers, serving staff, gardeners, and even the gong farmer!

I stink. I'm the gong farmer, that's why! My job is to clean out all the garderobes or toilets.

I am the constable and my main focus is security. The safety of the castle is my responsibility so I make sure the soldiers control who or what comes in and out of this place.

I am the marshal. I look after horses and carts, blacksmiths, stonemasons and carpenters.

I am the chamberlain. I look after my lord and lady's rooms and all their belongings. I also look after their clothes and make sure the servants clean them properly. I am trusted to look after all my lord's money and valuables. I make sure good accounts are kept of all the taxes paid and every penny spent.

Key Words

garderobe   gong farmer
oubliette

I am a forgotten prisoner who was kept in the oubliette, a tiny, secret dungeon with access only through a trapdoor in the ceiling. I stole from the baron. Now I'm on display as a warning to others. My body will stay here for months. Birds and maggots will eat my flesh until only bones are left.

There is so much work to be done around here and we are too busy to stop and explain exactly what we do. As servants, we are the ones who cook, clean, wash, serve, tidy, fetch and carry. Few of us even have proper rooms, so we just sleep anywhere we can.

I'm the jester. Sometimes people call me the fool. My job is to tell funny stories and sing rude songs. Even my clothes are silly!

My job as a sheriff is to arrest criminals, collect taxes and make sure people keep the laws. I don't live in the castle, but visit it often to meet with the lord.

I've got 21 days to go! As a knight, my main job is to protect my lord. I do this for 40 days a year because the baron gave me some land. I use men who live on my land as soldiers to help me. When my 40 days are over, another knight who lives nearby will come and do his duty.

We work for the knight. Our job as soldiers is to defend the castle and protect the baron when he travels.

Over to You

1 a Make a copy of the puzzle template and fill it in using clues 1 to 5.

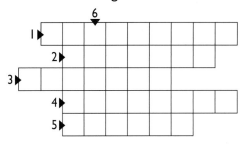

CLUES:
1 Where the forgotten prisoner is kept
2 Looks after horses and carts
3 Arrests criminals
4 Defenders of the castle
5 Works for the baron for 40 days

b Now read down the grid (clue 6) and write a sentence or two about this person.

2 Choose one of the characters from the castle. Imagine that they have fallen from the battlements by accident. It's your job to recruit someone to fill their post. Write a job advert to find a replacement. Remember to include a full job description and the skills required for this post. Hint: You can't apply to be the baron (the king will choose this man), or his wife… or the forgotten prisoner!

Who's the king of the castle?

Part of the reason for building a castle was to create an impression. The baron wanted to show everyone that he was in charge and there to stay. Imagine how impressive and powerful a new castle must have looked 800 years ago. It would have been the tallest building anyone had ever seen, and the huge towers and high stone walls would have been topped with menacing soldiers staring out over the towns, villages and fields below.

The castle was also a safe base from which the baron or lord could rule the local area. There was no fixed plan or shape for a castle, so each one varied according to how the baron wanted it constructed. This is why all castles look a little bit different. The castle in the diagram is typical of those built in the twelfth century.

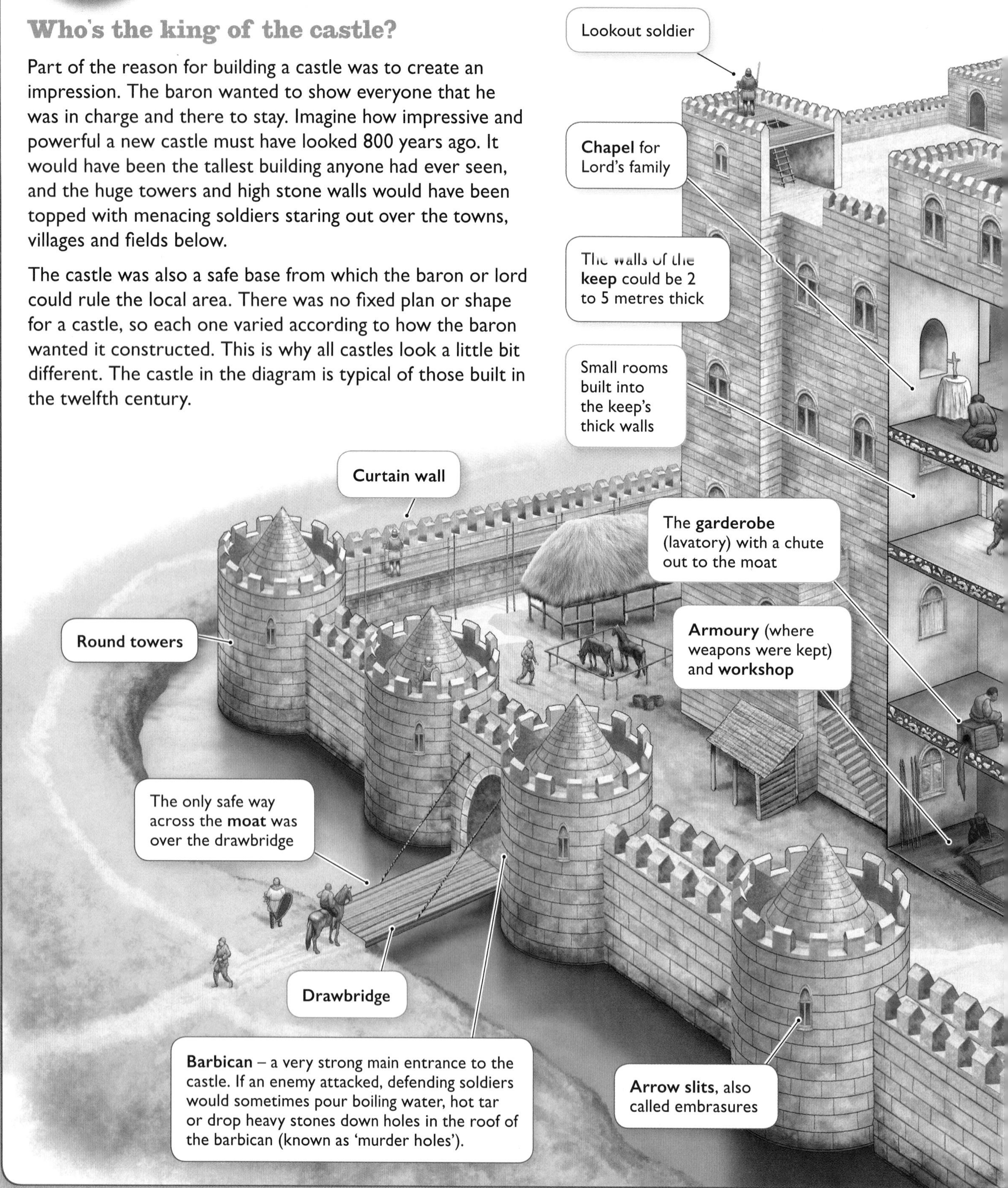

Lookout soldier

Chapel for Lord's family

The walls of the **keep** could be 2 to 5 metres thick

Small rooms built into the keep's thick walls

Curtain wall

The **garderobe** (lavatory) with a chute out to the moat

Round towers

Armoury (where weapons were kept) and **workshop**

The only safe way across the **moat** was over the drawbridge

Drawbridge

Barbican – a very strong main entrance to the castle. If an enemy attacked, defending soldiers would sometimes pour boiling water, hot tar or drop heavy stones down holes in the roof of the barbican (known as 'murder holes').

Arrow slits, also called embrasures

Tank for collecting rainwater

Merlons (raised stonework)

Crenels (the gaps)

Curtains for privacy

Solar – the baron's private rooms

Spiral staircase

The **great hall** where people would sleep as well as eat

Buildings inside the **bailey** might include stables, workshops, guardrooms, etc.

Guardsroom

Keep entrance

Well

Dungeon

Storeroom for flour, salt, salted meat, wine, etc.

Fact ✓

Staircases in castles almost always went up in a clockwise direction. This was so that defenders coming down the stairs would have space to swing their swords in their right hands, while the attackers would find it more difficult.

Over to You

1 Make a list of reasons why a baron would want to spend so much time and money building a huge stone castle.

2 **EITHER:** Imagine you are a wealthy baron about to build a new stone castle. Draw up a short list of requirements for your builder. Make sure you include:
- information about different parts of the castle – what key features must it have?
- details about the thickness of the walls and layout of the castle
- any special features you require – how many garderobes or wells?
- a rough, drawn plan to go with your list.

OR: Imagine the baron of the castle pictured on page 70 has asked you to show a very important guest around the keep. Write a two- to three-minute speech explaining the keep in detail, which you could use as you show around the baron's guest of honour.

Knowledge and Understanding

1 Match up the rooms or features found in a castle with the correct descriptions.
- well
- keep
- solar
- armoury
- drawbridge
- great hall
- round towers

- the largest, strongest, tallest part of the castle
- a room where everyone ate
- the only safe way across the moat
- there were several linked by thick stone walls
- provided water for drinking and washing
- the baron's private rooms
- where the weapons were kept

2 Describe two defensive features of a medieval castle.

4.3A The siege of Rochester Castle

By the 1200s, one of the finest castles in the country was Rochester Castle. It was a masterpiece of medieval castle design with the largest Norman keep in England. But in 1215, Rochester Castle became the scene of one of the most famous sieges in British history when a group of barons rebelled against King John. But what, exactly, is a siege? Why did the barons rebel? And what weapons, methods and tactics were used?

Objectives

- Recall the names of at least five weapons, methods or tactics used to get into a castle.
- Summarise how each of these weapons, methods or tactics was designed to work.
- Explain the weapons, methods and tactics King John used to get into Rochester Castle.

Rebellion against King John

King John was the great-great-grandson of William the Conqueror. In 1215, a group of rebel barons weren't happy with John because they felt he was a poor leader. He had spent a lot of his time fighting (and losing) wars in France – and to make matters worse, he kept asking the barons for more and more money in taxes to pay for these unsuccessful wars.

In June 1215, a group of rebel barons had forced King John to sign Magna Carta. This was a series of written promises that the king would follow certain rules, laws and customs (see Chapter 5). But King John wasn't happy that he had been forced to sign it, and a war broke out between the king and the barons.

In October 1215, the main rebel barons were in Rochester Castle in Kent. This was a very important castle because it guarded one of the main roads in and out of London. King John knew that if he wanted to regain full control over the country, he needed control of Rochester Castle.

The siege begins

Rochester Castle was very well defended. In 1206, King John himself had spent a fortune improving its ditches and keep – making it one of the strongest castles in the country. The outer walls were over 3 metres thick and the walls of the main tower were over 34 metres high. So, at first, the king decided to lay **siege** to the castle. From the French word 'sièger', meaning 'to sit', a siege is when attackers 'sit' down and wait. They stop anyone getting in or out of the castle – and when the food runs out, the people inside have to give up and surrender, or starve to death.

However, after a few weeks the king realised he was wasting his time. The barons had enough food and water to hold out for weeks, maybe months. So, the king scrapped the siege and instructed his army to use some of the latest weapons – **battering rams**, **mangonels** and trebuchets – to get in and defeat the rebellious barons. Look carefully at the drawing on the next page. It shows some of the key weapons King John used to try to get into Rochester Castle.

Fact ✓

King John lost so many battles in France that he was nicknamed 'Softsword'. He even lost Normandy, the birthplace of his great-great-grandfather, William the Conqueror.

▼ **SOURCE A** Rochester Castle, in Kent, was one of the most important and best defended castles in England at the time.

▼ **B** Some of the key weapons and tactics used by King John when trying to get into Rochester Castle.

Battering ram: A tree trunk hanging on a wooden frame, protected by a roof of animal skin, which does not burn easily.

Greek fire: A mixture of tar, oil and sulphur which could not be put out with water. However, it could be put out with urine!

Siege tower: A large wooden tower protected from fire by animal skins. The soldiers would climb up it and over the walls.

Sappers: Specialist soldiers who could dig under a wall or tower. The wooden cover they hid under was called a 'tortoise'.

Trebuchet: Could fire rocks or burning hot substances such as 'Greek fire'. Sometimes rotten animal corpses were fired into the castle. Why do you think this was done?

Mangonel: Another machine used to fire rocks.

Archers: A skilled archer could fire an arrow over 200 metres, or even straight through the arrow slits in the castle walls.

Slow progress

But as hard as they tried, King John's soldiers just couldn't smash down the castle's thick walls and get to the barons. After a few weeks, the king was getting desperate; he received news that another group of rebels were about to come and help the ones trapped inside the castle. He needed another plan… and quickly!

Over to You

1. Explain why the barons inside Rochester Castle were rebelling against King John.

2. Why was Rochester Castle so important to both the rebels and King John?

4.3B The siege of Rochester Castle

Dig, dig, dig!

By the beginning of November, after trying to regain the castle for several weeks, King John had achieved some success... but not much. His battering rams and trebuchets had managed to break down some of the outer walls, but he still couldn't get to the barons inside the great stone keep, protected by walls over three metres thick. So, John decided on a new tactic known as undermining.

Undermining involved a group of specialist soldiers, known as sappers, digging a tunnel under a castle wall or the corner of a castle's tower. They would then hollow out a huge cavern underneath the wall or tower, propping up the roof of their cavern with wooden supports as they went.

Then, when they felt the cavern was big enough, the wooden supports would be burned so that the cavern would collapse... and bring everything above down with it. **B** shows how undermining worked.

Feeling the heat

Undermining a castle's walls was a clever tactic, but it didn't always work. Sometimes the wooden supports didn't burn through properly and the walls didn't fall all the way down into the hole. So, King John decided to make sure the fire in the underground cavern was very, very hot, to be certain that the supports would be totally destroyed... so he sent for some extra fat pigs! (See **D**).

▼ **C** How undermining worked.

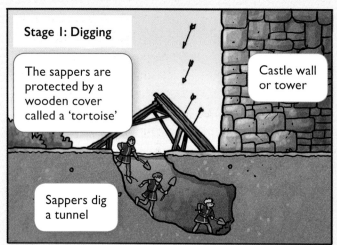

Stage 1: Digging

The sappers are protected by a wooden cover called a 'tortoise'

Castle wall or tower

Sappers dig a tunnel

Stage 2: Wooden supports

The cavern is supported by wooden supports or props

The sappers hollow out a huge cavern

Stage 3: Fire

A soldier with a flaming torch enters the cavern

The wooden supports are set on fire

Stage 4: Collapse

When the wooden supports collapse, the wall or tower falls into the hole.

The attacking army then runs through the gap left by the collapsing wall.

▼ **SOURCE D** King John's order to find 40 fat pigs, sent to one of his loyal supporters Hugh de Burgh on 25 November 1215. This has to be one of the strangest royal requests ever.

'Send to us with all speed by day and night forty of the fattest pigs of the sort least good for eating to bring fire beneath the tower.'

Pig power

As soon as the pigs arrived, John knew he'd have the walls of the keep down in no time. Pig fat burns at a very, very high temperature (up to around 500°C), so John piled up the (dead) pigs in the huge cavern dug deep below the castle walls… and set them on fire! The fat burned so well that the wooden supports collapsed, the cavern caved in and the foundations of the wall above began to crack. Eventually, the wall of the keep collapsed and the whole south-east tower fell into the hole. It was then that the king stormed in. On 30 November 1215, the siege of Rochester Castle was finally over – thanks to 40 fat pigs!

The aftermath

King John didn't punish the rebel barons as severely as many thought he would. He needed their money, after all, and decided it would be best if they were kept alive so that he could tax them heavily. However, he did get his revenge on one man who changed sides halfway through the siege and joined the rebels. What did King John do to the unfortunate man? He ordered his hands and feet to be cut off.

Over to You

1 Look at **Source D**.
   a What does King John request?
   b How does this request help John break into the castle?

2 It's time to put your knowledge of attacking and defending castles into practice:
   a In pairs, consider all the ways that castles can be both attacked and defended. Make two lists: 'attacking a castle' and 'defending a castle'. Hint: You might also want to revisit pages 76–79.
   b In your pair, one of you chooses to be the attacker of a castle, the other chooses to be the defender. Write a siege diary from the point of view of your character. How the siege turns out is up to you.

Cause and Consequence ⭐

The ability to write down the story of an event in the past is an important history skill. This is sometimes called a 'narrative account'. A narrative account often includes the causes and the consequences of an event, as well as lots of accurate detail about what happened (names, dates, facts). You are now going to work towards writing an account of the siege of Rochester Castle.

1 Match up the weapons and tactics on the left with their correct definitions on the right.
   • siege   • a huge catapult
   • trebuchet   • a covered ladder
   • battering ram   • from the French for 'to sit'
   • siege tower   • a special mixture that's set on fire
   • greek fire   • pushed against doors and walls to make a hole

2 Create a brief timeline identifying three to five of the most important events in the siege of Rochester Castle.

3 Write a narrative account of the siege of Rochester Castle. Use your answers from **1** and **2** to help you answer this question. You must also use the following terms: rebels, King John, Magna Carta, trebuchets, sappers, undermining, wooden supports, pig fat.

4.4A What was life like in a medieval village?

Most people live in towns and cities today. In the Middle Ages, things were different. Although towns existed, there weren't many of them, and the vast majority of people lived and worked in villages. So, what were these villages like?

Objectives

- Describe how a medieval villager spent their day.
- Examine village life during the Middle Ages.
- Compare a medieval villager's house with a modern house.

Village life

Around nine out of every ten people lived in villages and farmed the land. Life in a medieval village was tough. The peasant villagers (known as villeins) worked out in the fields from sunrise to sunset whenever there was work to do. Most of the land was owned by someone else (the lord of the manor) who was usually a knight or baron. The lord let the peasants live on his land in return for their obedience, their help when required, and several days of work from them per week.

The peasant families lived in small huts that they would build themselves. Each had a small garden where they grew vegetables and fruit. They might also keep sheep, pigs, goats and chickens.

Farming the land

The fields that surrounded the village were carefully divided up into strips and shared out among the villagers, so that no one peasant had all the good land or all the bad land. Peasants grew wheat for bread, barley for beer, and oats and rye to feed the animals. There were no shops or supermarkets as we know them today, so most of the food they needed had to be grown by the peasants themselves. If there was a bad harvest or their animals died, the villagers could starve to death.

Church

Woodland: peasants gathered firewood here, but only the lord (or the king, of course) could hunt in it

Common land: cattle were allowed to graze here

Carpenter's workshop: for making carts, axe handles and wheels

Blacksmith's workshop: for making pots, pans, chains and knives

Village green: used as a meeting place and for markets

Mill: people ground their corn into flour at the watermill. Peasants had to pay the lord to use it

River: villeins had to pay the lord to fish in the river

Specialist jobs

However, not everyone in the village farmed. Some had specialist jobs, for example blacksmiths, carpenters or cloth weavers. They would sell their goods and services to other people – or even travel to the nearest town or village to sell things on market days.

Fact ✓

How many people do you usually see in one day: 100, 300, perhaps even more? You probably see more people in one day than a medieval villager saw in their whole life.

Over to You ▪▫▫

1 If you could travel back in time and meet with someone who lived in the village pictured on these pages, what interview questions would you ask them? Make a list.

2 Briefly describe where you live to a medieval villager. What are the main differences? Are there any similarities?

Manor house: the landowner (a knight, for example) lived here with his family; all the peasants worked on his land and paid taxes when required. The manor house was strong, secure and comfortable

Castle: the baron lived here

Open fields divided equally into strips: each peasant had one or two strips in each field

Tithe barn: peasants had to give 10 per cent of what they grew to the priest; this was called a tithe and the produce was kept here

Village pub: a mug of ale and a sing-song was a popular way to pass the time

Beehives: honey was one of the only methods of sweetening things

Peasant houses

Peasant's vegetable patch

What were the villagers' homes like?

The villages varied in size. Some contained fewer than ten houses, but larger ones might have over 50 homes as well as a manor house, a church, a mill, and workshops for a blacksmith or a carpenter. Look at the diagram and sources on these pages to discover what a typical peasant cottage was like and how a peasant villager lived.

Where do they live?
In a one-room hut. The frame is made from wood and the walls are made from wattle (sticks woven together) and daub (mud, dung and straw – see A). The windows are holes in the wall covered by shutters. The floor is made of mud mixed with straw and ox blood to make it hard. There is a hole in the roof to let out the smoke from the fire inside. The animals live in the hut too… what a smell! Water for cooking and cleaning comes from a well or a river and outside is a hole dug in the ground that is used as a toilet.

Can the villeins leave the village?
No, they aren't allowed to because the lord controls what they do. They can't leave the land or even marry without his permission. And if they run away, they can be tried in court and punished. However, villeins are sometimes given their freedom by a kind or grateful lord – or they can buy their freedom if they save up enough money. When this happens, they are called 'freemen'.

What do they eat?
• Breakfast – 6am. Bread and ale to drink (water wasn't safe).
• Lunch – 10am. Bread, perhaps an egg, a piece of fish, or cheese. Ale to drink.
• Supper – 4pm. Bread and a thick vegetable soup called pottage. Ale to drink.

What about women in the village?
The women work as hard as the men. They cook, clean and look after the children. They fetch water, make and mend clothes, and help in the fields whenever needed. If a woman's husband dies, the lord usually wants the land to be kept within the family, so she holds onto the land for as long as she lives – and passes it on to her oldest son when she dies.

How do the villagers spend their days?
They get up when it's light enough to see and they work all day. In spring they plough the land and plant seeds. In summer they harvest the hay, weed the corn and scare the birds. In autumn (the busiest season), they harvest the corn, and kill some animals in order to preserve the meat for winter. In winter they clear away any wasteland, repair the hut and tools, gather nuts, wild fruits and herbs – and, most importantly, try to keep warm.

Does the village provide all the villagers' needs?
Villages are often cut off from each other. The roads between villages are very poor and almost impossible to travel along in bad weather. Large areas of woodland also contain wild animals (such as wolves). As a result, a village tends to look after itself. The villagers grow their own food, brew their own beer and make all their tools, clothes, carts and furniture. If they need anything else that they can't make themselves (glass, ribbons, spices and needles, for example), they might travel to the nearest town occasionally – with the lord's permission, of course.

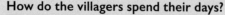

► **SOURCE A**
A photograph showing the medieval building technique of wattle and daub.

▼ **SOURCE B** An image from a medieval book, dated around 1340. The man on the left is throwing stones at birds to scare them away and stop them eating newly planted seeds.

▼ **SOURCE C** Adapted from *The Vision of Piers Plowman* by William Langland, a poet and priest, written around 1390. Langland was very critical of villeins' living conditions.

'The poorest folk are our neighbours... in their hovels [small, simple houses], overburdened with children... whatever they save by spinning they spend on rent, or on milk and oatmeal for food. And they themselves are often famished with hunger and wretched with the miseries of winter – cold, sleepless nights, when they get up to rock the cradle – and rise before dawn to spin the wool, to wash and scrub and mend, and wind yarn... while the monks feast on roast venison, they have bread and thin ale, with perhaps a scrap of cold meat or stale fish... I tell you, it would be a real charity to... comfort these cottagers along with the blind and the lame.'

Over to You

1 a Self-sufficiency is when a person or group of people can supply what they need for themselves. In what ways was a medieval village self-sufficient?

  b Why did the village need to be largely self-sufficient?

2 Look at **Source B**.

  a Describe what is going on in the picture.

  b In which season of the year would this be taking place?

3 Read **Source C**.

  a Sum up what the writer is saying about a villein's life.

  b Why might the writer have been so keen to make the villein's life sound so terrible?

Change and Continuity

1 Copy and complete the table below, putting the following headings in the column on the left: windows; number of rooms; cooking; floor; heating; water supply; toilets; washing.

	A villein's home	My home
Windows	Holes in wall, shutters	Glass, curtains
Number of rooms	One	

2 In what ways was a villein's home different from your home? Explain five ways.

4.5A What was life like in a medieval town?

People who didn't live in villages in the countryside, or in castles, lived in towns. When William conquered England in 1066 there were only about 15 towns with a population of more than 1000 people, and only about eight with more than 3000 living there. London was the largest with about 10,000 people, followed by Winchester and Norwich with about 3000 people each. Most people (about 90 per cent of the population) lived in small country villages, with no more than 50 to 100 people in each.

Objectives

- Explain what life was like in a medieval town.
- Identify how buying and selling was organised.
- Examine why towns grew.

Why towns developed

After 1066, towns began to grow. Some villages grew in size too – and became towns. Sometimes towns grew where major roads met, or near a bridge, where people came to buy and sell goods. Others grew near a castle or monastery. The local lord still owned these places, but, if the town continued to grow and the townspeople made lots of money, they might join together and offer money to the local lord or king to buy their land and freedom from him.

Town charters

A town's freedom was written down on a special piece of paper known as a **charter**. Charters gave towns the right to hold their own courts and run markets without paying taxes to the lord or king. A town's charter gave the townspeople the chance to run the town themselves and elect a **mayor** and a **council**. The council could collect taxes and spend this money on improvements – repairing town walls, cleaning up the streets or building a place where the council could meet, for example. In fact, by 1400, about 300 towns had received their charter and freedom. By this time, London's population had grown to over 40,000.

The diagram on these pages shows a typical town in about 1250. Look for the following:

1 Most streets are just dirt tracks
2 A pedlar selling goods as he walks through the streets
3 The castle – at one time only the castle was here, but over the years the town has grown up in front of it
4 Shops have picture signs to show what they sell because few people can read
5 Large private house, probably the home of a **merchant**
6 Defensive tower – a place where guards keep lookout
7 Entrance gate – guarded 24 hours a day, seven days a week

8 Having fun – all sorts of people entertain the townspeople in return for a few coins
9 A young apprentice being taught the skills of a trade by a master craftsman; the training lasts seven years
10 The market – held once or twice a week where people come from the countryside to sell eggs, cheese, butter, fruit and vegetables
11 Many houses have vegetable gardens
12 Market stalls – as well as local goods, merchants bring exotic goods, such as spices and silks, from abroad
13 Meeting rooms above the gateway where the town council and mayor meet

14 Traders bringing in goods by river
15 A wagon bringing goods to sell at the market
16 The Guildhall where the **guilds** meet. A guild is a group of traders and craftsmen that makes rules for its members to follow; they set prices, organise training and make sure goods are well made. There are different guilds for different trades (a Shoemakers' Guild, a Hatmakers' Guild and so on)
17 Town walls patrolled by guards
18 Town church

Fact ✓

Leeds and Liverpool received their charters in 1207. Kings were often short of money and sold charters as a way of making money. King Richard I and King John sold many charters.

Over to You

1 What is a charter?

2 What advantages were there in having a charter for:
   a the townspeople?
   b the local lord or king?

Causation

A 'cause' is the reason why something happens. Most events and developments have a number of different causes. The growth of towns, for example, has a number of different causes.

1 Explain two causes of the growth of towns.

Buying and selling

Most towns held a market once or twice a week. People from the local villages would come into the town and sell things they had produced themselves such as vegetables, milk, meat and corn. Merchants would also set up small stalls (a lot like a market today) and sell goods such as clothes, shoes, spices, pottery and knives.

As towns grew bigger, some of the traders built small shops to sell their goods. They often had a small workshop next door where the goods were made or prepared. Soon, some towns had specialist shops – a bakery, a butcher's shop, a shoemaker's shop and a fishmonger's, for example. The advantage of shops was that the traders didn't have to pack away at the end of the day (like on a market stall) and goods could be bought on any day, not only on days when the market was held.

Look through all the sources and images on these pages to discover what life was like in a medieval town.

▼ **SOURCE B** William Fitzstephen's 'Description of the city of London', from around 1174. Fitzstephen was an assistant and adviser to Thomas Becket, the Archbishop of Canterbury.

'Traders can be found in their particular areas each morning. There is wine for sale on the river bank. Every day you may find food, dishes of meat – roast, fried and boiled; fish; cheap cuts of meat for the poor and more expensive for the rich… Just outside the town there is a field called Smithfield. On every sixth day of the week there is a sale of fine horses… In another part of the field are things brought to market by the country folk – farming tools, pigs, milk, cows, large oxen and woolly sheep, mares to pull the plough and young foals.'

▼ **MAP A** A plan of Norwich market in the Middle Ages. By the 1300s, Norwich was one of England's largest and richest cities. The region (East Anglia) produced huge amounts of grain, sheep, cattle and poultry. Norwich itself was known for its textiles, leather and metalworking. The market was a major trading centre for these goods.

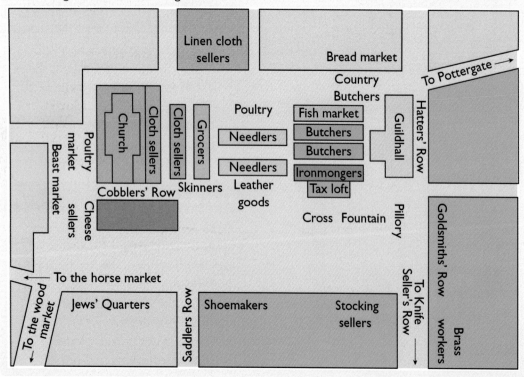

Fact ✓

Britain's most important **export** at this time was wool. It was sold by farmers and traders, both in Britain and abroad, where it was made into cloth. Fortunes were made from the wool trade and it has been estimated that by 1300 there were up to 18 million sheep in Britain (and around 3–4 million people).

▶ **SOURCE C**
Market stalls around a town wall, as shown in a manuscript from 1458. Can you see what customers are buying?

▼ **SOURCE D** Guild rules from a variety of towns.

- Poor workmanship will be punished by a fine and goods will be confiscated.
  Shoemakers' Guild, Chester
- No one shall make or sell hats within the city unless he has special permission.
  Hatmakers' Guild, London
- If the threads of the cloth are too far apart, the cloth and the tools used will be burned.
  Weavers' Guild, Bristol
- If by chance a member of the guild shall become poor through old age, accident or sickness, then he shall have seven pence (3p) from the guild every week.
  Tanners' Guild (leather workers), London

Key Words   export

Over to You .ıll

1 Read **Source B**.

   a Where in London would you be able to buy wine, horses or sheep?

   b In larger towns (such as London, Bristol and York), certain parts of the town were used by traders selling the same thing. For example, all the silversmiths might be in Silver Street. Which goods would you expect to be sold in the following streets:

   Baker Street, Cutler Row, Pudding Lane, Gold Street, Brewhouse Lane, Vine Street and Tanners Lane?

   c What advantages might there be in having all the traders close together, for the buyers – and for the sellers?

2 Look at **Source D** and label 16 on page 87.

   a What was a guild?

   b Why do you think some of the guild rules were so strict?

   c Why do you think one of the guilds chose to give money to its members who became poor because of old age, sickness or accident? Hint: Think how people might manage today if they were old, sick or had an accident.

3 🖊 Look at the picture of a town on pages 86–87 and read **Source B**. Imagine you live 16km (10 miles) away from town. For the first time ever, your parents are taking you into town, and it is the most exciting day of your life – there are lots of new (and strange) sights, sounds and smells. Describe your visit.

4.6 Could you have fun in the Middle Ages?

In the Middle Ages, ordinary people didn't really have holidays. Instead, there were several times through the year, such as Christmas Day, Easter Day, saints' days and Midsummer's Eve, where people would take a break from their hard-working lives to enjoy themselves. Most of these days were special religious occasions. On one of these days, after going to church, people would usually make their own fun, using home-made equipment. So how did ordinary people enjoy their holy days?

Objectives

- Analyse the similarities and differences between how the rich and the poor spent their time in the Middle Ages.
- Compare and contrast the sports and games played in the Middle Ages and now.

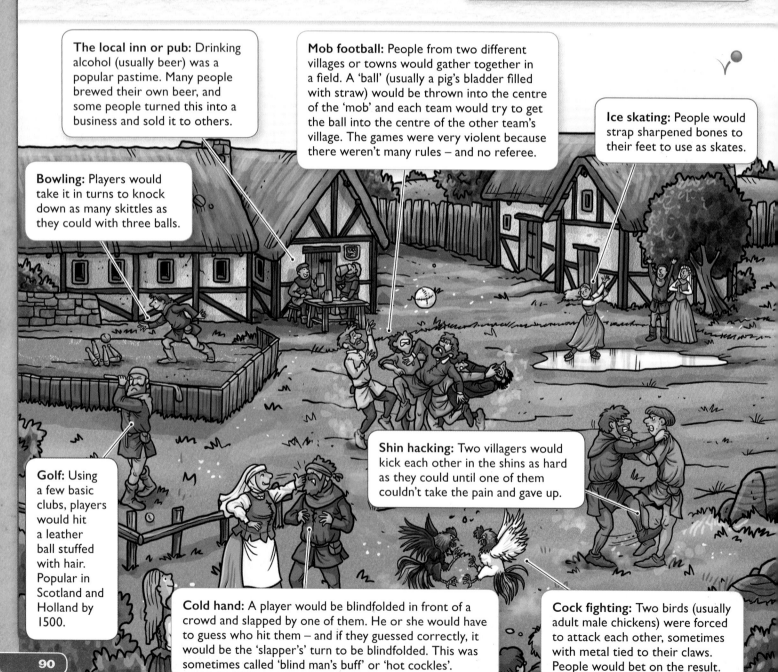

The local inn or pub: Drinking alcohol (usually beer) was a popular pastime. Many people brewed their own beer, and some people turned this into a business and sold it to others.

Mob football: People from two different villages or towns would gather together in a field. A 'ball' (usually a pig's bladder filled with straw) would be thrown into the centre of the 'mob' and each team would try to get the ball into the centre of the other team's village. The games were very violent because there weren't many rules – and no referee.

Ice skating: People would strap sharpened bones to their feet to use as skates.

Bowling: Players would take it in turns to knock down as many skittles as they could with three balls.

Golf: Using a few basic clubs, players would hit a leather ball stuffed with hair. Popular in Scotland and Holland by 1500.

Shin hacking: Two villagers would kick each other in the shins as hard as they could until one of them couldn't take the pain and gave up.

Cold hand: A player would be blindfolded in front of a crowd and slapped by one of them. He or she would have to guess who hit them – and if they guessed correctly, it would be the 'slapper's' turn to be blindfolded. This was sometimes called 'blind man's buff' or 'hot cockles'.

Cock fighting: Two birds (usually adult male chickens) were forced to attack each other, sometimes with metal tied to their claws. People would bet on the result.

What about the rich?

The most popular form of entertainment for the rich was a **tournament**. This was a series of competitions such as sword fighting, jousting and horse-riding, with prizes for the winners. They would also go hunting or enjoy feasting and dancing. A group of acrobats or jugglers might entertain the local lord and his guests. And if they got bored with the entertainers, they might play chess, draughts, cards, or throw dice.

In the Middle Ages a popular game for rich men was 'real tennis'. Two players had to hit a wooden ball over a rope with a racquet. Sometimes the ball was hit so hard that players could be killed if it hit them on the head. Falconry (also known as 'hawking') was also very popular for rich men and women. Specially trained birds of prey would fly off to catch and bring back smaller animals. Some of these sports were only enjoyed by the rich because the poor were either banned by law from taking part (the poor couldn't hunt in any of the Royal Forests, for example) or they simply couldn't afford to train the expensive birds of prey or own horses.

Archery: England's armies always needed archers. Boys were encouraged to practise from a very young age.

Stoolball: A young woman would sit on a stool and men would throw a ball at her. She would try to dodge the ball, perhaps using a bat to hit it away. If they hit her, they got a kiss.

Wrestling: People loved all sorts of fighting games – the more blood the better.

Bear baiting: A bear would be chained to a post while dogs attacked it. People would bet on the result – would the dogs or the bear win?

Key Words tournament

Fact ✓

Today we use the word 'holiday' to describe any special day of rest or relaxation where we don't go to work or school. The word comes from the medieval term 'holy day'. In medieval times, a 'holy day', such as a special religious day, was when people would go to church and then spend the rest of the day away from work enjoying themselves.

Over to You

1 Explain where the word 'holiday' comes from.

2 a Look closely at the illustration showing ordinary people enjoying their holy day. Make two lists: 'Things we no longer enjoy today' and 'Things we still enjoy today'.

b Choose one example from your list of things we no longer enjoy today. Explain why you think this pastime is no longer practised.

c Choose one example from your list of things we still enjoy today. Explain in what ways, if any, it has changed since medieval times.

Similarity and Difference

People's lives can be very different, even if they live in the same country in the same period of history. Compare the ways that rich people and poorer people had fun in the Middle Ages:

1 a List five leisure activities enjoyed by the rich in medieval times.

b List five leisure activities enjoyed by the poor.

c Explain why the poor did not take part in some of the same sports and leisure activities as the rich.

4.7 Has football changed much since the Middle Ages?

There are many different explanations about the origins of football. FIFA (the international organisation that controls football) says that the first version of the game with regular rules took place in China around 2000 years ago. According to FIFA, there were also football-type games played in Ancient Japan, Ancient Greece and Ancient Rome. There was also a British version, first mentioned by a monk in a book called *The History of the Britons* in the ninth century. It then became very popular in the years that followed. So, what was early British football like? Just how popular was it? How similar was football in the Middle Ages to the game we know today?

Objectives

- Explain the origins of football in Britain.
- Evaluate how football in the Middle Ages differs from football today.

Mob football

The earliest known games of what became known as 'football' were very violent. Known as 'mob football', it involved all the men (and sometimes women) of one village or town playing against another. They usually met up in a field once or twice a year on public holidays such as Shrove Tuesday (Pancake Day), and there could be as many as 500 players. A 'ball', usually a pig's bladder filled with straw, would be thrown into the centre of the 'mob' and each team would try to get the ball into the centre of the other team's village or town. In Workington, an old rulebook said that players could use any method to get the ball to its target 'except murder'! Sometimes a game was played with several balls – and there was no referee. A writer once described the game as 'a devilish pastime. More a bloody murdering practice than a sport.'

▼ **SOURCE A** Adapted from a description of mob football played in London on Shrove Tuesday, written by William Fitzstephen in 1174. He was an assistant and advisor to Thomas Becket, the Archbishop of Canterbury. A game of 'mob football' is still played in some parts of Britain today on Shrove Tuesday.

'After lunch all the youth of the city go out into the fields to take part in the ball game. The students of each school have their own ball. The workers from each city craft also carry balls. Older citizens, fathers and wealthy men come on horseback to watch the juniors competing, and to revive their own youth. You can see their inner passions aroused as they watch the action and get caught up in the fun.'

Banned

Football was regularly banned. In 1314, King Edward II banned it in London after a group of merchants told him it was damaging their businesses because 'the hustling over large footballs causes great uproar in the city'. However, the game had become so popular among so many people that the ban was ignored. In 1349, Edward III became the first king to officially ban football throughout the country by law. He said that people were playing it so much they were forgetting to practise their archery skills. The king was worried that if a foreign army invaded England, men would have forgotten how to use their bows and arrows properly.

Indeed, football became one of Britain's most banned games. Between 1314 and 1667, it was officially banned by more than 30 royal or local laws. Richard II, Henry IV and Henry V all tried to ban it, but people were so determined to play that they carried on regardless. In Scotland, King James I once famously ruled that 'na man play at the fute-ball', but the Scots loved the game so much they were playing football in Edinburgh the very next week.

▼ **INTERPRETATION B** A 1905 drawing of football in the Middle Ages, by artist Amedee Forestier. He worked in England and specialised in British historical scenes.

▼ **SOURCE C** A modern game of football. Can you spot any differences from mob football of the past?

Change and Continuity

1 Make a list of all the differences you can find between football in the Middle Ages and football today. Use the sources and the interpretation to help you.

2 What do you think the biggest difference is? Explain your answer.

3 In what ways has football changed since the Middle Ages?

Fact ✔

In 1321, the Pope issued a special letter of forgiveness to a player who had accidentally killed an opponent. A few days later a Londoner wrote that players used to 'retire home as from battle, with bloody heads, bones broken and out of joint, and bruises that will shorten their days'. By 1450, players in some towns introduced a new rule to try to reduce the number of accidents: the ball could only be kicked, not carried or thrown.

Over to You .ıl

1 Write these statements in the correct chronological order.
   - New rules were introduced in some towns saying the ball could only be kicked, not picked up.
   - An early version of football was played in China.
   - King Edward III banned football throughout the country.
   - Football was banned in London after traders complained it was damaging their businesses.
   - The Pope issued a special letter to forgive a player who had killed an opponent.

2 a Why do you think so many kings tried to ban football?

   b Why do you think the bans weren't very successful?

4.8 The story of the English language

In medieval Britain, several languages were spoken, including Welsh in Wales and Gaelic in Scotland. English was the main language in England, of course. But did you know that for many years after 1066, it was the third most important language in England? Why had English become less important after 1066? And how did English develop and become the number one language in England by the end of the Middle Ages?

Objectives

- Recognise the origins of the main language spoken in Britain today.
- Examine the difference between 'Old English' and modern English.

Before 1066...

Before William the Conqueror and his Norman followers invaded (and took over) in 1066, the people of England spoke a language called 'Old English'. This was a mixture of different languages taken from the various peoples who had invaded England over the years. The diagram below shows the ingredients that made up 'Old English':

Norse

From the 700s onwards, the Vikings attacked and settled in England. These 'Norse men', as they were sometimes called, added some of their own words to Old English. Many of these words were linked with place names, such as 'by', which is Norse for a settlement. As a result, we get Grimsby and Whitby. Norse for a village is 'thorpe', so we get Scunthorpe and Cleethorpes. Other Viking or Norse words include anger, dregs, flit, glitter, oaf, skin and ugly.

Latin

When Britain became a Christian land, several Latin words (mainly connected with the Church) came into use. Some Latin words that still survive today are saint, alter ego, factor, parent and et cetera (which we shorten to 'etc.').

Anglo-Saxon

Tribes called Angles, Saxons and Jutes from Germany and Denmark invaded Britain about 1500 years ago. The Anglo-Saxons were great storytellers. The language they spoke would be difficult for us to understand but some of their words still survive, including drink, father, ground, love, name, silly, son, the, was and wife.

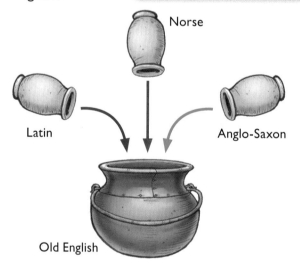

Old English

After 1066...

In 1066, William the Conqueror brought the French language to England. King Harold II, the man he had defeated at Hastings, was the last Old English-speaking king. All the important people William brought over from France spoke French – the queen, the barons and their families. They brought French words with them too – words that we still know today, such as army, baron, castle, enemy, grape, judge, prison, sausage, sugar and traitor.

The ruling Normans of England (and their lawyers, priests and secretaries) could also speak Latin – a living language in 1066. Latin was taught in schools and cathedrals, and was spoken by educated people all over Europe. So, after 1066, Old English was officially the third most important language in England. Nobody wrote English down any more and nobody seemed to care. Kings and their friends spoke French (and Latin); churchmen, teachers and merchants used Latin, and books were written in Latin too.

English survives

But Old English didn't die out because ordinary peasants and townspeople spoke it every day. They wouldn't and couldn't learn French or Latin, so they kept on speaking the language they had known all their lives – Old English.

In the mix

However, as the centuries passed, Old English and French began to mix (just as the people did). An Old English-speaking peasant who knew a worker up at the castle might use a French word; a French nobleman visiting the local town would also use a French word. He then might visit another town, pick up a few Old English words and use them with his friends. Latin was still the language of the Church, but in trade, business and the growing towns and villages, it was awkward to have different languages, so they gradually blended into one. By the 1400s, something very similar to modern English had emerged.

▼ **SOURCE A** A description of the change from teaching in French to teaching in English in a school. Written by John Trevisa in 1385, a writer who was translating an earlier book written by Ranulf Higden, a monk.

'John Cornwal, a grammar school teacher, changed from teaching in French to teaching in English; and Richard Pencrych learned the way of teaching from him, so that now, in 1385, in the reign of the second King Richard, in all the grammar schools in England, children are learning in English and translating Latin into English instead of French.'

Later on...

The English language continues to change. For example, new words and phrases are created as a result of new technology, new products and new experiences. A century ago, no one would have known about common words we use today such as Internet, texting and laptop. Also, different people from different places pick up new words and phrases from each other. We have all started to use words that our friends have used, or we have heard spoken on the TV or social media.

The English language continues to absorb words from other languages. Here are a few examples.
Arabic: admiral, alcohol, sofa
Japanese: judo, sushi, tycoon
Inuit: anorak, igloo, kayak
Turkish: coffee, yoghurt
Czech: pistol, robot
Welsh: corgi, flannel
Portuguese: cobra, marmalade, palaver
Norwegian: ski, slalom
Hindi: shampoo, chutney
Scottish Gaelic and Irish: slogan, trousers
Aztec: chilli, chocolate, tomato
Russian: mammoth, vodka

Fact ✓

Many medieval kings spoke French and couldn't read or write either. It was Edward III who realised that English, not French or Latin, was still spoken by millions of ordinary people and allowed English to be used in Parliament and in law courts. Soon after, Henry IV became the first monarch in over 300 years to make his first speech as a king in English.

Over to You

1 Explain what is meant by the term 'Old English'.

2 The English language is always changing. Think carefully and write down why you think the English language changes so much.

3 Make a list of words and phrases used today which your great-grandparents wouldn't understand. Try to explain why they wouldn't understand them.

4 Read **Source A**.
   a What changes in language and education are mentioned in the source?
   b Why do you think English eventually replaced French and Latin?

Cause and Consequence

1 Why did French replace Old English as the main language in the Middle Ages?

2 In what ways was language affected by the invasions of Britain up to and including the Middle Ages?

4.9 Medieval Masterchef

Think about what you have eaten over the last week. You may find that you've eaten chocolate bars, a few burgers or pizzas, chicken nuggets or maybe something healthier such as pasta, rice or fruit and vegetables grown locally or imported from abroad. Today, we have more choice in where we get all our food, what we eat, even how we cook it, than ever before. Things have certainly changed a lot since the Middle Ages. So, what was it like to eat in medieval Britain?

Objectives

- Compare food in medieval times with the food we eat today.

- Judge whether a medieval or modern diet is healthiest.

It ain't pleasant for a peasant

A peasant's food was rather dull and was the same – year in, year out. There was no tea, coffee, orange juice, or fizzy drinks and the water wasn't usually fit to drink, so they drank a watery kind of beer called **ale**. Look at **A** to see a typical peasant's diet.

Healthy diet?

Peasants grew a lot of strong-flavoured vegetables and herbs to make their dull food tastier. Onions, garlic, leeks, cabbage, carrots, parsley and mint were common. Apples, cherries, pears and wild berries were also eaten (and sometimes made into fruit pies), and honey was one of the few ways to sweeten anything. In fact, a peasant's diet was probably much healthier than most people's today. They didn't eat food that contained large amounts of sugar (like cakes, biscuits and chocolate) and they worked all day, so they got lots of exercise.

Later on...

Potatoes didn't reach Britain until the 1500s so there were no chips, potato wedges or crisps for the peasants to enjoy!

▼ **A** A peasant's daily meals.

4am to 6am — Bread and ale

10am — Bread, cheese, onion, eggs, ale or cider

4pm — Bread, fish, pottage (thick vegetable soup), ale or cider

What about meat?

If peasants did eat meat, it was usually bacon. This was the most common meat among peasants because pigs were very easy to keep. However, peasants sometimes ate food that people today would find unusual – squirrel, hedgehog, pike and eel, for example. There were no refrigerators to keep food fresh, so meat was usually salted or smoked. Peasants would rub salt into meat to stop it going bad or hang strips of meat from the roof of their cottage, so it would dry out and last longer.

Life in the manor house

For the richer folk, daily life was a lot easier than it was for the peasants. They had servants to do most things for them, including the cooking. They still ate a lot of bread, but it was of better quality. Like a peasant, a rich noble would eat three times a day, but would eat a lot more meat – and drink a lot more wine! Soups and stews were common, as were puddings such as fruit tarts or pancakes.

A medieval feast

For a special occasion, the lord and lady of the manor would hold a feast in their largest room – the great hall. A servant would lay out spoons, knives, drinking cups and bread. Forks were rare. The lord and his guests would probably have spent the day hunting for the meat about to be eaten – venison (deer), wild boar, ducks, swans, or even peacocks. Slices of stale bread called **trenchers** were used as plates. The juices from the meat and vegetables would soak into them and when the meal was over, they might be given to the poor – or thrown to the dogs (see **B**). Servants would then carry around warm bowls of water and bits of cloth so that guests could rinse and clean their fingers after eating.

Later on...

Today, many people have a taste for salty or smoked food. For example, some of you will put extra salt on your chips or enjoy 'smoky bacon' crisps or 'smoked' kippers. We like these things because humans have been preserving food like this for thousands of years and our taste buds haven't changed much in that time.

▼ **SOURCE B** An illustration of a medieval feast in a wealthy household, with entertainers and servants, from a manuscript created around 1310.

Over to You

1 a Look again at **A**, which shows a peasant's meals. Draw a similar diagram to show your meals during one of the days in the last week. Remember to include everything you have eaten, even snacks.

   b Write down at least two ways in which the peasant's meals are different from your meals. Then make a judgement – whose diet is healthier?

2   Produce a menu for a medieval feast. Try to include lots of food. Remember, most people couldn't read, so you'll need to illustrate your menu.

3 a List three examples of food and drink that a peasant would regularly eat.

   b List three examples of food and drink that a lord would regularly eat.

   c Explain one way in which a peasant's diet was different from a lord's.

Source Analysis

Look at **Source B**.

1 Can you see: the servants; the dog eating from the table; the man begging for food; the entertainers?

2 Describe what's going on in **Source B** in as much detail as you can.

3 How useful is **Source B** for an **enquiry** into a lord's food and entertainment in the Middle Ages?

4.10 Knight life

Have you ever held a door open for someone? Have you ever kicked the ball out of play during a football match to allow an injured opponent to receive treatment? Or have you given up your seat on a bus for an elderly person or pregnant woman? If you answered 'yes' to any of these questions, you have probably been told what good manners you have, or what a 'good sport' you are. The person you've helped knows you didn't have to do any of these things, but they (and you) feel much better for it. So why do we do this? Where does this sort of behaviour come from?

Objectives

- Examine the role of the knight in medieval society.
- Explain how aspects of medieval history still have relevance today.

From the Middle Ages?

Lots of sports today include these ideas about behaving properly and being polite. For example, when playing golf or snooker, there are no rules to stop you making a noise when your opponent is taking a shot, but players are quiet when their opponent is playing. This is because they don't want to distract them and be seen as unsporting. But this idea of behaving in the correct manner comes from the Middle Ages. And it all started with the best warriors in Europe – the knights.

The knight's code

The first knights were just soldiers on horseback. William the Conqueror brought them to England in 1066 to fight King Harold. As a reward for beating Harold, King William gave them land. In return, they promised to spend 40 days a year fighting for their king. This was called **paying homage**. From the twelfth century onwards, though, knights were expected to follow a code of honour, called **chivalry**. Inspired by Christian teachings, chivalry demanded that knights were kind, truthful, loyal, polite, and brave in battle. They had to spend money and choose friends wisely, never break a promise, and defend people who couldn't defend themselves.

The code also stated that knights had to treat women especially well. They should fight for a woman, do brave things for her, and even write her poems.

Fact ✓

If a knight was captured in battle he would rarely get killed – because he was valuable and his family would pay a ransom to free him.

How did you become a knight?

1 If you wanted to be a knight, having a rich father helped. Being a knight was expensive because you had to pay for all your horses and weapons – and you were expected to give expensive gifts to your friends.

2 A knight's training would start at seven years of age when he would be sent to a knight's home to serve him. The **page**, as the boy would be known, would clean dishes, serve meals and wash clothes, and might learn to read and write.

3 At about 14 years old, the page would become a **squire**. He would learn about chivalry, weapons, fighting, armour and horses. If the squire worked hard enough for another seven years, he might be ready to become a full knight.

4 The knight-to-be would spend the night before the ceremony in church, praying. He would promise to be a good and worthy knight. The white tunic shows he is pure; the red robe means he is prepared to spill blood for his king.

5 He would put on all his armour ready for the knighting ceremony. The squire kneels before his lord, or even the king, and promises to be loyal and brave and to protect the poor and weak. He is then **dubbed** (touched) on each shoulder with the flat of his own sword.

6 A knight is born! He is often presented with a set of spurs (used to control a horse), a sword and a new suit of armour. The priest will bless him, so he should always triumph in battle. He is also usually given land and reminded that he must spend 40 days a year fighting for his lord.

Key Words   chivalry   dubbed   page
paying homage   squire

▼ **SOURCE A** Adapted from a description of a squire in *The Knight's Tale*, one of 24 stories in Geoffrey Chaucer's book *The Canterbury Tales*, written between 1387 and 1400.

'With curly locks, as if they had been pressed.
He was some twenty years of age, I guessed.
In height he was of a moderate length,
With wonderful agility and strength.
He'd seen some service with the cavalry
In Flanders and Artois and Picardy...
Short was his gown, the sleeves were long and wide;
He knew the way to sit a horse and ride.
He could make songs and poems and recite,
Knew how to joust and dance, to draw and write'

Over to You

1   Explain the following words and phrases:
   - chivalry
   - paying homage
   - dubbed

2   Read **Source A**.

   a   Make a list of all the things the squire was able to do.

   b   This source is a work of fiction. What are the advantages and disadvantages of this source for a historian?

Knowledge and Understanding

1   What was the difference between a page and a squire?

2   Describe two features of a knight's training.

4.11 Welcome to the tournament

If there wasn't a war to keep a knight fit and his skills sharp, the next best thing was a tournament. This was a big, organised series of competitions – and a fun day out for visitors and spectators. It also gave a knight the chance to become rich and win prizes.

Objectives

- Explain why tournaments took place.
- Consider the different activities that took place in a medieval tournament.

So much to see!

Look at the picture of a tournament and identify all the different events and entertainments that took place.

1   Tents for visiting knights

2   An archery competition taking place

3   The tournament **marshal**. He was like a referee, making sure that everyone followed the rules correctly

4   A joust taking place. Knights on horseback would ride at each other and try to hit their opponent with a 3-metre lance. Three points were awarded if a knight knocked his opponent off his horse, two points if he hit him on the head and one point if he hit any other part of his body. A point would be lost if he hit the horse. Also, if a knight fell off his horse, the opponent got to keep his armour and horse

5   The **herald** announced the names of the knights in each contest

6   A sword fighting competition. Not all knights jousted – some preferred other tournament games

7   The **coat of arms** of each knight taking part in the tournament. In order to stand out when jousting in tournaments, or to avoid being killed by his own men during battle, the knight decorated his shield. The designs were made up of special pictures or patterns known as a coat of arms. A coat of arms was a knight's personal badge and had to be easy to recognise

8 The ale tent

9 A poor beggar, hoping that some of the crowd will throw him a few coins

10 Entertainers performing for the crowd

11 A stand for spectators

12 The local lord and lady who were hosting the tournament

13 Dog fighting – people would bet on the result

14 A beaten knight trying to buy back the horse he lost for falling off during the joust

15 Winner's prize. Often this was a golden cup or a silver plate, but it could be rather unusual – in London in 1216 the prize was a huge brown bear. Some knights made a living out of jousting, taking part in tournaments all over Europe

16 An injured knight. Although the competitions were not designed to hurt the knights, injuries, and even deaths, were common

Key Words   coat of arms   herald   marshal   tilt

17 A dancing bear – people would pay to watch this

18 The tilt. This barrier was introduced to stop the knight who had been knocked off his horse being trampled to death by his opponent's horse

19 Lance – these weren't sharp because the knights weren't trying to kill each other

20 A knight waiting to joust

21 Horses were protected with armour and padding

22 A grandstand for the richest and most important guests

Over to You

1 What is the difference between a marshal and a herald?

2 Why do you think tournaments were so popular among:
   a knights
   b spectators?

3 What was jousting? Make sure you explain the points system in your answer.

4 Re-enactments of medieval tournaments are a popular tourist attraction today at castles and palaces. Some of you might have seen one. Imagine you are designing a poster or flyer for a modern re-enactment of a medieval tournament. Outline what people will see. How would you attract people? What could you charge for entry? What explanations might you need to add to your poster to help people understand what they're coming to see?

4.12 Enough of history: what about *herstory*?

Men held nearly all the top jobs in the Middle Ages – kings, knights, lawyers, bishops, and even town and village officials. So what were the women up to? What were their rights and responsibilities? And, since half the medieval population was female, why don't we know a lot more about medieval women?

Objectives

- Examine the rights, opportunities and activities of medieval women.
- Explain why there was little written about the lives of medieval women.

Second-class citizens

In medieval Britain, there were limits on what women could do. A woman could not marry without her parents' permission. She couldn't own any property, such as clothing or jewellery, unless her husband died and she became a widow. Women had no legal rights either – they couldn't inherit land from their parents if there were any living brothers (even if they were younger) and divorce was almost impossible.

There were also restrictions on their careers. Women couldn't go to university, train to be a doctor or lawyer, join the army or navy, or become a priest. There were, however, some opportunities in the Church. Some women became nuns and dedicated their lives to God. A nun could take on an important role as the head of a nunnery. In the larger nunneries, the abbess in charge had responsibilities similar to a landowner, and had to manage not only the nunnery, but the surrounding land and workers as well. Like monks, nuns also copied out important texts and books so that they were preserved. Today, the British Library contains several important early manuscripts and documents which were copied by women during the medieval period.

Village women

Life was especially tough for an ordinary woman in a medieval village. Mothers would teach their daughters how to cook, sew and care for children and animals. The average age for girls to marry was 17, although some brides were as young as 13. If a woman lived in the countryside, she would either work in the fields or make cloth at home. As well as working all day, she was expected to cook all the food and care for the children. Also, men and women were not paid equally (see **A**).

▼ **SOURCE A** This table compares the daily wages for men and women in the Middle Ages.

Job	Men's wage	Women's wage
Reaper (cutting crops for harvest)	8 pence	5 pence
Hay maker	6 pence	4 pence
Clipper of sheep	7 pence	6 pence

Women in towns

There were some opportunities in towns for women to build a career. Some became cloth sellers, shopkeepers or even blacksmiths. It was not unusual for women to brew and sell ale, or run ale-houses (pubs). However, sometimes these opportunities were very limited. In York, for example, women were *only* allowed to be cap and glove makers, dyers, makers of parchment (a type of paper), bow stringers, tanners (makers of leather) or barber-surgeons (who did basic medical procedures).

Rich women

While many poorer women could choose who they wanted to marry (as long as the husband's family approved!), a girl from a wealthy family couldn't choose her husband – her family would choose for her. The husband received a **dowry** – a payment from his new wife's family – when he got married. These marriages were often arranged to strengthen the ties between two rich and powerful families.

For a wealthy woman, much of her time would be spent entertaining her husband's friends, hunting, dancing and playing games, running the family household and managing the servants.

Fact ✓

Rich women sometimes played a key part in medieval life when their husbands were away. The wives of lords would often help run the castle in their husbands' absence – and Richard I's mother helped him rule the whole country when he was away on the Crusades.

Missing history

A lot of the information we have about the Middle Ages comes from monks, who were one of the few groups that could read and write. They wrote about things that interested them, such as religion, rulers and fights between countries. Women didn't have a great deal to do with these things and most monks had no contact with women, so they were hardly mentioned.

Later on... 1928

The inequalities between men and women remained for many hundreds of years. British men and women only got equal voting rights in 1928.

Meanwhile... 1100s

In the Western world, opportunities in education for women were limited. It took until 1877 for the first woman to get a degree from a British university. But in the Islamic empire women could study, earn religious degrees and qualify as Islamic teachers as early as the twelfth century.

Key Words   dowry

▼ **SOURCE B** This picture of hardworking women appeared in the *Luttrell Psalter*. This book was written between 1320 and 1345 at the request of Sir Geoffrey Luttrell, lord of the manor of Irnham in Lincolnshire.

Over to You

1 Explain why historians don't know much about the lives of women in the Middle Ages.

2 Imagine you got to meet a woman from the Middle Ages. What three interview questions would you ask her? Also, what three pieces of information would you share with her about the role of women today?

3 a Look at **Source A**. Why do you think men and women were paid different wages? Suggest reasons.

   b How could you follow up **Source A** to find out more about the lives of women in the Middle Ages?

Similarity and Difference

1 Make a list of all the things that women were not allowed to do in medieval Britain.

2 Explain one way that the lives of women were different from the lives of men in the Middle Ages.

4.13 Matilda: the forgotten queen

It may not surprise you to learn that between 1066 and 1553 there were no female monarchs in England. Most people in medieval times believed that a monarch should be male. In 1135, all that nearly changed when Princess Matilda, King Henry I's daughter, was named as next in line to the throne. But why wasn't Matilda crowned queen? Who gained control of the country instead of her? Whatever happened to Matilda?

Objectives

- Recall why Matilda thought she should have been crowned queen in 1135.
- Explain the reasons why she wasn't.
- Examine how the struggle between Stephen and Matilda ended.

Henry's got no heir!

King Henry I was the son of William the Conqueror. Henry's older brother had been King of England before him until his death in 1100. By 1120, King Henry had been on the throne for 20 years and had two children – a son named William and a daughter named Matilda. His son was next in line to the throne... until disaster struck. On 25 November 1120, 17-year-old William drowned when the boat bringing him back from France sank. It is said that after Henry heard the news, he never smiled again.

King Henry was determined that the Crown should remain in his family, so before he died he made all the most powerful barons swear to make his daughter, Matilda, queen after he was gone. But many of them didn't think a woman should be the monarch. When Henry died, they broke their promise, and put the king's nephew, Stephen, on the throne. Look at the fact files for Stephen and Matilda.

Matilda

Background:
- Married a German king when she was 12, lived in Germany for ten years until he died in 1125.
- 26-year-old Matilda then married a 14-year-old French prince. They had three sons – Henry, Geoffrey and William.

Claim to the throne:
- Eldest child of Henry I and her father's choice as heir.
- The barons had sworn to make her queen.

Personality:
- She grew up in Germany and was not familiar with the English way of life.
- She could be rude and didn't make friends easily.

Stephen

Background:
- His father was killed fighting abroad when Stephen was just five years old. His mother was the daughter of William the Conqueror.
- He was brought up by his uncle, Henry I, and became a great favourite of the king.
- Henry gave him huge amounts of land. By the time the king died, Stephen was the richest man in England.

Claim to the throne:
- Despite swearing to support his cousin Matilda, Stephen had no intention of doing this.
- He was one of Henry's closest male relatives, and felt the Crown should be his.

Personality:
- Very mild-mannered and good tempered – sometimes accused of being too laid-back.

What happened next?

1 When King Henry I died in 1135, Stephen (who was based in England) raced to London and was crowned king. Matilda, who had been living in France with her French husband, was furious. She gathered together an army. Stephen rewarded his loyal followers, but he was weak and could not control some of the barons. The country was in chaos.

2 Matilda and her supporters landed in England and fierce fighting broke out. In 1141, Matilda's forces captured Stephen and she declared herself 'Lady of the English'.

3 Matilda's victory didn't last long. The people of London didn't like her (because she made them pay more taxes) and rose up against her. She had to run away to France for safety... and Stephen was declared king again.

4 Matilda didn't give up. After more fighting, she and Stephen eventually reached a deal. Stephen would remain King of England – but Matilda's eldest son (Henry) would take over after Stephen's death. So, when Stephen died in 1154, Matilda's son became King Henry II.

▼ **SOURCE A** Monks in the twelfth century wrote about how the barons took control when Stephen was king.

'In the days of this king [Stephen], there was nothing but strife, evil and robbery, for quickly the great men rose against him. When the traitors saw that Stephen was a good humoured, kindly man who inflicted no punishment, they committed all manner of horrible crimes. It grew worse and worse. They took tax, as protection money, from villages. When the wretched people had no more to give, they robbed and burned all the villages.'

▼ **SOURCE B** Written by an unknown monk in the 1100s.

'Matilda sent for the richest men and demanded from them a huge sum of money, not with gentleness but with the voice of authority. They complained they did not have any money left. When the people said this, Matilda, with a very grim look, every trace of a woman's gentleness removed from her face, blazed into unbearable fury.'

Over to You

1 Why do you think Henry I named Matilda and not Stephen as heir to England's throne?

2 Look at the claims to the throne of both Matilda and Stephen. Suggest reasons why the barons might have wanted Stephen as king, and not Matilda.

Source Analysis

Read **Source A**.

1 According to this source, what happened in England under Stephen's rule?

2 In what ways does this source criticise Stephen?

Read **Source B**.

3 Summarise what the writer says about Matilda.

4 If you knew that the man who wrote this source supported Stephen and not Matilda, how might this affect your view of what the writer says about her?

5 Study **Sources A** and **B**. How different are they?

⟳ Quick Knowledge Quiz

Choose the correct answer from the three options:

1 What was a barbican?

   a   a strong, stone gatehouse in a castle
   b   the outer wall of a castle
   c   a type of bridge that raised up and down

2 Who would clean a castle's toilets?

   a   the steward
   b   the constable
   c   the gong farmer

3 In a castle, what were a baron's private rooms called?

   a   dungeon
   b   solar
   c   garderobe

4 Which of the following was a medieval building method?

   a   cut and cover
   b   wattle and daub
   c   find and fix

5 In a medieval village, who would make pots, pans, chains and knives?

   a   the blacksmith
   b   the miller
   c   the chamberlain

6 A town's freedom, written down on a special piece of paper, was known as what?

   a   a guild
   b   a council
   c   a charter

7 What name was given to a group of traders and craftsmen who made rules for their members to follow?

   a   a council
   b   a charter
   c   a guild

8 Which sport involved specially trained birds of prey?

   a   stoolball
   b   falconry
   c   cold hand

9 Slices of stale bread were often used as plates. But what were they called?

   a   trenchers
   b   pewters
   c   tinkers

10 What was chivalry?

   a   a sport played by knights at a tournament
   b   a code of conduct that knights followed
   c   the name of the knighting ceremony

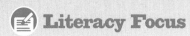 **Literacy Focus**

Linking words

When writing historical narratives, it's really important that the story *flows*. You already know that it's vital to get things in chronological order, but it's also useful to be able to use a variety of **connectives** (joining words used to connect one part of text with another) to form longer sentences and improve the flow of your writing.

Original answer:

> King Henry made all the important barons swear to make his daughter, Matilda, queen after he died. King Henry died in 1135. His nephew, Stephen, became king instead of Matilda. Matilda gathered an army. She went to war with Stephen. In 1141, Matilda's forces captured Stephen. She declared herself 'Lady of the English'.

TIP: This paragraph is simply a collection of short, sharp sentences. Look at the paragraph below to see how connectives have improved it.

Look at this answer with connectives added:

> King Henry made all the important barons swear to make his daughter, Matilda, queen after he died. Then, in 1135, King Henry died and his nephew, Stephen, became king instead of Matilda. Following that, Matilda gathered an army and went to war with Stephen. Eventually, in 1141, Matilda's forces captured Stephen and she declared herself 'Lady of the English'.

1 Now it's your turn. Add connectives to improve the flow of the paragraph.

> Matilda's victory didn't last long. The people of London didn't like her. She raised taxes and they rose up against her. Matilda ran away to France for safety. Stephen was declared king again. Matilda and Stephen went to war again. They reached a deal. Stephen would remain King of England but Matilda's eldest son would take over after Stephen's death. Stephen died in 1154. Matilda's son became King Henry II.

Word bank: connectives

If you want to emphasise something:
- Most of all
- Above all
- Especially
- Notably
- In particular

If you want to add something:
- And
- In addition
- Furthermore
- Also
- As well as

If you want to give an example or illustrate a point:
- For instance
- For example
- These include
- Such as
- As revealed by

If you want to show cause or effect:
- As a result
- Because
- Therefore
- This led to
- Consequently

If you want to compare:
- Equally
- Similarly
- Likewise
- In the same way
- Compared to

If you want to contrast:
- In contrast
- On the other hand
- However
- Alternatively
- Whereas

If you want to put a sequence together:
- Firstly
- Secondly
- Finally
- Then
- Subsequently

In History lessons, you must remember that even though there could be many similarities between people's lives in the past, there were probably big differences in their experiences too, even if they lived in the same period of history. Historians often call this diversity.

> **TIP:** For example, a farmer in a village or a town merchant might both have to follow the same laws and might suffer from the same illnesses.

> **TIP:** For example, they might have access to different foods or employment opportunities, or live in different types of home.

Comparing similarities and differences
Here is one way to answer a question on similarity and difference. Imagine you have been asked:

> Compare the ways in which rich people and poorer people enjoyed themselves and had fun in the Middle Ages. In what ways were they similar and different?

1 **Recap:** Start by recapping what you have learned about how people enjoyed themselves and had fun in the Middle Ages. Make some factual notes on the ways people enjoyed themselves and had fun. Think about these points:

- What were the common sports and types of entertainment in the Middle Ages?

- Note down how the sport and leisure activities enjoyed by the rich were different from those enjoyed by the poor. Suggest reasons for this.

- What was a tournament like? Was there a different experience for the rich and poor?

> **TIP:** Why not think about setting up a Venn diagram to help you make notes? You can turn to pages 90–91 and pages 100–101 to help you complete this.

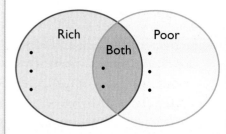

2 **Think deeper:** The idea behind step 1 was to get you thinking about the different ways in which people enjoyed themselves in the Middle Ages. You probably spotted that:

- **People had different experiences**, even though they lived in the same period of history. For example, the poor would have enjoyed different activities from the rich.

- **The poor did not always have access** to the same activities as the rich (such as hunting or hawking) because of the costs involved or the fact that they were not permitted to take part in some activities.

Sometimes it is possible to spot both similarities and differences in the same example:

- **Tournaments** are a good example of this. Both rich and poor could enjoy a tournament (so that is a *similarity*), but the poor were not allowed to take part (or even sit in the same place as the rich) – so their *experience* of a tournament was **different**.

- **Leisure time** is another example. Both rich and poor would enjoy drinking and playing with dice, for example – but the *difference* would be that this entertainment was done in different places. For the poor, they might enjoy drinking and gambling in their homes or in the local pub, but for the rich it would be at the manor house or castle.

3 **Write:** After identifying these similarities and differences, it is time to write your answer.

Here is one effective way to structure an answer, using some sentence starters:

> There were several differences in the way the rich and poor enjoyed themselves and had fun in the Middle Ages. One of the main differences is related to the types of activity they enjoyed.
>
> For example, poorer people would usually make their own fun, creating home-made equipment with whatever they had to hand. They would enjoy simple games and sports, played in or near their village or town on Holy Days. For example...
>
> The rich would enjoy different activities. For example...
>
> The reasons why the rich and poor enjoyed different activities were...
>
> There were some similarities in the way that the rich and poor enjoyed themselves. For example...

Your challenge is to answer this question on similarity and difference:

> Compare life in a town with life in a village in the Middle Ages. In what ways were they similar and different? (20)

The steps below will help you structure your answer. Use the tips and sentence starters to help you.

1 **Recap:** Start by recapping what you have learned about the way people lived their lives in towns and villages. Remember, this includes a lot of areas of life, so you will have to review several pages in this book.

- **Medieval villages:** What was a village like? Who mainly lived in villages – rich or poor? How would life in a village differ from life in a town? What were the common jobs in a village?

- **Medieval towns:** What were towns like? How did town life differ from village life? What were the common jobs?

- **Food and drink:** What were the common foods in medieval times? Did the rich and the poor eat the same things – or was it different? If so, why?

- **The role of women:** Make brief notes on the role of women in the Middle Ages. How did their rights and responsibilities compare to men? Were some women able to build careers?

> **TIP:** What was the main type of work in villages? Was this different from the main type of work in towns? You can use a Venn diagram to help you recap.

> **TIP:** Was a woman's role different in a village compared to a town? What opportunities were there?

2 **Think deeper:** In step 1 you wrote down what you know about life in towns and villages in the Middle Ages – and you noted the different kinds of lives, roles, homes and work opportunities that there were. This means you have considered the *diversity* of life at that time. Now it's time to start organising these notes into an answer. You could:

- Write about different *types of people*. You could start with the rich and write about where they lived, the foods they ate and so on. Then you might look at people in villages and so on.

- Or, look at different *areas of life* in the Middle Ages. So you might start with homes and write about the diversity of homes in the Middle Ages. And then move on to jobs, for example, and describe how jobs and opportunities were different.

Whichever way you choose, you need to have a structure to your answer.

> **TIP:** In History we make 'generalisations'. In other words, we sometimes talk about 'the rich' as one general group. A good historian will know that within the 'rich group', some will be richer than others and experiences will be different (that's diversity, after all), but generalisations are useful to us because they help us reach conclusions. However, it's always important that we back up these conclusions with evidence from what we have learned.

3 **Write:** It's time to start writing your answer. You may use the sentence starters below.

There were many differences in the way that people lived in towns and villages in the Middle Ages. One of the main differences is related to the type of **homes** they lived in. For example, in villages...

However, in towns...   (5)

Another difference was the type of **jobs** that people did. In villages, the main type of job was...

However, in towns...

In a village, a woman might...

In towns, a woman might...   (5)

There were some similarities in both **town and village life.**
For example...   (5)

Another similarity was...   (5)

> **TIP:** Were there similarities in the foods eaten? What about the rich and poor?

Crown vs Church: Murder in the Cathedral

We all know that kings and queens were very powerful and important people in medieval times. But did they always get their own way? The next few pages look at a well-known time in the Middle Ages when a king's power was tested... and which led to a vicious murder inside one of Britain's most famous cathedrals.

Objectives

- Summarise the events in the quarrel between Henry II and Thomas Becket in the correct chronological order.
- Evaluate King Henry's reasons for making Becket Archbishop of Canterbury.
- Examine the murder of Thomas Becket – and its consequences.

Best of friends

In 1154, Henry II became King of England. One of his best friends was a man called Thomas Becket. They hunted and got drunk together. They both enjoyed expensive clothes, magnificent palaces and the very best food and wine. Henry respected and trusted Thomas so much that he made him **Chancellor**. This was a very important job – he managed the king's money, wrote important documents and took charge of the country when Henry was away.

Henry the hot head!

King Henry was a popular ruler, but he did have one major fault – his temper. He liked to get his own way and, when he got angry, his eyes became bloodshot and he threw huge tantrums. He once got so angry that he ripped all his clothes off, threw himself on the floor and started chewing straw!

Controlling the country

Despite being king, Henry did not have complete control of the country. All the people who worked for the Church – bishops, priests, monks, nuns, for example – were under the leadership of the Archbishop of Canterbury, not the king. Also, the Church owned large areas of rich farmland throughout the country, and controlled the people living on the land. So, in the Middle Ages, the Church was both wealthy *and* powerful.

Henry's master plan

As well as owning lots of land and controlling lots of people, the Church had its own separate law courts. So, people who worked for the Church and broke the law went to these courts rather than the king's courts. This affected lots of people as, at this time, one in six people worked for the Church in some way. Henry was worried that there was too much crime and he thought that the church courts were too soft. For example, the king's courts might cut off the hands of thieves, but the church courts would probably fine them.

Henry wanted a clever and trusted friend he could put in charge of the Church. That way, the church courts would punish people how he wanted – and his power would be complete.

Archbishop Becket

In 1162, Henry made Thomas Becket the Archbishop of Canterbury, placing him in charge of the Church in England. Becket would be based at Canterbury Cathedral in Kent. Unfortunately for the king, though,

Becket took his new job very seriously indeed. He stopped getting drunk and wearing fancy clothes. He started to wear an itchy, goat-hair shirt and slept on the hard, stone floor. Religion became very important to Becket and he spent hours praying every day. When Henry spoke to him about changing the church courts, Becket refused. The two men began to argue, and after Henry lost his temper in one particularly nasty disagreement, Becket fled to France – for six years!

Guess who's Beck?

Becket eventually returned to Britain and the two men agreed to try to work together. But it soon went wrong again. Becket **excommunicated** all the bishops who had helped Henry run Church business while he was away. This meant that they were sacked from their jobs and were told they'd go straight to hell when they died.

When Henry found out, he was furious. In one of his rages he shouted, 'Is there no one who will rid me of this troublesome priest?' Four knights were standing nearby and they decided that they could rid their king of this priest. They set off to Canterbury without delay.

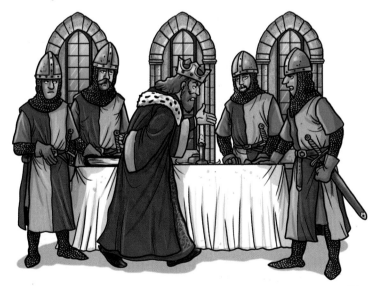

Meanwhile...

In 1154, the same year that Henry II became king, Nicholas Breakspear became Pope – the only English man ever to be chosen for the role.

Key Words Chancellor
excommunicated

Over to You

1 Before the four knights set out to kill Becket, the following events occurred. Write these down in the correct chronological order.
   - Becket ran away to France for six years.
   - Henry and Becket became best friends.
   - Henry made Becket Archbishop of Canterbury.
   - Henry made Becket Chancellor.
   - Henry was heard to say, 'Is there no one who will rid me of this troublesome priest?'
   - Becket excommunicated some bishops.

2 **a** Think of five adjectives to describe King Henry II.

   b Think of five adjectives to describe Thomas Becket after he became Archbishop of Canterbury.

   c Are any of your words the same? Using the words you have listed, write two paragraphs describing Henry and Becket.

Cause

1 Briefly describe the relationship between Henry II and Thomas Becket at the time Becket was made Chancellor.

2 Why was Henry unhappy with the Church?

3 Explain why Henry II made Becket the Archbishop of Canterbury in 1162.

The afternoon of 29 December 1170 was a dark and stormy one. Four knights had arrived outside Canterbury Cathedral. Some monks, sensing trouble, hurried inside to find Archbishop Becket and rush him to safety. The events that followed caused a sensation throughout medieval Europe. If it had happened today, it would have been a huge news story covered by lots of television channels and journalists. If there had been TV news in 1170, it may have been presented something like this…

TV reporter: I can confirm the news that Thomas Becket, the man in charge of religion in England, has been hacked to death inside our most important cathedral. I can also reveal that the four men officially linked with the murder are knights and were apparently acting under orders from King Henry! The knights – Reginald Fitzurse, William de Tracy, Richard Brito and Hugh de Morville – have fled into the stormy night. If they really are Henry's men, this will be the most sensational story of the century!

I have an eyewitness. His name is Edward Grim, a monk who claims to have seen it all. What can you tell us, Brother Edward?

Edward Grim (monk): It was truly awful – I'm still shaking with anger and fear. The murderers entered this house of God in full armour and with their swords drawn. Some of my brother monks had tried to bolt the doors to keep them out, but the archbishop ordered the doors to be reopened. He said, 'It's not right to make a fortress out of a house of prayer.'

In a crazed fury, one of the knights yelled out, 'Where is Thomas Becket, traitor to the king and country?'

TV reporter: What did Becket do?

Edward Grim: Becket stood in front of his attackers and said, 'I am no traitor and I am ready to die.' The knights then grabbed hold of the archbishop and tried to drag him outside in order to kill him. Becket clung to a pillar but, realising that his time on earth was nearly over, he bowed his head in prayer and made his peace with God.

The murderous knights brought a sword crashing down on Becket's head, nearly chopping my hand off as it passed. Then another sword slashed down, again at his head, but still Becket stood firm in his prayers. The third blow was swung with such force that it knocked him to his knees.

As he knelt, a fourth and final blow cut off the top of his head – that sword smashed to pieces on the cathedral floor with the force of the strike.

TV reporter: Did the knights then run away?

Edward Grim: No, these evil men weren't finished yet. One knight put his foot on the holy priest's neck and scattered his blood and brains all over the floor. I couldn't bear to look any more, but Brother William said he saw one of them scooping Becket's brains out of his skull with his sword. The last thing I heard was one of the knights saying, 'Let us away, this fellow will get up no more!' With that, they disappeared into the night.

TV reporter: This news will shock the country. The big question tonight is – the knights claimed to be acting on King Henry's orders, but how will the king respond?

Fact ✓

Edward Grim really was a witness to the events. He was visiting Canterbury on that day and wrote his account down soon after.

National sensation

Although this TV report is imaginary, the events it describes are recorded in witness statements and other evidence available to historians.

Henry II was horrified when he heard the news. He hadn't exactly ordered the knights to go to Canterbury, but he knew he was going to get the blame. He was terrified that he might be excommunicated by the Pope. So, he decided to say sorry – in a big way! Henry walked the streets of Canterbury barefoot and, when his feet were cut and bleeding, he approached the cathedral. He then prayed at Becket's tomb while monks whipped his bare back. He spent the night on the hard, stone floor – on the very spot where Becket was killed. It worked – the Pope forgave Henry. Also, more importantly for the Church, Henry stopped his plans to change the church courts, and they carried on as before.

The knights were not as fortunate as Henry. They were sent on a pilgrimage – all the way to the Holy Land. None of them survived the long journey.

Later on... `1173`

People started claiming miracles were taking place at Becket's tomb as soon as he died. Blind people claimed they could see, and deaf people claimed they could hear after visiting his tomb. In 1173, Becket was made a saint by the Pope, and before long, the journey to pray at Becket's tomb was one of the most popular pilgrimages in Europe.

Over to You .ıl

1 a Why do you think the knights tried to drag Becket outside the cathedral?

 b Why do you think Henry reacted to Becket's murder in the way he did?

2 a Look at **Interpretation A**. In your own words, describe what is happening in the picture.

 b What impression of Thomas Becket do you think the artist was trying to create? Give reasons for your answer.

Cause and Consequence

1 Make a list of all the different people who contributed in some way to Becket's death.

2 Write a narrative account analysing the death of Thomas Becket in 1170. You may use the following in your answer:
 • the role of the knights
 • the role of King Henry II.

5.2 King John: Magna Carta man

The job of a medieval monarch was often complicated. Although they lived a life of luxury, they also had a job to do – keep law and order, protect the country from attack, collect taxes, and more. And sometimes they made mistakes. They made poor decisions and upset those who helped them run the country. This lesson investigates a king who made several mistakes… and explains how his actions changed the country forever.

Objectives

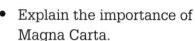

- Analyse the consequences of King John's mistakes.
- Explain the importance of Magna Carta.

King John's struggles

King John was the son of Henry II and younger brother of King Richard I. When his older brother died in 1199, John had little money left because Richard had spent so much of it fighting abroad. Unfortunately, King John soon did things that turned many people against him. The cartoon below sums up the main complaints of the barons and Church leaders.

What did the barons do?

By 1215, the barons had decided they'd had enough. Around 40 barons put together an army and marched towards London. Then they gave King John a choice – change the way he was running the country… or fight the army on its way to London!

King John gave in and asked the barons what they wanted. The barons made a list of 63 rights that they wanted. The main points are listed in **A**.

King John agrees

In June 1215, the barons met the king in a field at Runnymede, near Windsor. After four days of discussions, King John agreed to the list (known as **Magna Carta**, which means 'Great Charter'), and the barons agreed to be loyal to the king.

Fact ✓

Many copies of Magna Carta were made and sent out to important officials all over the country. Only four copies currently exist: two are in the British Library in London, one is in Lincoln Castle and one is in Salisbury Cathedral.

King John is a poor leader in battle. A few years ago, England ruled over lots of land in France… but not any longer! The French have defeated us many times and regained much of their land as a result of John's mistakes.

We have even lost Normandy in France, the birthplace of William the Conqueror. I hear some people use the nickname 'Softsword' to describe King John!

And he keeps demanding higher and higher taxes to pay for battles he keeps losing! He has even started taxing sons when their fathers die! It's all money, money, money with King John.

King John has argued with the Pope many times. He made the Pope so angry that he closed all our churches for seven years. No one could get married or have a proper Christian burial.

John can be cruel too, or so I hear. He left the wife of one of his enemies to starve to death in prison. And he murdered his nephew in a drunken rage… apparently.

▼ **SOURCE A** Adapted from Magna Carta, written in 1215. King John never actually signed it because he couldn't write, so he stamped it with his royal seal to show he agreed.

'I, King John, accept that I must run the country according to the law. I agree:

- not to interfere with the Church
- not to imprison freemen or nobles without a trial
- that trials will be held quickly and fairly
- to stop unfair taxes
- not to ask for extra taxes without consulting a council of Church leaders and landowners (known as a Great Council)
- to let merchants travel around the country to buy and sell without having to pay large taxes
- that 25 barons will be elected by the other barons to make sure I follow this agreement.'

Was Magna Carta important at the time?

King John never liked Magna Carta. He said he had been bullied into agreeing to it. People accused the barons of being selfish too. After all, Magna Carta didn't apply to the vast majority of the population (the peasants) – it listed the rights mainly for wealthier people, such as barons, knights, merchants and freemen. In fact, John tried to break his promises and he briefly went to war with the barons. However, just over a year after agreeing to Magna Carta, John caught dysentery (a nasty form of diarrhoea) and died.

Is Magna Carta important now?

Even though it didn't apply to all citizens at the time, as the years have passed Magna Carta has become more and more important. It introduced the idea that there are certain laws and rules that even monarchs must accept, and that they couldn't do whatever they wanted. After King John died, other kings signed Magna Carta too, and today it is known as one of the first steps towards Britain becoming one of the world's first democracies. In fact, some of the best-known parts of Magna Carta still apply to everyone today. For example:

- British people have the right to a fair trial before they can be punished.
- British people cannot be taxed unfairly.

Key Words

democracy   freemen
Great Council   Magna Carta

▼ **INTERPRETATION B** From historian Dan Snow's film on why Magna Carta was so significant (2015).

'Magna Carta survived and thrived over the centuries and its ideas have spread around the world. Its principles can be found in the American Bill of Rights and the Universal Declaration of Human Rights. The fundamental freedoms encoded in Magna Carta are as important now as they were 800 years ago, showing [the idea] that there are limits to the power of our rulers.'

Over to You

1 Think of three words that best describe King John. Say why you chose them.

2 Imagine you are a baron in England in 1214. Write King John a letter explaining why you're angry with him. Make sure you tell him what angers you most and why. Remember to set it out like a proper letter with the address of your castle and the king's address at the Tower of London at the top.

3 Create your own Magna Carta for your school. List at least seven changes you would like to see. These rules must apply to everybody, students and staff, and they must improve your school or education. Explain your reasons for each rule.

Significance

Historians sometimes try to judge whether an event or a person is significant. This is not about being famous or simply 'important'. Historical significance is about looking at the impact *at the time* (short term), its effects *over a long period* (long term), and whether it is still relevant *today*.

1 a Make a list of the main points in Magna Carta.
  b Which of the points are still important today?

2 Was Magna Carta a short-term or a long-term success? Explain your answer.

3 Explain the significance of Magna Carta. Include its short-term and long-term impacts and whether it is still relevant today.

Where did our Parliament come from?

Medieval monarchs had always asked rich, powerful landowners (the barons, earls, lords and nobles) for advice on things like raising money or going to war. When kings met with advisers it was often called a Great Council. Sometimes there were arguments at these meetings... but the king nearly always got his own way.

This all changed in 1215 when King John ruled. The rich landowners rebelled and forced him to sign Magna Carta, which said that the king couldn't do whatever he wanted. However, King John died in 1216 and his son became King Henry III when he was only nine years old. So, would young Henry also agree to follow the rules laid down in Magna Carta... or would he just ignore them and rule however he wished? And how is all this linked to **Parliament** and the way Britain is ruled today?

Objectives

- Examine why King Henry III argued with the barons.
- Identify the origins of Britain's Parliament.

The boy king

To begin with, young King Henry III regularly met with the Great Council and took advice. But Henry didn't stay a boy forever – and when he got older, and got married, he began to ignore advice and ran things how he wanted. As you might imagine, this annoyed members of the Great Council. The cartoon below sums up their complaints.

And just like his father, he's not a very successful soldier. He tried to take over large parts of France... and lost! And he expects us to provide soldiers and money for his expensive wars!

And who's paying for all this? That's right – us! Our taxes go up because he spends so much.

Henry is spending a fortune on living a life of luxury. He even tried to buy the Italian island of Sicily as a present for his son!

A Frenchman, Peter des Rivaux, has all the top jobs. He's got over 20 jobs! In fact, Henry seems to give all the best jobs to his wife's friends and relatives.

He doesn't even take our advice any more. He just listens to his French wife and her French friends and relatives!

And he's meddling with religion. Or rather, his wife is. She begged Henry to make her uncle – a Frenchman – the Archbishop of Canterbury.

▼ **SOURCE A** A picture from a medieval manuscript created during the time of Henry III showing him watching the building of a church. The king spent vast sums of money on church-building and on royal castles.

Key Words   Parliament

▼ **SOURCE B** Adapted from the Provisions of Oxford, signed in 1258. The word 'parliament' is from the French word 'parler', which means 'to talk'.

'The Provisions of Oxford

- The king cannot make decisions without the Great Council's agreement.

- The Great Council should choose the king's main advisers.

- A Parliament consisting of 15 members of the Great Council, plus 12 other barons, has to meet at least three times a year.

Signed,

Henry III and the Great Council'

Over to You

1 Write a sentence or two to explain the following terms:
   a Great Council
   b Provisions of Oxford.

2 a Make a list of things that made Henry unpopular with his barons.

   b Which of these things do you think upset the barons the most? Make another list, putting them in order. Start with what you think annoyed the barons the most.

   c Explain how some of the entries on your list are linked or connected.

Enough is enough!

By 1258, the barons had had enough. They were fed up with high taxes and the fact that Henry listened more to his wife than to them. So, the barons threatened to fight King Henry unless he agreed to meet to discuss things. At a meeting in Oxford, the barons showed Henry a document called 'The Provisions of Oxford' (see **B**). If Henry agreed to this, the barons would have a lot more power. Henry felt he had no choice, so he signed it.

However, the king's son, 19-year-old Prince Edward, was furious that his father had been treated this way, and swore to get revenge.

King Henry the prisoner

In 1264, King Henry III got an army together to fight the barons. He was unhappy that the barons had forced him to sign the Provisions of Oxford because it took away a lot of his power. The king's army was led by Prince Edward, Henry's son. The baron's army was led by Simon de Montfort, a powerful landowner who was married to King Henry's sister. On 14 May 1264, the two sides fought a battle at Lewes (near Brighton) in Sussex. The barons won, and King Henry and Prince Edward were taken prisoner.

What happened next?

In 1265, Simon de Montfort called a meeting of the Great Council. But this time, he didn't just invite important bishops and rich barons. He also included two ordinary wealthy people from each large town (known as burgesses) and two knights from each county. This was the first time that ordinary people had been included in any sort of discussion about running the country. This meeting is often called 'the first Parliament'.

De Montfort is doomed!

Not surprisingly, the king and the young prince fought back. Prince Edward escaped from prison and gathered another army together. In August 1265, de Montfort's army was defeated at the Battle of Evesham in Worcestershire. Source C shows the rather nasty way in which de Montfort was killed.

Parliament lives on

Although de Montfort had died, his idea lived on. When Henry III died in 1272, Prince Edward became King Edward I. He didn't want to risk more wars with the barons by scrapping Parliament, so he kept meeting with them (see D). Soon, the barons in Parliament realised that they were quite powerful. For example, if the king needed money (which he often did) he knew he couldn't go around collecting it all himself – he needed Parliament to get it for him. In return, Parliament could ask the king for permission to introduce new laws. So, although Parliament couldn't exactly tell the king what to do, it was certainly a powerful force in the country because it controlled the king's money and could make new laws… just like today.

By the mid-1300s, meetings of Parliament had settled into a pattern that lasted for centuries. By the end of the fourteenth century, the richer people from the towns and some of the knights (together known as the 'commons') had their own meeting place to discuss issues that directly related to them.

▼ **SOURCE C** This illustration from the 1200s shows the death of Simon de Montfort. It works a bit like a cartoon strip – first (on the left), de Montfort is stripped of his armour, then his body is cut to pieces. Later, his head was given to a baron who hated him, who sent it to his wife as a gift!

▼ **INTERPRETATION D** A fourteenth-century picture of King Edward I and his parliament. Edward's Parliament of 1295 is also known as the 'Model Parliament'. The king is on a throne at the top centre. This picture wrongly shows rulers from Wales (Llywelyn) and Scotland (Alexander) sitting to the king's left and right. They did not actually attend at the same time as King Edward. The barons, knights and burgesses are in front of the king.

▼ **E** The monarch and his two groups of advisors – the 'lords' and the 'commons'. Today, the British Parliament is still made up of the 'House of Lords' and the 'House of Commons'.

The Monarch
- The king decided when Parliament was to meet, usually for a few weeks a year.
- The king still thought of Parliament as being there to raise money for him – it couldn't stop taxes being collected even if it didn't like what he was doing.
- In return, the king allowed Parliament to help with the passing of some laws.
- The king was aware of the power of the barons and knights, and knew it was better to try to work together on some issues.

The Lords
- A number of rich barons and bishops met in the House of Lords. They advised the king.
- The right to attend passed from father to son.

The Commons
- They were invited by the king, and were usually the richer people of the town and landowning knights. Discussions and voting on issues took place.
- These people became known as the 'commoners' or 'Commons' and met in the House of Commons.

Over to You

1 What were the advantages of having a Parliament:
  a   for the king
  b   for the barons, bishops, knights and townspeople?

2 a   How did Simon de Montfort die?
  b   In what ways could de Montfort be seen as both a hero and a traitor?

3 Use pages 116–121 to help you draw a flow diagram showing the key steps towards holding a Parliament in England. Start with King John and the difficulties he had with his barons and end with Edward I's Parliament.

Later on...

TODAY

The British Parliament, made up of the House of Lords and the House of Commons, still meets like this today.

Cause and Consequence

1 Describe how events in each of the following years affected the development of Parliament:
  a   1264   b   1265   c   1272

2 Explain the following:
- The importance of Simon de Montfort in the development of Parliament
- The importance of King Edward I in the development of Parliament.

Why were peasants so angry in 1381?

In today's world, large groups of people sometimes gather together because they are angry about something. They might hold a big meeting or march through the streets carrying banners and shouting slogans to express what they are unhappy about. When this happens, it is called a **protest** and the people taking part are called protesters.

Objectives

- Examine why peasants were so angry in 1381.
- Evaluate the causes of the peasants' anger and make connections between them.

You may have seen scenes like the one in **Source A** on news reports. Protests like this have taken place in recent years in Britain and in the rest of the world over all sorts of issues.

Sometimes, though, the protesters are so angry about things that they are prepared to use violence, which is illegal in today's society. Some protesters might get weapons and tell the leaders of a country to change things… or else! When this happens, it is usually called a **revolt** or a **rebellion**.

One of the best-known examples of rebellion in Britain happened during the summer of 1381. Ordinary people were so angry about the way they were forced to live that thousands marched to London, set fire to houses, murdered some of the king's men, and demanded that the king make changes to their lives. This event became known as the 'Peasants' Revolt'.

So why were the people so angry?

▼ **SOURCE A** This photo shows people marching through the streets of London in protest against cuts to the NHS in 2013.

England has been at war with France since 1369, and we haven't been doing well. The king wants money to pay for the war, and he keeps demanding a tax – called a Poll Tax – from both rich and poor whenever he decides!

I don't own my own land – the local lord gives me some and I try to make a living from it by growing and selling crops. But I still have to work a few days a week for no wages. This is called 'work service' and I hate it. I just want to own my own land...

When we're not doing work service and actually get paid, our wages are very low. But it wasn't always like this! When the deadly disease called the Black Death killed lots of workers, there were not enough people to do all the jobs. So, we asked for more wages or else the work would not get done. For a time, our wages rose and rose. But then a new law called the 'Statute of Labourers' said we couldn't earn more money than we did before the Black Death. It's not fair!

The rich can afford the Poll Tax, but we can't. And it keeps going up! We paid 4 pence in 1377... and now, in 1381, it's 12 pence!

Richard II became the king in 1377, but he is only young. He is 14 years old now, and is badly advised by greedy evil men who care only about making themselves rich... or so I've heard!

I have been very interested in what a priest called John Ball has been saying. He has been travelling around the country since 1366, saying that all men are equal in the eyes of God, and that this country won't be right until there is no difference between rich and poor.

Short-term causes of the revolt?

On 30 May 1381, a group of King Richard's tax collectors arrived in the village of Fobbing in Essex to collect the hated Poll Tax money. The peasants refused to pay and attacked the tax collectors. Three of the king's men were killed but another escaped and rode back to London to tell the king. Soon, other tax collectors were attacked all over south-east England. Before long, a large group of up to 60,000 angry peasants decided to march to London to challenge the king about the high taxes and low wages – the Peasants' Revolt had begun...

Over to You

1 Explain the difference between a 'protest' and a 'protester'.

2 Working in a small group, imagine that you all live in a village in Essex or Kent in May 1381. Your small group is determined to be part of the Peasants' Revolt, but some of your fellow villagers aren't so sure. Your task is to convince other people in your village to join you and march to London.

   a Prepare a short speech outlining your reasons for taking part in the revolt. It should focus on why you are so angry about the life you lead. In your opinion, is one reason more important than the others? If so, focus on this point a bit more.

   b Design a poster that tries to persuade fellow villagers to support the revolt.

   c Make a list of slogans that you might sing, chant or write on banners that you might carry while marching to London.

Cause and Consequence

1 Give definitions for the following terms:
   a Poll Tax
   b Statute of Labourers
   c revolt

2 Explain the connections between two of the following:
   • the Poll Tax
   • the Peasant's Revolt
   • the Statute of Labourers
   • the Black Death.

Power to the people

In 1377, ten-year-old Richard II became king. Since 1369, England had been at war with France and the king desperately needed money for weapons. Richard got tax collectors to go around the country collecting money from anyone over the age of 15 to help pay for his costly war.

The new tax (known as the Poll Tax) was first collected in 1377, and then again in 1380. But it was hated, especially by the poor, who said they couldn't afford to pay it. Then, in 1381, Richard asked for even more money. For thousands of ordinary peasants, this was the final straw!

Objectives

- Examine what happened to the angry peasants when they took their revolt to London.
- Analyse evidence, and identify similarities and differences.

Chaos in the streets of London

The Peasants' Revolt started in May 1381 when peasants in Essex refused to pay the Poll Tax. This led to more attacks and the situation soon escalated.

1 Peasants began rebelling all over the south-east of England.

2 Peasants burned important documents, books and papers.

3 Some peasants broke into Maidstone prison and freed a priest called John Ball.

Ball had made speeches saying peasants deserved more from life. He preached fairness and equality. The Archbishop of Canterbury thought it was dangerous to make such speeches and had put Ball in prison.

4 In June 1381, up to 60,000 peasants marched towards London. They chose a former soldier called Wat Tyler as their leader. The gatekeepers at London let the peasants into the city, as they didn't like the rich lords either.

5 On 13 June, the angry mob ran riot in London. They burned down the houses of rich Londoners.

Let's go and attack the Tower of London!

6 Meanwhile, King Richard II watched the rioting from the safety of the Tower of London. But…

I must go and meet them.

But it's not safe, my lord!

I suggest you meet them in a place where they cannot get near you.

7 On 13 June, the king decided to meet the peasants and spoke to them on a boat on the River Thames.

We want you to be our king… but we cannot stand how we are treated any longer.

What do you want?

8 Tyler told the king that peasants wanted higher wages and didn't want to be forced to work for their lords for free for a few days a week.

Can we trust him?

Thank you for your demands, but I will not come ashore to discuss this today.

It is dangerous here, my Lord. Let's return to the Tower of London.

10 On 15 June, the king met the rebels once more. He agreed to their demands.

I will give you what you want, but the killing must stop!

9 Meanwhile, a group of peasants broke into the Tower of London and murdered both the Archbishop of Canterbury and the king's treasurer.

The king's not back yet, but the man who looks after the king's money is here… so is the Archbishop of Canterbury.

Die, you traitor!

Arghh…

After the bloodshed and havoc of 14 June, the king and the rebels decide to meet one last time.

Over to You

1 Match up the names with the correct descriptions.
- Wat Tyler
- John Ball
- Richard II
- Archbishop of Canterbury

- 14-year-old king
- killed by rebel peasants
- leader of the Peasants' Revolt
- priest who believed people were created equal

What happened next?

On 15 June 1381, the king once again met with Wat Tyler, this time at Smithfield, near St Paul's Cathedral. Tyler was joined by around 25,000 peasants, while the king had around 75 knights and nobles, including the Lord Mayor of London. Tyler asked the king to divide up all Church land among the peasants and make everyone, with the exception of the king, equal. The king agreed!

We are not exactly sure what happened next, as the only people who wrote about the event were on the king's side. However, the events of the next few minutes of the meeting were amazing. Read the following two accounts carefully to see if you can work out what happened.

▼ **SOURCE A** Adapted from the *Anonimalle Chronicle of St Mary's*, a detailed account written by monks in York at the time of the revolt. The monks were not there, but put together this account from what they were told.

'Wat Tyler, in the presence of the king, rinsed out his mouth in a very rude manner... One of the king's guards... said aloud that Wat Tyler was the greatest thief and robber in all Kent... For these words Wat would have killed him in the king's presence; but because he tried to do so, the Mayor of London, William of Walworth... arrested him... Wat stabbed the mayor with his dagger. But, as it pleased God, the mayor was wearing armour and took no harm... he struck back at Wat, giving him a deep cut in the neck, and then a great blow on the head. And during the fight a guard of the king stabbed Wat two or three times.'

▼ **SOURCE B** Adapted from text written by Jean Froissart, a French poet and historian for the royal family. He wrote this at the time of the revolt, but didn't see what happened. He based his account on interviews with eyewitnesses.

'Then Tyler saw a squire [one of the king's landowners] who was carrying the King's sword, and said, "Give me that sword." The squire said, "No, it is the King's sword." Tyler replied, "I'll kill you – or never eat again."
At that moment the Mayor of London appeared with twelve knights, all well armed. He said to Tyler, "How dare you speak like that in the King's presence? You are a lying, stinking criminal and you'll pay for those words."
The mayor then drew his sword and hit Tyler such a blow on the head that he fell to the ground. Then the knights gathered round Tyler, so the rebels couldn't see him. One of the King's squires, John Standish, stuck his sword into Tyler's stomach, killing him. Then the unruly mob saw that their leader was killed, so they said, "Our leader is dead. Let's go and kill them all." And they got themselves in battle order, with the bowmen in front.'

How did it end?

The rebels were shocked by Wat Tyler's death and some looked ready to attack the king. Despite this, the king rode out to them, alone, and said, 'Sirs, what is the matter? You shall have no leader except me. I am your king. Be peaceful.' (See C.) Almost immediately, the situation calmed down, and shortly afterwards the peasants began to go home.

Consequences of the revolt

King Richard didn't keep any of the promises he'd made. His army hunted down and killed many of the leaders of the revolt. John Ball, the priest, was cut into pieces in front of the king and his head was stuck on a spike on London Bridge. It was joined by the head of Wat Tyler. However, the hated Poll Tax was scrapped, and taxes were never as high again.

Also, over the next 50 years the peasants ended up getting most of the things they asked for. Eventually, Parliament stopped trying to control peasants' wages and they were allowed to work for the best wages they could get.

▶ **INTERPRETATION C**
This picture is taken from an account of the murder of Wat Tyler and was painted 60 years after it happened. It is in two parts. On the left, Richard II sees the murder; on the right, he rides out to speak to the rebels.

With increased wealth, some peasants bought or rented land from a landowner. Having their own land meant they didn't have to rely on a lord to give them land – which meant they didn't have to work for him for free for a few days a week in return. Gradually, peasants became more independent and relied less on a lord to run all aspects of their lives – which is what the peasants who took part in the Peasants' Revolt really wanted!

Over to You

1　EITHER: Imagine you were one of the peasants who marched to London with Wat Tyler. The revolt is over and you are back in your village, but the villagers who didn't go with you want to know what happened. Write down what you would tell them – and remember to make it accurate and exciting!

OR: Finish off the cartoon strip on pages 124 and 125. The final cartoon ends with Richard II meeting with the peasants on 15 June 1381. But, as you know, such a lot happened at that meeting... and afterwards. Complete the cartoon by adding another two to five pictures to explain what happened next.

2　a　Look at **Interpretation C**. Describe what is happening.

　　b　What do you think the painter did to research what they were about to paint?

Source Analysis

The people who wrote about the revolt were either monks or rich people who had little sympathy for the peasants. Both monks and rich people needed peasants to farm for them – and didn't want to pay them higher wages. As a result, they often portrayed the peasants as vicious and rude. However, there are still many differences in the accounts of the revolt.

Read **Sources A** and **B**.

1　Why do you think no peasants wrote down what happened on 15 June 1381?

2　The two sources were written by the king's supporters. How might that affect what was written?

3　How different are the two sources? Name at least three differences in your answer.

4　How similar are the two sources? Name at least three similarities in your answer.

Keeping law and order

The topic of crime and punishment is big news in today's world. We often hear about murders or big robberies on our television screens and on news websites. TV programmes are dedicated to catching criminals or showing how the criminal justice system works. The police investigate crime and try to catch lawbreakers. The courts decide if a person is guilty or not and apply punishments including fines and imprisonment.

But what law and order systems were in place in the Middle Ages? Who was responsible for catching criminals? And how were people punished?

Objectives

- Identify how law and order was maintained in the Middle Ages.
- Compare medieval types of punishment with modern methods.

Keeping the peace

In the Middle Ages, one of a monarch's most important roles was to keep law and order, to maintain a peaceful kingdom. It was important to make sure that everyone obeyed the laws, but there were no policemen. If towns and villages wanted to keep law and order they had to do it themselves. If you saw someone committing a crime you had to raise the **hue and cry**. This meant that you had to shout loudly, and people would come to help you catch the criminal. You would be fined if you failed to do this (see **A**).

In some areas, all men and women over the age of 12 were put into groups of ten – called **tithings** – and were responsible for each other's behaviour. If a member of the tithing broke the law the others had to take them to court and pay their fines.

Some places set up a **watch** – a group of people who patrolled the streets each night – and a **constable** was chosen to coordinate them. But these weren't particularly popular jobs. People didn't get paid... and you lost sleep while walking around the streets all night. As a result, constables and watchmen didn't always do their jobs properly – if they did, they might be chosen again!

Because there was no police force, criminals must have got away with very serious crimes, as they were rarely caught. So sometimes even the king himself got involved in investigations.

constable

four-man watch

▼ **SOURCE A** From Wakefield Manor court records, October 1315.

'The township of Stansfield did not raise the hue and cry on the thieves that burgled the house of Amery of Hertelay, nor ever found or prosecuted them. They are to be fined 40 shillings.'

Fact ✓

In the Middle Ages there weren't any prisons as we know them today. Some towns had a small stone building (called a 'cell') where criminals were kept until they were punished.

Punishment fits the crime

When a criminal was caught, they would usually be taken to the local lord's manor house. The lord would then decide on a punishment, which would usually be a fine. Sometimes, he would try to make the punishment fit the crime. So, a person who sold bad wine might be forced to drink some while the rest was poured over their head. Sometimes thieves had fingers cut off and people who told lies had their tongues cut out (see **B** and **C**).

▼ **SOURCE B** Adapted from descriptions of crimes and their punishments from the 1335 records of Rochdale Court. 'd' was a medieval way of writing 'p' for 'pence'. Two pence was a lot of money in the Middle Ages.

> Nicholas Hopwood for hitting Magota, daughter of Henry – fined 2d.
> Margaret Webb for breach of peace [such as fighting or making too much noise] – fined 2d.
> Amos Walter for theft of his lord's pigs. Also carrying a bow and arrow in his lord's wood – two fingers on right hand struck off; fined 2d for bow and arrow.

▼ **SOURCE C** This baker, seen in a book written in 1266, has been found guilty of breaking a law which controlled the sale of bread. The baker is being dragged through the streets with the bread tied around his neck while people throw rotten food and shout abuse at him.

Stocks and pillory

Two of the best-known punishments were the stocks and the pillory. They were often carried out in the middle of town to publicly humiliate the guilty person – and make other people think twice about committing crimes themselves. The difference between stocks and pillory was simple – criminals could sit down in the stocks, but they had to stand up in the pillory. Sometimes a prisoner's ears were nailed to the wood or a large stone was hung around their neck; naughty children might be taken to a finger pillory, which trapped just the fingertips!

Key Words   constable   hue and cry   tithings   watch

Over to You

1 Complete the sentences below with an accurate term:
   a A group of ten people who are responsible for each other was called a _____.
   b The _____ were a group who patrolled the streets each night.
   c When you saw someone committing a crime you had to raise the _____ and _____.
   d A _____ was an official who coordinated the watch.

2 Explain the difference between the stocks and the pillory.

3 Suggest reasons why so many punishments were carried out in public.

Source Analysis

Look at **Sources A, B** and **C**.

1 Why were the people in the town of Stansfield fined?

2 a What crimes had Walter Amos committed?
   b Why do you think Amos was punished in this way?

3 a What is meant by the term 'the punishment fits the crime'?
   b In what way does this apply to the baker in **Source C**?

4 How useful are **Sources A, B** and **C** to a historian studying crime and punishment in the Middle Ages?

pillory   stocks

Most minor crimes were dealt with by the local lord. So, for example, a villager who let his pigs wander into another person's crops might be fined. Fines were a good way for the lord to raise money. But sometimes crimes were so serious that they were dealt with by one of the king's special courts – crimes such as murder, violent assault or major theft. These courts were known as Shire Courts or Royal Courts.

Objectives

- Examine the medieval trial system.
- Judge the effectiveness of 'trial by ordeal'.

Serious stuff

A judge, appointed by the king, would travel to each county (perhaps twice a year) to deal with serious crimes. Working with advisers, the judge would look through the evidence, listen to witnesses and come to a decision. If a judge thought a person was guilty, he could punish them any way he chose… and some of the punishments were brutal. The diagram below shows you the types of punishment a guilty person could expect for serious crimes.

▼ **A** Serious crimes were dealt with brutally.

Serious assault, forgery, repeated stealing

Whipping

Fingers, hands, ears cut off

Murder, very serious assault, stealing anything worth a lot of money

Hanging (richer people often had their heads cut off)

Treason

Men usually hanged, drawn and quartered

Hanging

Drawing (pulling out a criminal's insides)

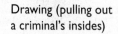

Quartering (cut into pieces)

Trial by ordeal

Sometimes judges couldn't make up their minds about whether a person was guilty or not, so they would order a **trial by ordeal** as a way of letting God decide someone's guilt. Trial by ordeal, the judge felt, was a good way for God to help the innocent and punish the guilty. The most common trials by ordeal were fire, water and combat.

Ordeal by fire

Step 1 The accused carries a red-hot iron bar for three steps, or takes a stone from the bottom of a pot of boiling water.

Step 2 The accused's hand is bandaged, and he returns to court three days later.

Verdict If the wound has healed, God must think the accused is worth helping because he is innocent. If the wound is infected, God must think the accused is not worth helping and so he must be guilty. The accused must be punished by being put to death.

Women usually burned

Ordeal by water

Step 1 The accused is tied up.

Step 2 She is thrown into a lake or river.

Verdict Water is pure, just like God. If the accused floats, the water doesn't want her, nor does God. If God has rejected the accused, she must be guilty, and must be put to death. If the accused sinks and drowns, God must want her in heaven. She must be innocent.

Ordeal by combat

Trial by fire and water had been around since Anglo-Saxon times. The Normans introduced a new one – trial by combat. This was a trial for nobles and barons. The accuser would fight the accused. It was possible to get someone called a 'champion' to fight for you. Some people did this for a living, earning huge amounts of money fighting on behalf of different lords.

Step 1 Both sides should select their weapons. These would be made from wood and bone.

Step 2 The accuser and the accused (or their champions) must fight for as long as possible, starting at sunrise.

Verdict People believed God would give the person telling the truth extra strength. The first person to surrender was thought to be guilty and therefore must be punished by being put to death.

Fact ✓

As you can see, God featured heavily in the criminal justice system. In fact, if you could read a verse from the Bible you were allowed to go on trial in a church court (usually reserved for naughty priests) and these often ordered lighter punishments than other courts. It was over these church courts that Henry II (who made some important changes to the law system) and Thomas Becket quarrelled (see pages 112–113).

(see pages 112–113)

Key Words

jury   treason
trial by ordeal

Trial by jury

Trial by ordeal was used less and less from the mid-twelfth century onwards. Henry II, who was king from 1154 to 1189, wanted a fairer justice system and felt that trial by ordeal was not suitable for serious crimes. Instead, it was gradually replaced by a system still used today – trial by jury.

The jury was a group of 12 local people who had the job of saying whether they thought the accused was telling the truth or not. The judge then decided if the person was guilty. In later years, the jury would decide on a guilty or innocent verdict – something that still happens in today's crown courts.

Over to You

1 Write down what sort of punishment these people might have received:
  a A woman who made fake coins
  b A wealthy male murderer
  c Someone who tried to kill the king
  d A man stealing vegetables from his neighbour
  e A poor female murderer.

2 Why do you think many of the punishments were so tough?

3 Imagine you work for one of the king's judges and you are about to visit a town for a series of trials. **EITHER** write a short speech **OR** design an information leaflet explaining how the judge will try to find out whether a person is guilty or not.

Change and Continuity

1 Why do you think so many people in the Middle Ages believed that ordeals were a good way to find out if a person was guilty or not?

2 What was trial by jury?

3 Do you think this was fairer than trial by ordeal?

4 Explain two ways in which trial by ordeal and trial by jury were different.

◎ Quick Knowledge Quiz

Choose the correct answer from the three options:

1 What was the first important job given to Thomas Becket by King Henry II?

 a Chancellor
 b Archbishop of Canterbury
 c Foreign Secretary

2 Thomas Becket was murdered in which cathedral and in which year?

 a Canterbury Cathedral in 1070
 b Durham Cathedral in 1170
 c Canterbury Cathedral in 1170

3 Which king agreed to the terms of Magna Carta?

 a King William
 b King John
 c King Henry

4 'Magna Carta' is the Latin for…?

 a list of rights
 b magnificent list
 c. great charter

5 Who led a baron's army against King Henry III's army in 1264 and 1265?

 a Simon de Montfort
 b William de Tracy
 c Hugh de Morville

6 Richard II introduced a new tax to pay for England's ongoing war with France. What was the tax called?

 a Council Tax
 b Peasants' Tax
 c Poll Tax

7 What was the name of the former soldier who led the Peasants' Revolt of 1381?

 a John Ball
 b Wat Tyler
 c Reginald Fitzurse

8 A group of ten people responsible for each other's behaviour was known as what?

 a the hue and cry
 b the constable
 c a tithing

9 Which one of the following statements is true?

 a Criminals could sit down in the stocks, but they had to stand up in the pillory
 b Criminals could stand up in the stocks, but they had to sit down in the pillory
 c Criminals could sit down in both the stocks and the pillory

10 Which of these punishments was usually reserved for treason (a crime against the king or country)?

 a whipping
 b hanging, drawing and quartering
 c having your hand cut off

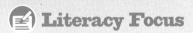 **Literacy Focus**

Note-taking

Note-taking is a vital skill. To do it successfully, you must pick out all the important (key) words and phrases in a sentence. The important words and phrases are those that are vital to the meaning (and your understanding) of the sentence. For example, in the sentence:

> 'King John gave in and asked the barons what they wanted. The barons made a list of 63 rights that they wanted to have.
>
> In June 1215, the barons met the king in a field at Runnymede, near Windsor. After four days of discussions, King John agreed to the list (known as Magna Carta, which means 'Great Charter'), and the barons agreed to be loyal to the king.'

....the important words are: June 1215; barons met King John; Runnymede (Windsor); four days of discussions; John agrees 63 rights barons wanted; Magna Carta (Great Charter); barons loyal to king.

The original sentence was 68 words long – but the shortened version is fewer than 30. Being able to take notes will help both your understanding of events and provide you with a great revision exercise.

1   Write down the important words/phrases in the following paragraphs. These important words/phrases are your notes.

   a   In 1154, Henry II became King of England. One of his best friends was a man called Thomas Becket. Henry respected and trusted Thomas so much that he made him Chancellor. This was a very important job – he managed the king's money, wrote important documents and took charge of the country when Henry was away.

   b   Despite being king, Henry did not have complete control of the country. All the people who worked for the Church – bishops, priests, monks, nuns for example – were under the leadership of the Archbishop of Canterbury, not the king.

   c   People who worked for the Church and broke the law went to church courts, rather than the king's courts. The church courts were not as strict as the king's courts. Henry was worried that there was too much crime and he thought that the Church courts were too soft.

   d   In 1162, Henry made Thomas Becket, the Archbishop of Canterbury, placing him in charge of the Church in England. The king hoped that Becket would allow him to change the church courts. Unfortunately for the king, though, Becket took his new job very seriously indeed. When Henry spoke to him about making changes to the church courts, Becket refused.

   e   The two men began to argue, and after Henry lost his temper, Becket fled to France – for six years! Becket eventually returned to Britain, but they soon argued again. After one particularly nasty disagreement Henry shouted, 'Is there no one who will rid me of this troublesome priest?'

   f   Four knights were standing nearby while the king ranted and raved. They decided that they could rid their king of this priest – and set off to Canterbury without delay. On 29 December 1170, the four knights killed Thomas Becket in Canterbury Cathedral.

History skill: Consequences

A good historian needs to be able to describe what caused an event, and what consequences (impacts) there were as a result of the event.

Sometimes, historians also like to divide causes and consequences into long-term and short-term ones:

- **Short-term:** A short-term cause is one that has existed for just a short time. This could be an hour, days or weeks (depending on the event). A short-term consequence is something that happens soon after the event.

- **Long-term:** If it's a long-term cause, it means that the cause of an event has built up over a long time, perhaps a year or several years. A long-term consequence is one that lasts for a long time.

Gardening

Short-term consequence

Long-term consequence

Exercise

5 Km   15 JANUARY

Short-term consequence

42 Km   23 SEPTEMBER

Long-term consequence

Great Fire of London, 1666

Short-term consequence

Long-term consequence

Responding to statements about consequences

This chapter's assessment is going to get you to think about the **consequences** of an event – the Peasants' Revolt. The question will ask you to **respond to a statement** about the consequences of the Peasants' Revolt. Here is one way to answer this type of question.

1 **Plan:** Your task is to think about the short-term and long-term consequences of an event. A good way to start would be to write down all the consequences of an event, and categorise the consequences as short-term or long-term. Remember, a consequence is the result or the impact. You might want to draw a table like this:

Consequences (short-term)	•
	•
Consequences (long-term)	•
	•

2 **Short-term and long-term consequences:** Once you have thought about the different consequences, you need to decide:

- Which do you think was the most important short-term consequence? List in bullet points the reasons for your choice.

- Which do you think was the most important long-term consequence? Explain your choice.

TIP: Can you explain why you have put them in this order?

TIP: Why is this consequence more important than the others?

3 **Answer:** Remember – this question type is focused on your response to a statement! So, you must actually give your response to the statement. After steps 1 and 2, do you agree with the statement you have been given? You could start by saying:

I agree that.../I disagree that...

4 **Explain:** You now need to add reasons to support your response. Use your plan to help you add detail and so on.

TIP: Write why your choice is the *most* important – and why you don't think the others are as important.

TIP: Don't simply write about your choice only. Firstly, back it up with factual detail. Then add information about the other consequences.

5 **Conclude:** Remember to include a concluding sentence stating your overall point of view.

Now, considering all these points, look at the next page and try putting this into practice!

Your challenge is to answer this statement question about consequences:

> 'In the short term, the peasants lost, but in the long term they won.' Do you agree or disagree with this statement about the consequences of the Peasants' Revolt? (20)

Make sure you:

- explain the different short-term and long-term consequences, and discuss how important they are

- respond to the statement – do you agree or disagree with it? Explain your choice.

- include information from the coloured boxes below and your *own knowledge* of the revolt.

Steps 1–3 below will help you structure your answer. Use the example sentence starters to help you begin each point.

1   **Plan:** Look at boxes A to H. Decide which of the boxes are **causes** and which are **consequences**. Remember, a 'cause' is a reason why something might happen – and a 'consequence' is the result or the impact. Copy the table below and fill in the letters A to H.

Causes (reasons which led to the revolt)	
Consequences (impact/results of the revolt)	

A RELIGIOUS

Since 1366, a priest called John Ball had travelled around the country preaching new ideas about all men being equal in the eyes of God, and that there should be no difference between rich and poor. He was thrown in jail several times for stirring up trouble, but he continued to encourage the poor to rebel against their lords.

B ECONOMIC/ WARFARE

When the young Richard II became king in 1377, he needed to raise money for England's ongoing war with France. The war was expensive and was not going well, so to raise money everyone over 15 had to pay a Poll Tax of 4 pence to the king.

C ECONOMIC

In May 1381, the peasants in Essex refused to pay the Poll Tax. More peasants began to rebel all over south-east England. In June 1381, 60,000 peasants under the leadership of a former soldier called Wat Tyler marched towards London to challenge the king and his government about the high taxes and low wages.

D ECONOMIC

For hundreds of years peasants, who belonged to their lords (landowners), had very few freedoms, and could not move away for better wages. The Black Death in 1348 killed many people and reduced the number of workers. The remaining workers asked for more wages or else the work would not get done, so for a short time, wages increased. But in 1351, the government passed a law saying that wages could not be higher than before the Black Death. The peasants felt this was unfair.

E ECONOMIC

In 1380–1381, Richard II demanded a new tax that was much higher than the one in 1377. Richard II's tax collectors were sent in May 1381 to collect the new Poll Tax of 12 pence. The tax was hated by the peasants, who could not afford to pay it.

F ECONOMIC

After 1381, things gradually got better for the peasants: the hated Poll Tax was scrapped and they were allowed to work for more money. Over the next 50 years, peasants also became more independent of their lords, and could buy or rent land themselves.

G POLITICAL

In June 1381, the peasants' leader, Wat Tyler, met with the king and his army in London. Wat was killed in front of the peasant army during this meeting.

H POLITICAL

Soon after the revolt, the leaders were tracked down. John Ball was cut to pieces in front of the king.

2 **Short-term and long-term consequences:** Look at your table in step 1 and answer the following questions:

- Which consequences were short-term consequences? Underline them.

- Which consequences were long-term consequences? Circle them.

- Which do you think was the *most important consequence* of the Peasants' Revolt? Explain your choice.

3 **Time to apply what you have learned:** Now you've thought about causes and consequences, it's time to apply this knowledge to the question.

You could follow the basic answer template:

Introduction

I (agree/disagree) with the statement that 'in the short term, the peasants lost, but in the long term they won'. The Peasants' Revolt of 1381 was a rebellion that started because...

What happened in 1381 was that... (5)

Short-term consequences

These events resulted in several consequences. An immediate consequence was that...

Another immediate consequence was that... (5)

Long-term consequences

There were some consequences that took a while to happen. For example...

Another long-term consequence was... (5)

Conclusion

Overall, I (strongly agree/agree to a certain extent/disagree) with the statement because, in the end, the peasants won/lost. This is because the most important consequence was... (5)

TIP: It's OK to disagree with a statement, or only agree with it a little, as long as you back up your argument with facts and reasons.

How smelly were the Middle Ages?

Today, we know about germs. We're taught to avoid them by washing our hands, clearing up rubbish, flushing toilets, brushing our teeth, and keeping ourselves clean. Our houses are full of cleaning products designed to make our clothes cleaner and our surfaces germ-free! However, medieval people knew nothing about germs. They didn't have microscopes through which they could have seen them, and scientists had not proven they existed. As a result, people in the Middle Ages were a lot less fussy about living in smelly, dirty places than we are today. So, just how smelly were the Middle Ages?

Objectives

- Identify how and why standards of cleanliness and personal hygiene were very different from today.

- Examine ways in which some people tried to keep themselves and their homes clean.

An open ditch ran down the centre of the street to carry away water and waste.

Sewage piled up in streets.

There were some toilets (called **privies**), but these were just small sheds outside houses, or buildings with a **cesspit** underneath where the sewage was collected.

Few streets were paved, so it got very muddy when it rained.

Wealthier people might get servants to sweep outside their homes.

Gong farmers were sometimes paid to clear away the filth.

Bakeries and breweries used the rivers to remove their waste.

Butchers dumped their waste in the rivers.

Many people used the rivers to remove their own sewage and other waste.

Smelly homes

In the countryside, villagers struggled to keep clean. Homes had no floorboards or carpets, just earth covered with straw. Windows (if they had any) were holes in the wall with wooden shutters to keep out the wind. In the centre of the room was a fire, its smoke escaping through a hole in the roof. Medieval peasants must have always smelled of smoke – or worse during the winter when they brought their animals inside, out of the cold! There were no taps to provide clean water for washing or drinking; water had to be fetched from a stream, a river or a well. And there were no toilets, just a bucket in the corner of the room or a hole dug outside.

A load of rubbish

In the towns, life was just as smelly. There was no rubbish collection in medieval times. Instead, people just tipped it into the streets or dumped it into a pit to rot away. There were no drains or sewage pipes to carry away dirty water either. There were a few public toilets in most towns, but at night people usually went to the loo in pots. The next day they tipped the waste out of the window into the street below. In London, there was a public toilet on London Bridge that emptied straight into the River Thames below!

▼ **SOURCE A** Adapted from notes from a court case in 1321. Thomas Wytte and William de Hockele were taken to court because of their toilets.

'Next case: the lane called Ebbegate. This was a right of way [a public footpath] until it was blocked by Thomas Wytte and William de Hockele. They built toilets which stuck out from the walls of their houses. From these toilets human dung falls onto the heads of passers-by.'

Getting better?

Although houses didn't have bathrooms or running water, it would be wrong to think that all people were permanently filthy. Some towns had public 'bath houses' where people could have a wash for a small fee, and a few places hired gong farmers to remove the filth. Some people also began to make the connection between rubbish and disease, although they still didn't know about germs – they thought it was the bad smells from rubbish that carried infection. This led to some town councils introducing laws to try to keep the environment cleaner. In 1374, for example, a London council made households that used the local stream pay a fee to have it cleaned each year.

▼ **SOURCE B** Part of a letter written in 1349 from King Edward III to the Lord Mayor of London.

'The human waste and other filth lying in the streets and lanes in the city must be removed with all speed. The king has learned that the city is so foul with the filth from out of the houses that the air is infected and the city poisoned to the danger of people.'

Fact ✓

Public health refers to the general state of health and cleanliness of the whole population, in a particular place at a particular time. This chapter looks at Britain's public health in the Middle Ages.

Over to You .ıll

1 a Make a list about your own personal hygiene – what have you done over the last few days to keep yourself clean, tidy and as germ-free as possible?

  b Underline the things in your list that people in medieval times would not have been able to do.

  c Use your list to help you write 3–5 reasons why people in the Middle Ages were not as clean as we are today.

2 Read **Source A**. What offence has been committed?

3 Read **Source B**.

  a Why does the king want the streets to be cleaned?

  b What do his reasons tell us about what some people thought caused disease at this time?

Knowledge and Understanding

1 What did medieval people think caused illness and infection?

2 Outline two ways in which medieval people tried to keep themselves healthy.

6.2A The Black Death: we're all going to die!

In the spring of 1348, the people of Britain were gripped by fear. A killer disease was spreading across Asia and Europe and killing thousands and thousands of people. Whole villages were being wiped out and no one seemed able to stop it. This disease was known as 'the Black Death' and it would go on to kill around one out of every three people.

Objectives

- Identify the main symptoms of the Black Death.
- Explain what people thought caused the disease at the time and how they tried to protect against it.

Read the following accounts of the impact the disease had on people. Victims of the Black Death really did suffer from the **symptoms** described by the villagers pictured here. Also, the various causes of the disease were all genuinely believed by people at the time. As you will discover, it is no wonder people were so scared…

2

Eleanor Carter, who works for the local landowner
- 26 years old
- Married, two children

Seven more families in the village are ill today. My mother has found red, tender, painful lumps called **boils** under her armpits and in her groin. I've been told that some people have found boils as big as apples. Father Peter has been mixing up some soothing ointments to smear over the boils, so perhaps that will help. He has also told us to pray to God to help those infected — and to keep the rest of us safe.

1

Emma Langdale, a baker
- 28 years old
- Married, three children

It's 12 August 1348 and I am so worried. Father Peter has visited most of the houses in the village and says that lots of people have been unable to work today. He says many people are hot and sweaty, like they have a fever, and that their muscles and bones ache. We are to pray that it is not the terrible disease that everyone is talking about. My friend Eleanor tells me that her mother has the fever.

3

Father Peter, local priest
- 38 years old

More and more people are becoming ill. And it attacks anyone — rich and poor, good and bad. Just yesterday, I was called to Emma Langdale's bakery because her little boy has a fever. Why him, O Lord? What harm has he ever done? And Eleanor Carter's mother is now covered in a red and black rash. She says she tried to stick a needle into one of the boils last night but it wouldn't burst. Nothing seems to work.

4

Sir James Bickley, local landowner who owns lots of land that the villagers work on
• 45 years old
• Married, three children

It's 15 August today and it's like the whole village is ill. It seemed to start three or four days ago after the weekly market in the centre of the village. I wonder if anyone from other villages who came to buy and sell here that day was poorly too. The Langdale family, who run the bakery, have been badly hit. They're all poorly, but their little boy is particularly ill. Boils have appeared on his body and his breath smells foul. What sins have we committed? Have we danced or drunk too much? God is punishing us all!

5

Adam Smith, village blacksmith
• 48 years old
• Married, three children, grandfather

People are dying! Twelve died during the night and three more already today, including Eleanor Carter's mother. Before she died, she was screaming for water. Eleanor gave her some, but her throat was so swollen that she couldn't swallow. Perhaps God punished her for drinking ale on Sundays. Eleanor said that the boils under her arms burst as she died and smelly black pus dripped onto the deathbed. All the Carters are ill now, and I fear for their lives.

6

John Edwards, works for Sir James
• 27 years old
• Married, four children

It's been a week since Eleanor Carter's mother became ill... and now she's dead. Someone told me that Eleanor herself has huge boils as big as onions under her arms. The Langdales are suffering too. The young boy has been covered in a rash for a few days now and his boils are getting bigger. Perhaps he's close to death.

I know Emma Langdale and her older daughter are in bed today with a fever and even Father Peter is ill. I'm worried about my youngest son who was up all night sweating and sneezing. We have decided to dig a large pit just outside the village in which to bury all the dead. But will it be big enough? Will anyone survive? Perhaps we're all going to die!

Over to You

1 Write a sentence to explain the word 'symptom'. Use a modern-day example of a common symptom of an illness in your answer.

2 a From what you have read in the accounts on these pages, identify at least five symptoms of the Black Death. Try to put them in the order in which a victim might get them.

 b Explain why the disease was called 'the Black Death'.

3 a List the ways in which some people thought you might catch the disease.

 b Describe three ways in which the people on these pages tried to treat the disease.

What actually caused the Black Death?

The Black Death of the fourteenth century was a **plague** – a disease that spreads quickly. In fact, experts who have studied the illness think that the Black Death was two different plagues that struck at the same time.

Bubonic plague

- This was caused by germs that lived in the blood of black rats and in the fleas on their bodies. The fleas would hop onto humans and bite them, passing on the disease.

- Victims would get a fever and large boils (called 'buboes') in their armpits, groin and behind their ears. Then the victim would develop a rash of red and black spots.

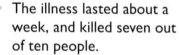

Ow! Something bit me!

- The illness lasted about a week, and killed seven out of ten people.

- Today, we know that fleas can also live on other animals, such as cats and dogs.

Pneumonic plague

- This was caused by the same germ from black rats and fleas, but the symptoms were different and more deadly. It was caught by breathing infected air – it attacked the lungs, causing victims to cough up blood and to spread deadly germs as they sneezed.

aaaachoo!!

- The victims' breath would smell as their lungs rotted inside them.

- Victims would die within a week.

A deadly combination

Bubonic and pneumonic plague combined to make the Black Death. It was possible to get one plague without the other, but pneumonic plague was so deadly that if you caught it you'd probably die anyway. About 30 per cent of people who caught only bubonic plague survived. However, millions of people across the world caught both plagues at the same time and stood no chance.

What did people think caused the Black Death?

At the time, people didn't understand infections or how diseases were passed from one person to another. They came up with a wide variety of ideas, some correct and some incorrect, to explain what was happening. **A** to **C** show some of the different ways in which people at the time tried to explain the causes of the Black Death.

▼ **SOURCE A** Adapted from a letter sent to the Bishop of London in 1348. It was written by Robert Hathbrand, a prior (leading churchman) at Christchurch Abbey, Canterbury.

'God uses plagues, famines, wars and other forms of suffering to terrify and torment people, and so drives out their sins. In England, because people are behaving increasingly badly and committing many sins, they are punished by plague.'

▼ **SOURCE B** Based on a report written by doctors at the Paris Medical Faculty in October 1348.

'The long-term cause is the position of the planets. It is also caused by evil smells which mix with the air and spread on the wind. When you breathe in the bad air you catch the plague.'

▼ **SOURCE C** Written around 1348 by Jean de Venette, a French monk and traveller.

'The disease was spread by contagion. If a healthy man visited a plague victim, he usually died himself.'

How did people try to deal with the Black Death?

Many different treatments were suggested to try to 'cure' the Black Death, and to prevent the disease spreading. It's easy to laugh at some of them but remember that people were scared – not stupid – and were prepared to try anything.

Key Words bubonic   contagion   flagellant   plague   pneumonic   provenance

Drinking vinegar and mercury (a silvery, liquid metal)

Locking plague victims in their homes

Praying

Lighting fires and spreading perfume in the air to drive away 'bad smells'

Plucking a chicken and strapping it to the boils

Some of the ways people tried to deal with the plague

Avoiding contact with people

GO AWAY!

Groups of people called **flagellants** walked around whipping themselves. They hoped this would show God how sorry they were for their sins – so he would spare them

Popping the boils

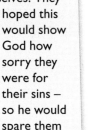

Killing cats and dogs

Moving away if they thought plague was coming

Killing a toad, drying it in the sun and holding it on the boils

Over to You

1 Explain the differences between bubonic and pneumonic plague.

2 a Look at the ways people tried to deal with the plague. Why do you think people tried so many different ways?

   b Knowing what you do about the real cause of the Black Death, do you think any of these ways would actually work? Give reasons why.

Source Analysis

1 Read **Sources A** to **C**. Make a list of all the different explanations that people gave for the cause of the Black Death.

2 Now look at the captions. They give details of who wrote each source, and when. Information about the origins of a source is known as **provenance**. Summarise the information given in the captions alongside your list.

3 How useful are **Sources A** and **B** to an enquiry about the Black Death? Consider the content of each source (what it says), the information in the caption (to give you an idea of who wrote it, and when), and include your own knowledge of the Black Death.

How deadly was the Black Death?

The Black Death was perhaps the worst disaster of the Middle Ages. Worldwide, it killed around 75 million people. In Europe, about 25 million people died (around half of the population). In Britain, at least two million people died in just one year, which was about one third of all people in the country. Where did the Black Death come from? How did it spread? What was its impact?

Objectives

- Outline how the plague spread throughout the world.
- Examine the impact of the plague on Britain at the time.

Map A shows how the plague spread through Europe. Historians think that the disease probably started in Asia and was carried by fleas, rats and people on ships and along trade routes that were transporting goods like spices and cloth into Europe. The sources on these pages show the impact of the disease in England, Italy and France.

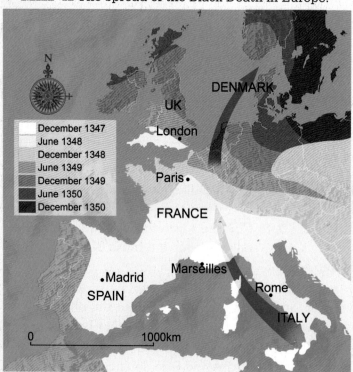

▼ **MAP A** The spread of the Black Death in Europe.

December 1347
June 1348
December 1348
June 1349
December 1349
June 1350
December 1350

DENMARK
UK
London
Paris
FRANCE
Marseilles
Madrid
SPAIN
Rome
ITALY

0 _____ 1000km

▼ **SOURCE B** Adapted from a letter written by an Italian writer, Francesco Petrarca, in 1349.

'Wherever I turn my frightened eyes, I see funerals: the churches groan, the dead bodies of the rich and the poor lie alongside each other. I recall the many dear friends who have died, the sweet faces which suddenly vanished, and the church yards now too full for more burials. This is what the people of Italy weep over, weakened by so many deaths; this is why France is grieving, exhausted and stripped of people; the same goes for other peoples, under whatever skies they live.'

▼ **SOURCE C** Robert of Avesbury, a writer at the Archbishop of Canterbury's court, 1349.

'The pestilence [disease], which had first broken out outside of Europe, became much stronger. It visited all the countries and brought sudden death. In England, it began in Dorset, immediately advancing from place to place and attacking without warning. Very many of those who were attacked in the morning were dead before noon. And no one it touched lived longer than three or four days. When it reached London, it took many lives every day, and increased so greatly from February till April 1349 that there were more than 200 dead bodies a day buried in the new Smithfield cemetery. The grace of the Holy Spirit finally arrived about May 1349, and it stopped in London.'

▼ **SOURCE D** This medieval graffiti was scratched onto a wall in a church in Ashwell, Hertfordshire. Written in Latin, it reads: '1349 the disease. 1350 pitiless, wild, violent, the surviving people live to tell the tale'.

Why did the plague spread so quickly in Britain?

There were several reasons why the Black Death spread so quickly:

- In towns, cities and ports people lived close together and knew nothing about how diseases spread. As a result, the plague passed easily among the crowds.
- The people who buried the bodies spread the disease still further because they did not protect themselves in any way when they handled the bodies.
- In villages, bodies were buried quickly in shallow pits – and these were often dug up by wild animals that then spread infected body parts around.
- The filthy streets gave rats the perfect environment in which to breed. Some town councils had simple laws about keeping streets clean, but these laws were often ignored. As a result, the rats kept multiplying – and spreading the disease!

Later on...

The plague never really died out completely – it came and went a few times. Smaller outbreaks of plague hit Britain in 1361, 1368, 1371, 1373 and 1390. One outbreak in 1665 killed around 100,000 people in London and was known as 'the Great Plague'.

The Black Death disaster

The Black Death affected all sorts of people – rich and poor, adults and children. No one was safe. Sometimes whole villages were wiped out. In some places, fields and streets were littered with bodies. Houses stood silent and empty. But there were other consequences, too:

- There were not enough people to look after farm animals and harvest crops. This led to food shortages – some people starved.
- There were fewer workers to do the jobs, so they began to demand more money to do the work. Peasants began to move around more because they were needed across the country.
- The king passed laws to stop wages going up, so poor people became very angry. Some historians think this was one of the key causes of the Peasants' Revolt of 1381 (see Chapter 5).

Over to You

1 Outline how the Black Death spread around the world.

2 Create a timeline of the Black Death's journey around Europe. Use **Map A** and an atlas to help you discover the different countries that were infected at different times.

3 Explain why the Black Death was able to spread so quickly in Britain.

4 Read **Source C**. Outline three things you can learn from this source about the Black Death.

5 Read **Source B**. Describe the impact of the Black Death, according to the author.

Cause and Consequence

A consequence is a result or an effect of something. An event can have many consequences, and these can be short-term (soon after) and long-term (over many years, decades, or even longer).

1 Write a list of consequences of the Black Death.

2 Divide the list into short-term and long-term consequences.

3 Describe two consequences of the Black Death.

6.4A Who healed the sick in the Middle Ages?

It is 1350 and you feel ill. If you are poor, you might ask the local **wise woman** or man in your village if they can help. They will probably tell you to try strange herbs, plants and potions. Some might even make you feel a bit better. You might also visit church a few more times and pray a bit more, or plan a pilgrimage to a holy place in the hope that God might cure you. As a last resort, you might take what money you have and travel to the nearest town to see the doctor. So, what did people think caused illness and disease at this time? What would a doctor do to try and make you feel better? How successful would the treatments be?

Objectives

- Identify the variety of medical treatments in the Middle Ages.
- Assess the theories behind causes of disease and treatments for them.

Popular theories about the causes of disease

In the Middle Ages, people didn't know that germs and viruses make us ill. In fact, they didn't know much about the real causes of illness at all. However, there were several popular theories...

> The position of the planets is to blame for most common illnesses. The study of how the stars and planets might make an impact on our lives is called astrology.

> The body contains four 'humours' — or liquids. If these get out of balance, you become ill.

> God sometimes sends disease to punish a person.

> Bad smells are the cause of some diseases.

> Tiny worms cause disease.

> Evil spirits cause disease.

Getting treatment

Visiting a doctor would cost a lot of money. Most people tended to treat themselves and their families in the same way as they had done for many years, using traditional treatments. The local wise woman was someone you could turn to for advice because they had learned about natural herbal remedies and first aid. Their knowledge was passed down by word of mouth, and some was written in books.

Earlier on... c400BC

A common theory about the cause of illness in the Middle Ages at this time was the theory of the four **humours** — it was developed by the Ancient Greeks. The idea was that a person's body contains four liquids (or 'humours') — blood, yellow bile, black bile and phlegm. When all four are present in equal amounts, then the body is healthy. When they are out of balance, you become ill.

Apothecaries were specialist medicine makers who experimented with plants and herbs (such as poppies, willow leaves and garlic) to treat people. Today, we know that they must have had some real successes. Modern scientists recently analysed a medieval apothecary book and concluded that over half of the herbal remedies prescribed to ease pain and help fight infection would have actually worked. Poppies and willow leaves, for example, contain a natural form of painkiller, while garlic is known to kill bacteria.

Beware!

Some people took advantage of people's lack of knowledge – and their fear – of disease. They tried to trick people into buying treatments that didn't work. These con artists were known as **quacks**. They sold their potions and remedies at fairs and as they travelled through villages and towns (see **A**).

▼ **INTERPRETATION A** A picture of a medieval quack selling medical 'cures' by the roadside, drawn by artist and popular historical writer Paul Lacroix in 1878.

Some apothecaries and wise women knew lots of effective ways to treat illness. However, some treatments were bizarre and unhelpful:

▼ **SOURCE B** Adapted from a treatment book from the eleventh century that was widely used in the Middle Ages.

'For swollen eyes, take a live crab, poke out its eyes and put it back in the water. Stick the eyes onto your neck and you will be well.
For wheezing and shortness of breath, kill a fox and take out its liver and lungs. Chop them up and mix it with wine. Then drink the mixture out of a church bell.
If you are bitten by a snake, smear ear wax on the bite, then ask the priest to say a prayer for you.
If you accidentally drink an insect in the water, find a sheep, cut into it and drink the blood while it's still hot. If you take good long gulps, all will be well.
For warts, hold a live toad next to the skin and soon your skin will soften, and the warts will disappear. Or, rub a mixture of dog urine and mouse blood onto the warts.'

Key Words

apothecary   humours   quack   supernatural   wise woman

Over to You

1 Describe the difference between a wise woman and a quack.

2 Suggest reasons why most ordinary people would:
 a not visit a doctor
 b choose to be treated by a wise woman or an apothecary.

3 a Make a list of different theories about the cause of disease in the Middle Ages.
 b Divide the causes into natural (ones relating to the natural world and the human body) and **supernatural** (relating to God, evil spirits, magic or astrology).
 c Explain why you think there were so many supernatural theories about the cause of disease.

Interpretation Analysis

1 Look at **Interpretation A**. In your own words, describe what is happening in the picture.

2 If you were asked to do further research on the quacks shown in **Interpretation A**, what would you choose to find out?

Trust me, I'm a doctor

A visit to a doctor would cost money – so it was really only the rich that would ever see them. The doctor would have spent at least seven years studying at a university. They would have learned mainly by listening to lectures and debating what they had read about in books. Some doctors left university without ever actually treating a patient! As well as reading many of the books written by the Ancient Greeks, who were advanced in medical thinking, they would study ideas from the Muslim, Indian and Chinese worlds.

Medieval doctors based most of their treatments around the theory of the four humours, which was developed by the Ancient Greeks. A doctor would carefully examine a patient (using all sorts of methods) and use special charts to work out a treatment – and get the 'balance' right again.

Investigating illness

To find out what was wrong with you, the doctor would probably ask you to urinate in a clear glass bottle.

He would then examine it three times – once when it's fresh, again when it has been cooling for about an hour, and finally when it has gone completely cold. He might even taste it to see if it was sweet or sour, bitter or salty.

▼ **SOURCE C** Adapted from a medical book that was used during the Middle Ages.

'A doctor must know how to read so that he can understand medical books. He must know how to write and speak well so that he can explain the diseases he is treating. He must have a good mind to investigate and cure the causes of disease. Arithmetic [maths] is also important, so that he can be a great help to the sick... Lastly, he must know astronomy so that he can study the stars and the seasons, because our bodies change with the planets and stars.'

Bad blood

After examining a patient's urine and taking their pulse, many doctors would usually conclude that the cause of illness was in some way connected to a patient's blood (which was one of the four humours).

He would probably examine your blood too, look at your tongue and take your pulse... although he wouldn't really know what he was looking for!

Doctors used this ancient theory to explain most illnesses.

'THE FOUR HUMOURS'

HOT — Yellow Bile — DRY
Fire
Blood — Black Bile
Air — Earth
Phlegm
WET — Water — COLD

Your doctor would then go off to look at his charts and flick through his books. The colour of your urine would be matched against the shades on a special diagram – doctors thought that every shade had a different meaning.

He might examine your faeces... but, again, he wouldn't really know what he was looking for!

As a result, many doctors thought the answer was to make the patient bleed, so that their 'bad blood' would disappear and their body would be in balance again. This was called bloodletting, and special tools and bowls were used to cut open a vein and bleed a patient (see **D**). Sometimes leeches were used to suck the blood out too. If you were selected for a bleeding session, you would hope your doctor was skilled enough to know when to stop before you lost too much blood (see **E**).

> ▼ **SOURCE D** Bloodletting in the 1800s. This image of a doctor, a nun and a patient shows that bloodletting continued to be used as a medical treatment for hundreds of years after the Middle Ages.

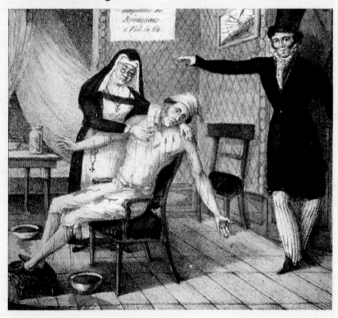

> ▼ **SOURCE E** Doctors had a mixed reputation. This person's opinion of a doctor, written by medieval author John Froissart in 1380, is not very positive.

> 'Doctors possess three special qualifications and these are: to be able to lie without being caught out; to pretend to be honest; and to cause death without feeling guilty.'

Terrifying treatments

Some doctors might conclude that purging was the best way to get your humours back in balance. This meant that they would give you something to eat to make you vomit or go to the toilet a lot. The idea was to get the 'badness' out of your body. Some doctors believed that it was important to check the positions of stars and planets before starting a treatment (see **C**).

Key Words	barber-surgeon	bloodletting
	leech purging	trepanning

Could women become doctors?

Women couldn't go to university, so they weren't able to train as doctors. Instead, women took on the role of main carer in most homes in medieval times and continued to act as midwives. Wise women also played a key role in healthcare in their local communities.

What were barber-surgeons?

Doctors were expensive – so a cheaper alternative was to visit the barber-surgeon. They could remove a nasty boil or rotten tooth, and you could have your hair cut at the same time (sharp knives, you see!). They would also be skilled at bloodletting, and even a treatment that had been around for many thousands of years – trepanning. This involved drilling a hole in your skull to let out evil spirits that were giving you a headache and making you feel unwell. A barber-surgeon's shop would be easy to spot because it had a red and white pole outside (red for blood, white for bandages). Some barbers still have poles like these outside their shops today.

> ## Over to You .ᴵᴵ
>
> 1 a What is bloodletting?
>   b What is purging?
>   c Explain why a medieval doctor would use either of these treatments.
>
> 2 **Sources C to E** tell us something about health and medicine in the Middle Ages. For each source, write a short sentence explaining when it was created, who created it, and what it shows. For example: *Source C is a from a medical book that was used in the Middle Ages. It outlines the qualities and skills that a doctor should have.*

> ## Change and Continuity
>
> 1 a When was **Source D** created?
>   b Approximately how many years after the Middle Ages (c1066–1500) was this source created?
>
> 2 Explain one way in which medical treatment in the Middle Ages was similar to the 1800s.

6.5 Was it dangerous to be the king or queen?

Would you like to have been a king or queen of England during the Middle Ages and Tudor times? Surely it was one of the best jobs in the world – a luxurious lifestyle with the best clothes, the finest homes and the tastiest food. You would have all the brightest and most hard-working people in the land to attend to your every need. But could a king or queen's great status, wealth and power buy them a long and happy life? Or, was it actually dangerous to be a king or queen of England?

Objectives

- Identify the ways in which medieval and Tudor kings and queens died.
- Judge whether you think England's monarchs were a particularly healthy bunch

King Harold II of England (1066)
Killed fighting at the Battle of Hastings.

William I (AKA the 'Conqueror', 1066–1087)
Killed in France when his bladder burst in a riding accident.

William II (1087–1100)
Son of William I. Shot and killed by an arrow in a hunting accident. Some historians think he may have been murdered, though!

Henry I (1100–1135)
Younger brother of William II. Spent a lot of time fighting. Died of eating too much.

Stephen (1135–1154)
Grandson of William I, nephew of Henry I. Spent most of his time fighting for the throne against his cousin Matilda (who ruled briefly in 1141). Died of a stomach infection and internal bleeding.

Henry IV (1399–1413)
Cousin of Richard II. Had lots of illnesses during the last few years of his life, possibly including leprosy (a disfiguring skin disease).

Henry V (1413–1422)
Son of Henry IV. Died of dysentery while fighting in France.

Edward IV (1461–1470 and 1471–1483)
Great-great-grandson of Edward III. Fought in the Wars of the Roses. Caught a fever after going to bed because he'd eaten too much.

Henry VI (1422–1461 and 1470–1471)
Son of Henry V. Fought the Wars of the Roses. Suffered with mental health problems, lost his throne twice and was murdered in the Tower of London.

Henry VIII (1509–1547)
Second son of Henry VII – the eldest son (Arthur) had died from a mystery illness. Henry is best known for marrying six wives, and for the religious changes that took place during his reign. Became obese later in life and suffered poor health, but died from natural causes.

Edward V (1483)
Son of Edward IV. Disappeared aged 12. Possibly suffocated or died of a mystery illness.

Richard III (1483–1485)
Brother of Edward IV, uncle of Edward V. Killed while fighting at the Battle of Bosworth Field.

Henry VII (1485–1509)
Great-great-great-grandson of Edward III. Ended the Wars of the Roses by marrying Elizabeth of York, a member of the opposing family. Died of tuberculosis (a lung disease).

Historians give names to the different groups or families who ruled England at this time. The Tudor period, for example, is named after the Tudor family, who ruled between 1485 and 1603.

KEY

 Harold – Anglo-Saxon

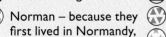 Norman – because they first lived in Normandy, France

Plantagenet – family name

Lancaster – family name

York – family name

Tudor – family name

Note: The dates in the timeline are the dates of the king or queen's reign, not their life.

Over to You .ıll

1 a Create a chart or list of how many kings and queens were killed by the following:

- battle
- murder
- accident
- illness
- eating too much

b Draw a bar chart to show your findings.

c What was the biggest cause of death? Why do you think this?

2 Which cause of death surprises you the most? Explain your answer.

3 'Being a medieval or Tudor king or queen was a dangerous job.' Do you agree or disagree with this statement? Give reasons for your answer. Use your chart from question **1** to help you.

Henry II (1154–1189)

Son of Matilda, grandson of Henry I. Died from a bleeding stomach ulcer while fighting in France.

Richard I (AKA the 'Lionheart', 1189–1199)

Son of Henry II. Shot in the neck by a crossbow bolt while fighting in France. The wound became infected when doctors tried to treat him. Died as a result of the infection.

John (1199–1216)

Brother of Richard I. Spent a lot of his time fighting wars in France and arguing with his barons. Died from dysentery, a nasty form of diarrhoea.

Henry III (1216–1272)

Son of King John. Thrown in prison by rebel barons in 1264, but regained his throne. Died of old age, possibly a stroke.

Edward II (1307–1327)

Son of Edward I. Lost all the land in Scotland that his father had won. Hated by his wife Isabella, who wanted their son (also named Edward) to be king instead. She eventually killed him by ordering two men either to suffocate him or to stick a red-hot piece of iron up his bottom! Historians still disagree over how he died.

Edward I (AKA the 'Hammer of the Scots', 1272–1307)

Son of Henry III. Died of dysentery on his way to fight the Scots.

Richard II (1377–1399)

Grandson of Edward III. Had no children. His cousin Henry (also the grandson of Edward III) fought him for the throne. Henry eventually beat Richard and became Henry IV. Richard was put in prison at Pontefract Castle and starved to death.

Edward III (1327–1377)

Son of Edward II. Ruled during the Black Death. Died of a stroke.

Edward VI (1547–1553)

Youngest child of Henry VIII (but the only male). Caught measles and smallpox in 1552, but probably died from tuberculosis, aged 15.

Mary I (1553–1558)

Oldest child of Henry VIII, older sister of Edward VI. Died of cancer.

Elizabeth I (1558–1603)

Youngest daughter of Henry VIII. Younger sister of Mary I (and older sister of Edward VI). Ruled England for 44 years during what many historians call a 'Golden Age'. Historians are still unsure about the cause of her death (aged 69), but say it could have been either blood poisoning, pneumonia or cancer.

Quick Knowledge Quiz

Choose the correct answer from the three options:

1 Which of the following jobs involved removing filth and sewage?

a costermonger
b gong farmer
c debt collector

2 In what year did the Black Death first arrive in Britain?

a 1348
b 1338
c 1358

3 Approximately what proportion of Britain's population were killed by the Black Death?

a three quarters
b one quarter
c one third

4 The Black Death was two types of plague, attacking at the same time. Which ones?

a bubonic and iconic
b pneumonic and epidemic
c pneumonic and bubonic

5 What name was given to the medical practice of giving a patient something to eat to make them vomit or go to the toilet a lot?

a bloodletting
b trepanning
c purging

6 Which medieval monarch ruled at the time of the Black Death?

a Edward III
b Henry III
c Richard II

7 Which of the following was a common theory in medieval times?

a theory of relativity
b theory of the four humours
c theory of five humours

8 Where did the theory originate?

a Tudor England
b Ancient Rome
c Ancient Greece

9 For how long did a doctor train?

a 5 years
b 6 years
c 7 years

10 Which of the following was a specialist medicine maker who experimented with plants and herbs to treat people?

a barber-surgeon
b apothecary
c pilgrim

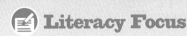 **Literacy Focus**

Spelling, punctuation and grammar

1 The sentences below don't make much sense. Some words are misspelled, and some sentences need capital letters, full stops and apostrophes.

a Copy out each sentence, adding punctuation as you write.

- in medeval villages there was often a wize woman or man to turn to for advise
- Medieval doctors based most of there treatments on a theory that was developed by the Ancient greeks
- Bloodleting was the moist painful treatment
- The black Death was the scariest disaese ever to hit britian
- In total historans think that the Black Death killed around 25 milion people in europe
- doctors were mor expensive than barber-surgons

> **TIP:** Remember, a fact is definitely true and can be backed up with evidence. For example, 'the Battle of Hastings was in 1066'. An opinion is how someone feels – it is their belief about something. For example, 'King William was the best king ever'.

b Underline the factual sentences in blue and the sentences that contain opinion in red.

Writing in detail

2 Look at the paragraph below. It is a very basic answer to the question: **What was the Black Death and how did it spread?**

However, the answer does not contain many specific, factual details. Rewrite the paragraph to include more detail – adding names, dates, examples and facts where possible.

> Could you add detail about the route of the disease? What countries did it travel through, and when?

> Can you add detail about fleas and bacteria here?

> The Black Death was two different types of plague attacking at the same time. The Black Death travelled along trade routes into Europe. It was brought to England by a ship carrying plague-infected people and rats.

> What were the names of the two plagues? What were the main symptoms?

> When did it arrive in England – and where exactly?

History skill: Source analysis

What is the usefulness of a source?

Historians often have to think about how useful a source is. The usefulness of a source is what it could tell you about the history of the time. A source might be useful because:

- it reveals something new
- it explains why events turned out the way they did
- it reveals why people acted or thought in a particular way at the time.

Judging how useful a source is

Here is one way to judge how useful a source can be. Think carefully about each step:

1 **Content:** Look carefully at what is actually written or pictured in the source. What does the source say – or show? What does it tell us about the event or the person? What does it *not* tell you?

2 **Caption:** If there is a caption or label with the source, it will tell you about where the source comes from, or where it originates from (also known as the 'provenance'). When reading the provenance, think: Was the person there at the time (an eyewitness), or has someone told them about the events? What are their views or background? Do you think they missed out any information? Do you think the person was exaggerating things? Is it one-sided? If so, why? Use the provenance to get you thinking about the reasons why the source was created.

> **TIP:** A source may not always seem trustworthy, but it can still be valuable to you because of the origin of the source and the message it carries.

3 **Context:** This is where you think back to what you already know about the topic. Is the source accurate? Does it match with what you have learned about the person or event it describes?

4 **Conclude:** Now use your answers from steps 1–3 and judge: How useful is the source to a historian studying the topic? Did you learn a little or a lot from the source? You can conclude by saying:

The source is... to a historian studying... because...

> **TIP:** You can pick one of the phrases below that you think fits best in the sentence:
>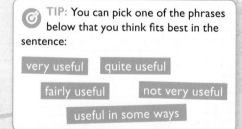
> very useful   quite useful
> fairly useful   not very useful
> useful in some ways

Now spend some time looking through this source. Imagine you have been asked:

 How useful is **Source A** to a historian studying health and medicine in the Middle Ages?

TIP: You are specifically asked to judge how useful the source is 'for a historian studying health and medicine in the Middle Ages', so make sure you link your answer to what you know about health and medicine at this time.

Caption: These two men are in England at the time of the Black Death – they are well-placed to know about both the Black Death *and* the state of health and medicine at this time. I believe the king of England and the Mayor of London would act to the best of their knowledge to improve things.

Content: This tells me the conditions in the streets.

Content: This tells me that people at the time were starting to make links between poor living conditions and poor public health.

▼ **SOURCE A** Part of a letter written in 1349 from King Edward III to the Lord Mayor of London. It was written while the Black Death was still killing thousands of people in Britain.

> The human waste and other filth lying in the streets and lanes in the city must be removed with all speed. The king has learned that the city is so foul with the filth from out of the houses that the air is infected and the city poisoned to the danger of people.

Context: I know that at this time, people believed that infected or poisonous air could make you ill. Many different remedies were used to try and clear the poisonous air – such as lighting fires or carrying strong-smelling herbs with you.

Content: This tells me that the king was taking an active role in improving public health.

Context: I know that in 1349, the Black Death epidemic was in its second year. This letter may help me understand the king's response at this time, and medieval views on disease.

Caption: The source is from the time of the Black Death. I have no reason to doubt that it is a reliable description. Why would the king write to say he wanted the streets cleaned if they were already clean? They *must* have been filthy.

After you have gone through this process with a source, you will finally have to make a **conclusion** and decide how useful it is to a historian studying health and medicine in the Middle Ages.

Now turn to the next page to have a go at answering this type of question.

Conclusion: This source is very useful because it gives detail about public health conditions in towns like London. This matches with what I know about the filthy conditions of towns at this time with their overflowing cesspits. It also tells me what people thought might be a cause of disease (infected air) and that the king was concerned about this and thought that the infected air (as a result of the filth) was a danger.

Your challenge is to answer this source analysis question:

> How useful is **Source A** to a historian studying the impact of the Black Death? (20)

▼ **SOURCE A** Adapted from an account written by William Dene at the time of the Black Death. He was a monk at Rochester Cathedral in Kent who was writing a biography of the Bishop of Rochester. He has first-hand experience of the things he describes.

'In 1348 and 1349 a plague that had never been seen before devastated England. The Bishop of Rochester, who didn't keep many servants or helpers, lost four priests, five gentlemen, ten serving men, seven young clerks and six pages, so that nobody was left to serve him.

During the plague, many religious men would only work if they were paid large salaries. Priests hurried off to places where they could get more money than in their own areas.

There was also a shortage of workers of every kind. More than a third of the land in the whole country was left unfarmed.'

The questions on the next page will help you structure your full answer. You can use the example sentence starters to help you get started.

aaaachoo!!

1 **Content:** What does the content of **Source A** tell you about the impact of the Black Death?

One thing I learned from the content is... (2)	These things are useful because... (2)
Another thing I learned from the content is... (2)	

2 **Caption:** What does the caption tell you? Who made the source? Why do you think they made it? Do you believe them? If so, why? If not, why not?

One thing the caption tells me is... (2)	These things are useful because... (2)
Another thing the caption tells me is... (2)	

> **TIP:** Your answers here mean you are thinking about the provenance of the source.

3 **Context:** Does the information in the source match with what you already know about the impact of the Black Death? If yes, how does the source help historians to understand the impact?

One thing I already know about the impact of the Black Death is... (2)	So the source is useful because... (2)
This (matches / doesn't match) with what Source A says about... (2)	

> **TIP:** You can pick one of the phrases below that you think fits best in the sentence:
>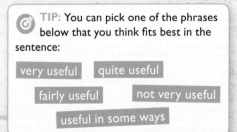

4 **Conclude:** Now make a judgement and answer the main question: how useful is **Source A** to a historian studying the impact of the Black Death? You can use the following sentence starters:

In conclusion, I think that Source A is... to a historian studying the impact of the Black Death. I think this because...   (2)

> **TIP:** Don't forget to mention some of the things you wrote about in steps 1–3 to justify (give reasons) how you decided this source's usefulness.

England and its neighbours: Wales

Do you know anyone who has argued with their neighbours? Do you know why they quarrelled? Was it about house or garden boundaries? Or perhaps they just didn't get on with each other?

England has two neighbours with whom it shares a border – Wales and Scotland – and Ireland is not very far away by sea, either. It may not surprise you to know that England has not always got on with its neighbours. In fact, in the Middle Ages, English kings tried to take over and control them. But why? How did they try to do it? And how successful were they?

Objectives

- Examine how and why England tried to conquer Wales.
- Judge how successful these attempts were.

England and Wales

In 1066, William the Conqueror won the Battle of Hastings and became King of England. At this time, Wales was a completely separate country from England. It had its own laws, customs and language. Wales didn't have a king, but instead each region or area was controlled by a chief or prince.

King William of England wasn't very interested in conquering Wales, but he did worry about the Welsh attacking England! So, he gave some of his most trusted barons land along the Welsh Marches (the border area) and told them to make England safe from attack. These **Marcher Lords**, as they were known, built castles to control the border lands and stop the Welsh attacking England. As time went on, some of the English barons attacked the Welsh and took more land. By the early 1200s, much of the land in the south of Wales was controlled by the English. However, land in the west and north of Wales was still in the hands of lots of Welsh chiefs and princes.

The 'Prince of Wales'

In the mid-1200s, the Welsh in the north began to unite under one leader, Llywelyn ap Gruffudd, who began calling himself the 'Prince of Wales'. The Welsh began to take back land in north and mid-Wales. In fact, Llywelyn became such a powerful force in Wales that the English king (Henry III) officially accepted him as 'Prince of Wales' in 1267, as long as Llywelyn stayed loyal to him (known as paying homage).

A new English king

King Henry III of England died in 1272 and his son, Edward, became king. The new English king didn't like the growing power of Llywelyn and the Welsh. When Edward instructed Llywelyn to swear his loyalty to him, Llywelyn refused – so Edward invaded Wales.

Invasion No. 1

In 1277, three separate English armies marched into the Welsh mountains in the north while English ships cut off Llewelyn's supplies of food from the island of Anglesey.

▼ **MAP A** Areas of control and castles in Wales.

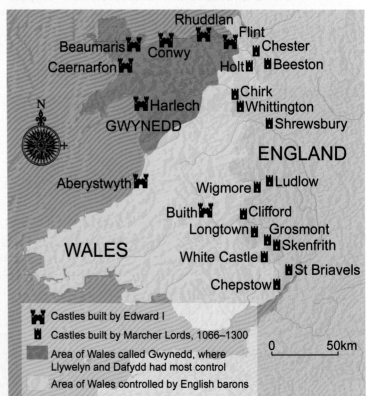

The Welsh prince was soon forced to ask Edward for peace and, although he lost much of his land, he was allowed to keep his title of 'Prince of Wales'.

Invasion No. 2

In 1282, Llywelyn (and his brother Dafydd) rebelled against the English. Once more Edward's army invaded Wales, but this time Llywelyn was killed. His head was stuck on a pole outside the Tower of London. A few months later Dafydd was also captured and executed. His head was displayed alongside Llewelyn's.

Edward's 'Iron Ring'

Edward wanted to make sure that the Welsh didn't rebel again. He gradually conquered the whole of Wales and divided it into counties (as in England). He introduced English laws, courts and sheriffs. He also built lots of large stone castles to keep the Welsh under control and remind them of the power of their rulers. These were the strongest castles ever built by the English. The most impressive ones were built in the north, around the area where support for Llywelyn and Dafydd had been strongest. The castles there, and the towns near to them, were filled with English people, and were known as the 'Ring of Iron'. By 1284, all of Wales was officially under English rule… and it is still a part of the UK to this day.

Prince of Wales

King Edward I introduced a new tradition. In 1301, he gave his son (the future Edward II) the title 'Prince of Wales', so that no Welshman could claim the title for himself. Ever since, the eldest son of a British king or queen is given this title.

▼ **SOURCE B** A photograph of Conwy Castle. James of St George, a European master castle designer, was employed to build the 'Ring of Iron'. Most of the castles were concentric in design (see pages 72–73), a style Edward I had seen when he fought on the Crusades.

▼ **INTERPRETATION C** The head of Llywelyn ap Gruffudd being paraded through the streets of London in 1282. This image appeared in a history book written by William Russell in the late 1700s.

Over to You

1 In what way is each of these dates important in the history of 'England versus Wales'?
  * 1066 * 1272 * 1277
  * 1282 * 1284 * 1301

2 a What was Edward I's 'Ring of Iron'?
  b Why do you think Edward chose to build his strongest castles in the north of Wales?

3 Give reasons why Edward I's decision to make his young son 'Prince of Wales' might be:
  a hated by the Welsh?
  b liked by the Welsh?

Change and Continuity

1 Make a list of ways that Edward I tried to make sure that the Welsh would not pose a serious threat to his rule.

2 Explain what was important about Edward I's conquest of Wales in 1277 and 1282. In your answer, include what changed between these dates. Did anything stay the same – was there any continuity?

England and its neighbours: Scotland

In the early Middle Ages, Scotland was ruled by its own kings and was a separate country from England. But all that changed when, after conquering Wales, King Edward I of England decided that Scotland should be brought under his rule.

Objectives

- Analyse how and why England tried to conquer Scotland.
- Assess how successful these attempts were.

The king dies

In 1286 Scotland's king, Alexander III, died in a riding accident. He had no clear heir to take his place. Thirteen Scotsmen all wanted to be king, so the Scots asked the English King Edward I to choose for them. In 1292, Edward picked a man named John Balliol, a distant relative of a past King of Scotland, to be king. However, Edward forced Balliol to make a promise – Balliol could be king, but he had to pay homage to Edward at all times. Balliol agreed… but the leading Scottish landowners hated this, and Balliol changed his mind.

The Scots made their feelings against the English clear when Balliol signed a friendship pact (called the 'Auld Alliance') in 1295 with France. The Scots did this just when England had started a war with France!

Scotland is attacked

Edward was furious that Balliol refused to obey him, and had also made a deal with France, so he decided to teach him a lesson. In 1296, Edward gathered a huge army in Newcastle, in northern England, and marched into Scotland. The Scots were beaten, and Balliol was thrown into prison. Edward then removed the 'Stone of Destiny', an ancient rectangular block of stone on which Scottish kings sat when they were crowned. The stone was taken to London and made part of a specially built throne on which English kings and queens were then crowned. Like Wales, Scotland was now controlled by the King of England.

Later on... 📅 1996

In 1996, the 'Stone of Destiny' was returned to Scotland. However, it will be returned to London every time a new British monarch is crowned.

▼ **MAP A** A map of Scotland and Northern England showing some of the key places featured on these pages.

Scottish rebellion

When Edward returned to England the Scots rose up in rebellion. Their new leader was a knight named William Wallace. The Scots defeated an English army in a famous battle at Stirling Bridge in 1297 and drove the English back over the border. It is said that Wallace had a long strip of skin from one of the leading English nobles killed at the battle turned into a sword belt.

Wallace is defeated

Edward returned to Scotland the following year and defeated the Scots at the Battle of Falkirk. Wallace was captured later on, in 1305, and was executed. His head was put on a spike on London Bridge, and an arm and a leg were each sent to Perth, Stirling, Newcastle and Berwick.

A new leader

In 1306, the Scots found a new leader in Robert the Bruce. He was a Scottish earl, and the grandson of one of the 13 people who originally claimed the throne after Alexander III's death. Edward once again marched north to invade Scotland, but died on the journey. His tomb in Westminster Abbey in London reads, 'Here is Edward I, the Hammer of the Scots: keep my faith'.

A new English king

King Edward's son was crowned King Edward II in 1307, but he was a weak king, a poor leader, and not interested in military glory like his father. Robert the Bruce, a brilliant soldier, took full advantage of this and captured many of the English controlled castles in Scotland. Eventually, in June 1314, Edward II sent a huge army of up to 15,000 men to Scotland to fight Robert and his army of 7000. At Bannockburn the Scots defeated the English in just two days. Robert the Bruce remained King of Scotland while Edward II and his battered army returned to England. Scotland remained a separate country for the next 300 years.

▼ **INTERPRETATION B** An illustration of Edward I during the capture of Berwick in 1296. This is from a book called *British Battles on Land and Sea, Vol. III* by James Grant, 1880.

▼ **INTERPRETATION C** Adapted from an account of Edward I's capture of Berwick in 1296, a town on the border of Scotland and England, from a fifteenth-century chronicle by the Scottish historian Walter Bower.

'When the town had been taken in this way and its citizens had submitted, Edward spared no one, whatever the age or sex, and for two days streams of blood flowed from the bodies of the slain, for in his rage he ordered 7500 souls of both sexes to be massacred... So that mills could be turned round by the flow of their blood.'

Over to You

1 Write a short paragraph on the following three figures from Scottish history. Explain who they were, their role in Scottish history and what happened to them:
   * John Balliol
   * William Wallace
   * Robert the Bruce

2 a Why was Edward I known as the 'Hammer of the Scots'?

   b What was the 'Stone of Destiny'?

   c Why did Edward I place the Stone of Destiny under his throne in England?

   d How was Edward II different from his father?

3 Create a timeline covering 100 years, from 1250 to 1350. Add the key events (with a short explanation) in the relationship between England and Scotland.

Interpretation Analysis

1 Look at **Interpretation B**. What impression do you get about Edward I when looking at this interpretation? Make a list of the words you think of.

2 Read **Interpretation C**. What impression do you get about Edward I when reading this interpretation?

3 How does **Interpretation B** differ from **Interpretation C** about the role of Edward I in the capture of Berwick?

England and its neighbours: Ireland

During the Middle Ages, England fought many wars against two of its nearest neighbours – Wales and Scotland – in an attempt to conquer them. Sometimes the English forces were successful, and England took control in these areas. Sometimes, however, the English were beaten and driven back. But what about Ireland? Did English kings try to control Ireland too?

Objectives

- Examine how the English tried to control Ireland.
- Explain why medieval kings failed to conquer Ireland.

Medieval Ireland

By the Middle Ages, Ireland was divided into several small kingdoms. There was no single ruler of Ireland, and rival Irish kings or chiefs fought each other for control of the different areas. It had been like this for centuries. Sometimes the Vikings invaded Ireland – and some settled there and created small villages.

The English kings get involved

Some of the early Norman kings (like William the Conqueror and Henry I) showed no interest in conquering Ireland. The Irish Sea was rough and difficult to cross. In addition, Ireland wasn't particularly rich, so English kings felt they wouldn't gain much from taking it over.

But in 1166, the Irish leader of an area called Leinster asked King Henry II of England for help. His name was Dermot MacMurrough and he was busy fighting the leader of another Irish kingdom. Henry allowed English barons to go and help... but they just took Irish land for themselves. Within a few years, English barons controlled more land in Ireland than the Irish! Henry II visited Ireland in 1171 and declared himself its 'overlord'. Eventually, the Irish kings accepted Henry's rule and agreed to obey him (see **B**).

English control weakens

But English kings didn't really have full control over Ireland. It was too far away, and the Irish often attacked the English settlements in Ireland. Both Henry II and King John built castles there to try to protect the English settlers and control the Irish, but the attacks continued, and no English king felt properly in control there (see **C** and **D**).

▼ **MAP A** This map shows the main Irish 'kingdoms' in the Middle Ages – Ulster, Connaught, Leinster and Munster and the castles built by the English from the 1170s onwards. By the end of the Middle Ages, English power had shrunk to the area known as 'the Pale'.

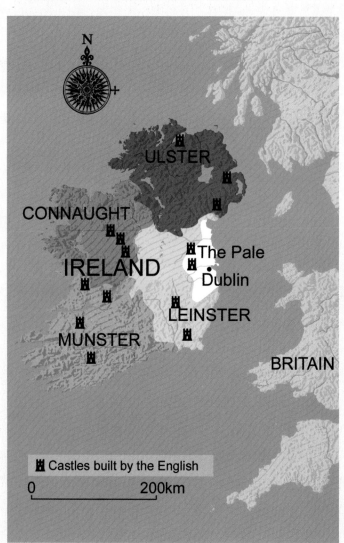

Castles built by the English
0   200km

In 1394, Richard II tried to take full control of Ireland. He was the first English king to go there since King John in 1210. He led a large army to victory over the Irish chiefs – but after his return to England, the man he left in charge soon lost control. Richard II went back to Ireland in 1399, but with little success.

By the end of the Middle Ages, English power in Ireland had shrunk to a small area around Dublin. This was called 'the Pale' and had to be defended with high walls, ditches and castles. Some English settlers married into Irish families, took Irish names and adopted Irish ways. Scottish settlers moved into the northern part of Ireland too.

Fact ✓

'The Pale' – the area of Ireland directly under the control of the English – was heavily fortified. 'Beyond the Pale' is a saying that is still used today to describe something that is completely uncivilised or uncontrollable.

Later on... 1492

The English struggles in Ireland are an early example of Europeans trying to explore and increase the number of places they controlled and traded with. This really kicked off in 1492, when Christopher Columbus discovered the 'New World' of America.

▼ **SOURCE B** Written by Ralph de Diceto, an English monk, in 1172.

'When the Irish understood that King Henry only meant peace and that he wished to bring law and order to Ireland, they met him to discuss peace. Since they had trouble keeping peace amongst themselves, they handed power over to Henry II so that they should have peace.'

▼ **SOURCE C** Trim Castle, one of the castles built over a 30-year period by Henry II in the twelfth century. It was the largest Norman castle in Ireland.

▼ **SOURCE D** The Irish chiefs and kings sent a letter to the Pope in 1317, explaining why they couldn't get on with the English settlers.

'The Irish have become wicked through mixing with the English. Different from us in language and customs, all hope of staying peaceful with them is out of the question.'

Over to You ▪▪▪

1 Complete the sentences below with an accurate term:
   a In the Middle Ages, Ireland was divided up into several small _____.
   b _____ _____ was the Irish leader of Leinster.
   c Henry II visited Ireland and declared himself its _____.
   d Both Henry II and _____ _____ built castles in Ireland.
   e The _____ was the area of Ireland directly under the control of the English.

2 Read **Source B**.
   a What can this source tell us about why King Henry II went to Ireland?
   b Why did the Irish kings accept him?

3 Compare **Sources B** and **D**.
   a How had the Irish attitude to the English changed since the time of Henry II?
   b Can you suggest reasons why this change in attitude happened?

England and its neighbours: France

William the Conqueror, who fought at the Battle of Hastings, was from Normandy in France. Ever since that time, the kings of England had controlled various parts of France. However, King John had lost most of these lands during his reign, and by the start of the 1300s, only a small area in the north of France and part of a rich wine-making area called Bordeaux remained under English control. In 1327, England's new king, Edward III, vowed to gain back the lost land. His actions led to one of the longest wars England has ever been involved in – the Hundred Years War.

Objectives

- Identify the causes of the Hundred Years War.
- Summarise the key events of the Hundred Years War.

Reasons for war

By 1337, Edward III had been on the throne for ten years. He was 24 years old and determined to be a stronger ruler than his father, Edward II. The young king enjoyed fighting and viewed a war with France as a way of achieving glory on the battlefield. But there were other reasons why war broke out:

A lot of wine was made in the southern part of France that England controlled. When the wine was brought over to England it was taxed, and King Edward made lots of money from this. However, the French threatened to take over this wine-producing area.

England sold lots of wool abroad. Areas near France (such as Flanders) turned this wool into cloth. Both the English and the people in places like Flanders made lots of money doing this. But the French threatened to take over these areas. If the wool trade was stopped it would make England poorer... and people wouldn't be able to afford to pay King Edward as much tax.

Edward III himself was closely linked to France. His grandfather had been King of France. He thought he had a better claim to the throne of France than the actual French king at the time, Philip VI.

Edward was also trying to conquer Scotland at the same time. The French promised to help the Scots, which made Edward furious!

Fighting the French

In 1337, England and France started fighting. There were battles at sea, but most of the fighting was on French land. No fighting happened in England. The Hundred Years War features one of the most legendary victories in military history, where around 10,000 English soldiers beat around 40,000 Frenchmen at the Battle of Agincourt, 1415. The war lasted, on and off, until 1453 – a total of 116 years. However, historians chose to call it 'the Hundred Years War', which sounds a bit better than 'the One Hundred and Sixteen Years War'!

▼ **MAP A** England held land in France at the start of the war, and traded wool and wine with France and other areas.

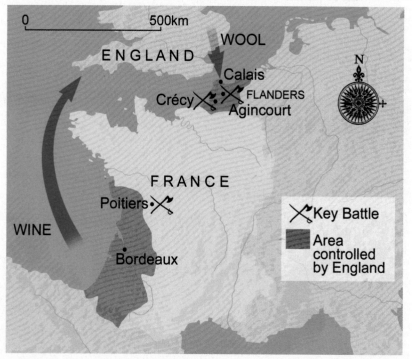

Every English king between 1199 and 1461 married a French princess or noblewoman.

▼ **SOURCE B** From *Froissart's Chronicles*, a history of the Hundred Years War written in the fourteenth century by Jean Froissart, a French-speaking medieval poet and historian from the area we now call the Netherlands.

'The English will never love or honour their king unless he is victorious in fighting. The English fight with their neighbours, especially those who are richer than themselves. They thoroughly enjoy battles and slaughter and they are always jealous of other people's riches.'

▼ **INTERPRETATION C** An image of King Henry V of England (wearing the crown) defending a fallen soldier under attack by the French Duke of Alençon at the Battle of Agincourt, 1415. This image appeared in an English history book published in 1864.

1 Read **Source B**.

   a What reason does this give for the cause of England's wars with France?

   b Do you think this is a satisfactory explanation for the cause?

2 Look at **Interpretation C**.

   a What impression do you get about Henry V when looking at this image?

   b Can you suggest reasons why the English king was drawn like this? (Hint: Look at the caption to help you.)

Cause and Consequence

1 Create a spider diagram that shows each of the causes of the Hundred Years War.

2 Number the causes in order of importance – the cause you think was the most important should be number 1, and so on.

3 Compare your order of causes with a partner's order. Do you agree or disagree? Explain your reasoning to each other.

4 'The most important reason why the Hundred Years War started was because the French were threatening English trade.' Do you agree with this statement? Explain your answer with reference to other reasons.

Gains and losses

Like most wars, the Hundred Years War had a series of ups and downs for each side. First one side did well and was on the up, and then the other side did well, and so on. Read the timeline of the war carefully.

1340: Battle of Sluys

England wins the Battle of Sluys. The English surprise French ships while they are anchored. Although the battle takes place at sea, it is fought by soldiers jumping from ship to ship and fighting as if they are on land. The French defeat means England controls the English Channel and can invade France more easily.

1347

Edward makes it a hat-trick of victories by capturing the French port of Calais. This is the closest port to England and was to remain in English hands for over 200 years.

1346: Battle of Crécy

Edward enjoys another clear victory on land. At the Battle of Crécy, his 12,000 archers and 2400 knights smash 12,000 French knights, 6000 crossbowmen and 20,000 ordinary foot soldiers. The English archers prove that they are far superior to the crossbowmen.

1356: Battle of Poitiers

English victories continue at the Battle of Poitiers, led by Edward's son, the Black Prince. John II is captured and held to ransom for £500,000. That's five times more than Edward normally earned from taxation in a year!

Winning battles... but losing the war

Despite famous victories at Sluys, Crécy, Poitiers and Agincourt, the English armies were never strong enough to defeat the French once and for all. By 1453, the French had pushed the English out of France almost completely. The small port of Calais was the only part of France still under English control.

The legend of the 'V sign'

The English archers were known for their brilliant accuracy and speed. They were greatly feared by the French. A good English archer could fire ten arrows a minute and kill a person up to 200 metres away. At the Battle of Crécy, King Edward's archers shot 72,000 arrows in 90 seconds, killing thousands.

If an English archer was captured, the French would often mutilate their limbs. Sometimes fingers or hands were cut off. Some historians believe that this is the origin of using the 'V sign' as an insult. It has been suggested that some English archers, when they saw a captured Frenchman, would run up to him and stick up their two fingers to show that they still had them, and they were still a threat! Over time this gesture became known as an insult.

▼ MAPS D TO G These maps show the changes in territory during the Hundred Years War. Areas in white show English territory, areas in orange show French territory.

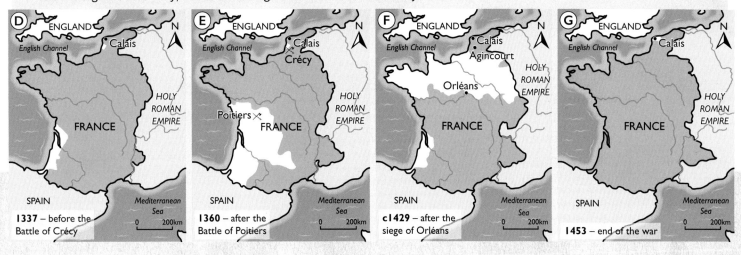

D ENGLAND | N
English Channel | •Calais
HOLY ROMAN EMPIRE
FRANCE
SPAIN | Mediterranean Sea
0   200km
1337 – before the Battle of Crécy

E ENGLAND | N
English Channel | •Calais
Crécy
HOLY ROMAN EMPIRE
Poitiers ✕
FRANCE
SPAIN | Mediterranean Sea
0   200km
1360 – after the Battle of Poitiers

F ENGLAND | N
English Channel | •Calais
Agincourt
HOLY ROMAN EMPIRE
Orléans
FRANCE
SPAIN | Mediterranean Sea
0   200km
c1429 – after the siege of Orléans

G ENGLAND | N
English Channel | •Calais
HOLY ROMAN EMPIRE
FRANCE
SPAIN | Mediterranean Sea
0   200km
1453 – end of the war

1370

The French start to fight back and, when the Black Prince falls ill, they win back some of their land.

1415: Battle of Agincourt

The new English king, Henry V, decides to renew the English claim to the French throne. He invades France and wins a famous victory at Agincourt. The French king lets Henry marry his daughter and agrees that Henry should be the next King of France when the current one dies.

1453

The French regain all their land except for the tiny area around Calais.

1377

The Black Prince dies in 1376 and his father dies the following year.

The French take advantage of the lack of strong English leadership and attack with force. They use cannons to recapture English castles in France.

1422

Disaster for the English! Henry V dies before becoming king of both England and France! His son is only nine months old. The French strike back under the leadership of a teenage peasant girl called Joan of Arc. (Find out more about her on pages 168–169.)

Over to You   .ıll

1 a How long was the Hundred Years War?

   b Why do you think historians have called it the 'Hundred Years War' when it didn't last for 100 years?

2 Look at the four maps on this page. For each map, write a brief description that outlines the differences in the land controlled by the English and French at the different points of the war. For example: **D** shows the land held at the beginning of the war. The English only control…

3 Who won the Hundred Years War? Use the information on these pages to help you – and support your opinion with evidence from the pages.

Change and Continuity ★

In History, it is important that you can spot 'turning points'. This is an event or development that changes things completely. A 'turning point' makes things different from how they were before.

1 Write a brief sentence describing what happened in each of the following years:
   • 1340   • 1356   • 1415
   • 1346   • 1370   • 1422
   • 1347   • 1377   • 1453

2 'The death of the Black Prince was the major turning point in the Hundred Years War.' How far do you agree? Explain your answer

Joan of Arc: the teenage girl who led an army

In the 1420s, during the Hundred Years War, England was on the verge of conquering the whole of France. But that all changed when a 16-year-old peasant girl went to see the French king and persuaded him to let her lead one of his armies. What made the French put a young girl in charge of an army? What made her such an inspirational leader? And what happened to the greatest heroine in French history?

Objectives

- Recall who Joan of Arc was and how she affected the course of the Hundred Years War.
- Examine why she is still a national hero in France today.

1 Joan was born in Domrémy around 1412. At the age of 12, she claimed that St Catherine, St Margaret and St Michael 'visited' her and told her to attend church regularly.

2 In 1428, with France on the verge of defeat, Joan claimed that the saints visited her again, and told her to go to the king and tell him to let her drive the English from France.

3 A determined Joan saw the desperate French king, who had been praying for a miracle. She told him that she knew he had asked God to save the French people from suffering. The king was amazed. He hadn't told anybody about his prayers – she must have spoken to God!

4 Joan was questioned about her visions by a panel of holy men for three weeks. They told the king that she must be telling the truth and to put her in charge of one of his armies.

5 Joan believed it was God's wish for her to go to Orléans, which was being attacked by the English. She wore a suit of armour and immediately made the soldiers go to church, give up swearing and stop stealing. People said she was sent by God and men flocked to fight for her.

6 Joan led an attack on the English in Orléans in 1429. Despite being injured, she inspired the French to victory with her strong beliefs. Soon, the English armies were being pushed back by the French. Never again would the English control so much of France.

7 Joan continued to lead the French to victory in other battles. When the new French king was crowned, Joan stood next to him, carrying her banner.

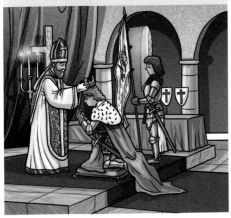

8 Joan continued to fight for France but was captured in 1430 at the town of Compiègne when she fell off her horse. She was taken to a nearby town controlled by the English. The French were devastated; the English were overjoyed!

9 Joan was put on trial by a group of mainly English churchmen for being a witch, but there was not enough evidence. In the end, they found her guilty of dressing as a man, which was against Church law. She was burned at the stake on 30 May 1431.

What happened next?

The fact that such a young, poorly educated peasant girl was able to inspire an army to such important victories is remarkable. Soon after her death even some English people began to feel that the execution had been a mistake. Even while Joan was burning, an English onlooker is said to have cried out, 'We are lost, for we have burned a saint.' An official of the English king even hurried back from the execution and said, 'We are all ruined, for a good and holy person was burned.' By 1453, England had lost all of its land in France apart from a tiny area around Calais.

Later on... `1920`

Twenty-five years after her death, the Church said that Joan of Arc should never have been killed and that she was not a witch. In 1920, she was made a saint after French soldiers in the First World War reported miracles after praying to her.

Over to You

1 Describe ways in which Joan of Arc was different from the kind of people who usually led armies in the Middle Ages.

2 Why do you think so many people followed Joan of Arc into battle?

3 Why do you think that Joan of Arc is a heroine in France today?

4 ✏️ You have been asked to contribute to a children's history book called *Who's Who in French History*. You are to write the entry for Joan of Arc but have been told there is only enough room for five sentences. Write the five sentences for the book.

▼ **INTERPRETATION A** 1912 poster advertising the newspaper of the Suffragettes, an organisation that campaigned for equal voting rights for women at this time. It shows Joan of Arc with the Suffragette colours: purple, green and white.

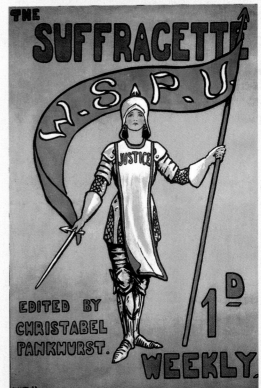

Interpretation Analysis ⭐

1 Suggest one reason why **Interpretation A** gives this view of Joan of Arc.

Choose your weapons!

Medieval warfare was a horrific experience. Archers and crossbowmen could stand 150–250 metres away from their enemy and fire arrows or crossbow bolts with savage accuracy. But sometimes soldiers would have to get close to each other and fight hand-to-hand. As a result, you'd be close enough to smell what your enemy had for breakfast. You would feel your weapon slice through flesh and crunch through bones. At any moment, you could lose an arm or a leg or be stabbed straight through the chest and left to die an agonising death on the battlefield. Some of the most common (and feared) weapons are featured on these pages. Find out how they were used – and how some of them changed and developed during the Middle Ages.

A English longbow
One of the deadliest weapons on the battlefield, the longbow could be quickly fired from over 200 metres away. It was almost two metres long and made from wood, with a linen string. The longbow was developed in Wales in the twelfth century – and when the English conquered Wales in the late thirteenth century, they were so impressed that they began using longbows themselves. The design remained largely unchanged throughout the Middle Ages.

B Crossbow
Crossbows were mini wooden catapults used to fire bolts through armour at a range of over 100 metres. They were used by European armies from about the eleventh century. Crossbows were easier to use than longbows but couldn't fire as far. Also, they couldn't be used as quickly as an archer could use a longbow – a crossbowman could shoot only two bolts per minute, for example, versus 12 or more arrows from a skilled archer! However, by the end of the medieval period, crossbows became more powerful – and could fire a little further.

C Mace
Around 1300, the mace became more commonly used. It was a heavy metal club with short, thick blades – or 'flanges'. It was brought crashing down onto opponents, shattering bones and crushing skulls. A mace could be used by both a soldier on foot and on horseback.

D Caltrop
These iron spikes were thrown on the ground and stabbed through the feet of charging horses and men.

E Pike

One of the most basic weapons on the battlefield, pikes (long sticks tipped with steel) were used by foot soldiers facing knights on horseback. Charging knights could be brought to the ground by large groups of pike-wielding men who stabbed the horses. Soldiers were ordered to gather together into large groups and point their pikes towards attacking cavalry. The English simply couldn't get through the wall of pikes! This battle formation was called a **schiltron**.

F Battleaxe

Battleaxes were devastating weapons that could slice a person in half with a single blow. A lot of space was needed to swing them, though, and they had to be held in both hands.

G Flail

Flails appeared in around 1500. Because of the chain they could be swung much faster and with greater force than a mace. They were often used to stick into armour and drag knights from their horses.

H Gunpowder

Earlier on...

Gunpowder was used in China from the ninth century, but it wasn't until the fourteenth century that it became commonly used in Europe. The Chinese are also known for inventing paper, the compass, silk, umbrellas and the first mechanical clock.

At first, cannons used gunpowder to fire large metal balls at an enemy – but they weren't very accurate or reliable. Handguns started to appear on the battlefield by the fifteenth century. Although useful for scaring horses, guns and cannons didn't become really effective until the very end of the Middle Ages, when they could fire further and more accurately.

I Swords and daggers

At the beginning of the Middle Ages, swords were large chopping weapons with a razor-sharp double-edged blade. As armour became stronger, shorter swords with extremely sharp points became more popular. Many men also chose to take a small dagger with them into battle. It came in useful when things got up close and personal and was often used to finish opponents off!

J Billhook

A billhook was a flat, curved razor-sharp piece of metal, around 30 centimetres long, attached to a wooden handle. It was used as a cutting weapon that could cause major injuries as it was forced between the gaps in a knight's armour.

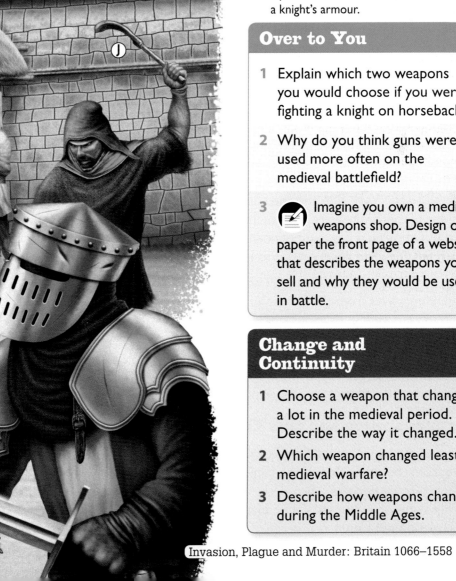

Over to You

1 Explain which two weapons you would choose if you were fighting a knight on horseback.

2 Why do you think guns weren't used more often on the medieval battlefield?

3 Imagine you own a medieval weapons shop. Design on paper the front page of a website that describes the weapons you sell and why they would be useful in battle.

Change and Continuity

1 Choose a weapon that changed a lot in the medieval period. Describe the way it changed.

2 Which weapon changed least in medieval warfare?

3 Describe how weapons changed during the Middle Ages.

Families can be very complicated. They can be very large and full of people of different ages and personalities. Sometimes certain relatives don't get on with each other – and there are often step-parents and half-brothers and half-sisters to deal with too! Also, families usually have different 'sides' to them. There's often a 'mother's side' and a 'father's side', which have different surnames. And sometimes one side might fall out with the other side.

> ## Objectives
>
> - Examine why England went to war with itself in the fifteenth century.
> - Investigate why England came to be ruled by Henry Tudor.

A right royal row

Don't think for a minute that royal families are any different from ordinary families when it comes to falling out with each other. Throughout history, kings and queens have argued (and even fought) with brothers, half-brothers, cousins, wives and sons. Edward II, for example, was murdered on the orders of his own wife so that their son could be king. And Richard II was put in prison and starved to death by his cousin. The cousin then became King Henry IV!

Lancasters and Yorks

In the early 1400s, members of England's royal family began arguing among themselves over who should be king. The argument involved two different sides of the same family – the York side and the Lancaster side. Both sides of the family were directly related to King Edward III (who ruled England between 1327 and 1377) and both felt they had good reason to rule.

The argument began when Henry VI was King of England. Henry was from the Lancaster side of the family. He was a gentle, religious man who struggled to control the country – and he was a poor military leader too. He also suffered from periods of mental illness and would sit silently for hours in a dark room, unresponsive to anything that was going on around him.

An opportunity for the Yorks

During one of Henry's mental breakdowns, a distant relative from the other side of the family (the Yorks) was chosen to be England's 'Protector' in Henry's place. His name was Richard, Duke of York, and he ruled England until Henry recovered.

When Henry was well again, Richard lost his power… but he wanted it back! So, he gathered an army to fight King Henry. Henry was beaten, and Richard became 'Protector' again. Henry was forced into hiding but his wife, Margaret of Anjou, gathered her own army and beat the Yorks. Richard was killed and Henry was now in control again.

However, Richard's son, Edward, was devastated by his father's death and swore revenge. And so began a series of violent and bloody battles between two sides of the same family – Edward and the Yorks versus Henry and the Lancasters.

> ## Fact ✓
>
> The fighting between the York family and the Lancaster family later became known as the Wars of the Roses. This is because the two families had different coloured roses as emblems for their shields and banners. The Lancasters chose a red rose and the Yorks chose a white one.
>
>

The Wars of the Roses, 1455–1485

The two sides fought each other for 30 years. First one side would win a battle and choose a king to rule the country, then the other side would win and choose their own king. **A** shows the locations (and winners) of the key battles.

▼ **MAP A** The locations of battles in the Wars of the Roses.

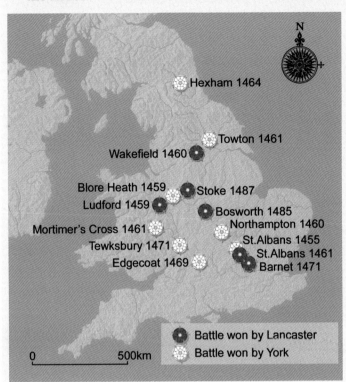

In 1591, William Shakespeare wrote a famous history play, *Henry VI, Part I*. In one scene (Act 2, Scene 4), a number of noblemen pick red or white roses to show their loyalty to either the Lancaster or York families.

▼ **INTERPRETATION C**
From a history book published in 1930.

'The nobles threw themselves eagerly into the struggle, and many battles were fought in England. It was a dreary war, for everybody was fighting for their own reasons and men changed sides shamelessly when it suited them. Everyone rejoiced when the Wars of the Roses were over, for indeed it was an unhappy, lawless time.'

▼ **INTERPRETATION D**
From *The Wars of the Roses: A Concise History* (1976) by historian Charles Ross.

'For the ordinary English person the effects of civil war were much less than for the nobles. English life in general was very little affected by the war. There was very little devastation, little pillaging and plundering. There was no general collapse of law and order.'

▼ **SOURCE B** A portrait of King Henry VI, who came from the Lancaster side of the family.

Over to You

1 a Who were the Lancasters?
  b Who were the Yorks?

2 How did the Wars of the Roses get their name?

3 Explain the role played by each of the following people during the Wars of the Roses:
  a Henry VI   c Margaret of Anjou, Henry VI's wife
  b Richard, Duke of York   d Edward, Richard of York's son.

Interpretation Analysis

1 Do **Interpretations C** and **D** agree on any details?

2 The two interpretations both comment on the impact of the Wars of the Roses on English people. How do they differ? What do they disagree about?

All change

As a result of each side winning different battles, the throne changed hands many times. Look at the diagram below. It illustrates how the role of 'King of England' swapped between the York family and the Lancaster family during the Wars of the Roses.

 1461 Henry VI (Lancaster) wins some of the early battles but is defeated at Towton by Edward (York). Edward becomes King Edward IV... and Henry flees.

 1470 Henry beats Edward IV and becomes king again. Edward escapes to the Netherlands.

 1471 Edward returns and beats Henry's armies. Edward is re-crowned. Henry is taken prisoner this time – and killed in the Tower of London.

1471–1483 Edward IV rules until his death in 1483.

 1483 Edward's son (also called Edward) becomes King Edward V. He is 12 years old and is helped by his uncle (Richard) who becomes 'Protector'. However, Edward V mysteriously disappears and Richard becomes King Richard III.

 1485 The last important member of the Lancaster family challenges Richard III for the crown. His name is Henry Tudor (Henry VI was his half-uncle). At the Battle of Bosworth Field, Henry Tudor and his Lancaster supporters beat Richard III and the Yorks. Henry Tudor becomes King Henry VII – the first Tudor king.

▼ **SOURCE E** A picture of Edward IV (seated, with his two sons next to him) receiving the first ever book to be printed (rather than copied out by hand by monks).

What happened next?

Most people thought Henry VII – a Lancaster – would soon be attacked and killed by supporters of the York family. But Henry held onto the throne and went on to rule England well. One reason why Henry was able to do this was because he cleverly married Edward IV's daughter, Elizabeth. This meant that the king was from the Lancaster family and the queen was from the York family, so their children would be both Yorks and Lancasters (see **F**). The marriage united the two families and ended the wars. The new king even united the York and Lancaster roses to create a new national symbol – the Tudor rose.

▼ **INTERPRETATION F** This double portrait of Elizabeth of York and Henry VII shows the red and white roses of Lancaster and York uniting because of their marriage. It was painted in the early 1800s by English artist Sarah Capel-Coningsby, Countess of Essex.

▼ **G** The Tudor rose is a combination of the roses of Lancaster and York.

▼ **SOURCE H** The Tudor rose can be seen today in all sorts of places. You probably didn't realise that there were ten of them on the England football badge!

Fact ✓

King Richard III's bones were found in 2012, buried underneath a car park which was built on the site of an old church in Leicester. The bones showed that Richard suffered from a crooked spine and was probably killed by a heavy blow to the head (the back of his skull was sliced off). There were eight wounds on his skull in total.

Over to You

1 a Who was Henry Tudor?

b Which battle did Henry Tudor win?

c Which king did Henry Tudor defeat?

d After Henry Tudor was crowned King Henry VII, how did he end the fighting between the families of York and Lancaster?

2 In 2012, researchers found the body of Richard III, the York king killed at the Battle of Bosworth Field by Henry Tudor's army in 1485. Imagine you've been asked to produce a short report for a children's news programme on the Wars of the Roses. The report is to be no more than 60 seconds and must contain everything a young historian would need to know.

Consequence

1 Place the following years in the correct chronological order, and write a short sentence summarising what happened in that year:
   - 1470
   - 1471
   - 1483
   - 1485
   - 1461

2 Write a narrative account of the Wars of the Roses. You must include specific details (names, dates, etc.) of events, *and* link the events together to form a well-organised story (narrative).

7.8 The Princes in the Tower

Edward IV died suddenly in April 1483. His 12-year-old son, also called Edward, travelled to London to be crowned. His brother, nine-year-old Richard, joined him. In the summer of 1483, they were seen playing in the gardens of the Tower of London. After that, they were never seen again. What had happened to them? Could they have been murdered? If so, who did it? The History Mystery detectives need to investigate!

Objectives

- Evaluate evidence about the deaths of the princes in the Tower.

Princes Edward and Richard stayed in the Tower of London while Edward prepared for his coronation. The boys' uncle, also called Richard, had been asked to look after the princes and help young Edward until he could rule the country on his own.

In June 1483, Uncle Richard announced that his brother (the dead King Edward IV) had not been legally married to the princes' mother. This meant that Prince Edward couldn't become king. Two weeks later Uncle Richard, was crowned king instead. He became King Richard III, and over the summer, his two nephews mysteriously disappeared!

You are about to learn about one of history's greatest mysteries, which has puzzled historians for over 500 years. When you have looked at the evidence, see if you can draw any conclusions.

Did Uncle Richard order the killings?

▼ **SOURCE A** Adapted from an account written in 1483 by an Italian named Domenico Mancini. He was visiting London at the time. The writer's English was very poor and the book he wrote on Richard was full of factual mistakes.

'Prince Edward and his brother were taken to the inner rooms of the tower, and day by day began to be seen less behind the bars and the windows, until they stopped appearing altogether... So far I have not discovered if he has been killed, nor how he might have died.'

▼ **SOURCE B** Adapted from the *Croyland Chronicle*, 1486, written by monks from Northamptonshire. Not much is known about the writers, but historians think the monks might have got their information from Bishop John Russell, trusted friend of the princes' father, Edward IV, and enemy of Richard III.

'For a long time the two sons of King Edward remained under guard in the Tower. Finally, in September 1483 people began to think of freeing them by force... but then a rumour was spread that the princes had died a violent death, but no one knew how.'

▼ **INTERPRETATION C** Adapted from an account written in 1513 by Sir Thomas More. More was only five when Richard III became king so he wouldn't have witnessed these events. More was brought up by John Morton, who had been imprisoned as an enemy of Richard III.

'King Richard wanted Sir James Tyrrell to carry out his wishes. Tyrrell decided that the princes should be murdered in their beds. He picked Miles Forrest and John Dighton to do the job.

About midnight Forrest and Dighton entered the room where the children lay in their beds and forced the feather pillows hard into their mouths until they stopped breathing.

Then Sir James got the murderers to bury them at the bottom of the stairs, deep in the ground under a heap of stones. Later a priest dug up the bodies and moved them to a place which only he knew.'

▼ **INTERPRETATION D** This nineteenth-century engraving is an artist's interpretation of what happened to the princes. Does the image match any of the evidence on these pages so far?

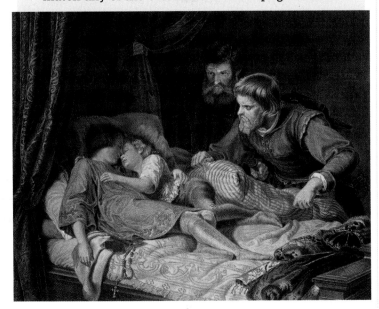

King Richard's defence

Many historians think that Richard III was connected to the disappearance of the princes in some way. Rumours of their death were going round within weeks of their disappearance, but Richard never tried to prove they were alive by having them seen in public. To some historians, this suggests that they were probably dead – and as king, he *must* have known about their deaths.

However, there are different theories about the mystery:

• Richard III had nothing to do with the disappearances. In the Croyland Chronicle of 1486 it says that Elizabeth Woodville (the princes' mother) sent her daughters to live with Richard III in 1486, three years **after** the disappearance. This shows that she trusted Richard III – she would not send her daughters to live with someone she suspected of killing her sons.

• In 1485, Richard III was killed in battle. He was beaten by a rival for the throne named Henry Tudor. Henry was crowned King of England and became Henry VII. Therefore, Henry VII might be involved in the murders in some way. Perhaps the children were alive when Henry became king and he had them killed soon after. Henry VII gave land and important jobs to James Tyrrell, John Dighton and Miles Forrest – this was perhaps a reward for their murderous actions (see **E**).

▼ **INTERPRETATION E** Historian Philip Lindsay writing in a magazine, 1972.

'I am certain that the princes were alive when Henry came to London in August 1485. He issued a list of all Richard's supposed crimes – and the list does not include the killing of the princes. That, to my mind, is proof that they were not even missing. Richard had no reason to kill them; Henry had every reason. If they lived, all he had fought for would be useless because Prince Edward had more right to be king than Henry Tudor. Henry spread the word that Richard had done the killing. Henry Tudor, murderer and liar – it is time the truth was known!'

Later on...

In 1674, men working on a staircase in the Tower of London found a box containing two sets of children's bones. The box was roughly where Thomas More said the princes were first buried. Charles II, who was king at the time, gave the bones a full funeral. In 1933, two doctors examined the bones and reported that the skeletons were not complete, they belonged to two children aged about 10 and 12, and a stain on one of the skulls may mean that they were suffocated. In 1955, different doctors looked at the 1933 report. They weren't allowed to look at the bones but studied pictures instead. They said that the bones were from children younger than the two princes and the stain was not caused by suffocation.

Over to You

1 Use only **Sources** and **Interpretations A** to **D**.

a What do you think happened to the princes?

b What makes you think this? List the evidence that led you to this decision.

c Do you trust all the evidence? Can you think of reasons why some of the things you've read so far might not be totally reliable?

d After reading the rest of the evidence about the disappearance of the princes, has your answer to question **1a** changed? Explain your answer.

2 Write a short paragraph explaining what you think happened to the princes.

Quick Knowledge Quiz

Choose the correct answer from the three options:

1   What name was given to King William of England's trusted barons who were given land along the Welsh border?
    a   Welsh Princes
    b   Border Knights
    c   Marcher Lords

2   What was the 'Ring of Iron'?
    a   the ring worn by King Edward after he had conquered Wales
    b   the name of a series of English castles built during King Edward's rule in Wales
    c   a type of punishment given to those who betrayed King Edward

3   Which Scottish king died in 1286 leaving no clear heir to take his place?
    a   Edward I
    b   Alexander III
    c   William IV

4   Removed to London by King Edward I, what was the name of the ancient rectangular block of stone on which Scottish kings sat when they were crowned?
    a   Stone of Royalty
    b   The Crown Stone
    c   Stone of Destiny

5   Who led the Scots to a famous victory over the English in June 1314 at Bannockburn?
    a   John Balliol
    b   Robert the Bruce
    c   William Wallace

6   Which two kings of England built castles in Ireland?
    a   King Henry II and King John
    b   King Edward III and King Stephen
    c   King William the Conqueror and King Henry VIII

7   The Battle of Agincourt took place in which year?
    a   1348
    b   1415
    c   1453

8   How long was the Hundred Years War?
    a   100 years
    b   106 years
    c   116 years

9   During the Wars of the Roses, what colour was the famous rose symbol of the York family?
    a   red
    b   white
    c   blue

10 Who defeated Richard III at the Battle of Bosworth Field in 1485?
    a   Henry Tudor
    b   Robert the Bruce
    c   Richard of York

Literacy Focus

Punctuation

1 The passage below doesn't make much sense. It needs capital letters, commas, apostrophes, paragraphs and full stops. Copy out the passage, adding punctuation as you write.

> in the early 1400s members of englands royal family began arguing amongst themselves over who should be king the argument involved two different sides of the same family the york side and the lancaster side both sides of the family were directly related to king edward III who ruled england between 1327 and 1377 and both felt they had good reason to rule the two main leaders of each side of the family were edward and henry edward was a york and henry was a lancaster the lancasters chose a red rose and the yorks chose a white rose as their symbol as a result the series of violent and bloody battles between two sides is known as the wars of the roses

Vocabulary and knowledge check

2 In each group of historical words, phrases or names below, there is an odd one out. When you think you have identified it, write a sentence or two to explain why you think it doesn't fit in with the other words in its group. The first one has been done for you:

   a Caernarfon   Conwy   Rochester   Beaumaris

   Rochester: This castle is in England, the others are in Wales.

   b John Balliol   Alexander III   Robert the Bruce   Edward I

   c Bannockburn   Stamford Bridge   Falkirk   Stirling Bridge

   d Gwynedd   Ulster   Leinster   Munster

   e Agincourt   Poitiers   Falkirk   Crécy

   f Domrémy   Orléans   Compiègne   Sluys

   g billhook   battleaxe   flail   schiltron

   h Henry VI   Richard III   Edward IV   Edward V

History skill: Causation

As you know, a **cause** is a reason why something happened. Most major historical events that you study will have a number of different causes. And even though events can have several different causes, there is often one cause that is more important than the others.

A good historian needs to be able to debate with others about *how much* they agree or disagree about the causes of an event. For example, they might respond to a statement that contains a judgement or a point of view, and argue which is most important.

Responding to statements about causation

This chapter's assessment requires you to think about the **causes** of an event – the Hundred Years War.

'The main reason why the Hundred Years War started was because the French threatened English-controlled land in France.' How far do you agree with this statement? Explain your answer.

> **TIP:** 'How far do you agree' simply means how much you agree with the statement. Do you totally agree with it? In other words, was the main reason for the start of the war because the French threatened English-controlled land in France? Or were there other reasons that were more important? This question asks you to think about the *extent* to which you agree with the statement.

The question will ask you to **respond to a statement** about the causes of the war and how much you agree with the statement. The steps on the next page show one way to answer this type of question.

1 **Plan:** Study the statement. Do you agree or disagree with it? What do you know about the topic? Also, make some notes about *other* reasons that led to the event. There may be several reasons for the cause of an event. So, what other reasons were there? You could make a mind-map to help you.

TIP: Look back at your notes or pages 164–167 of this book to remind yourself of the causes of the Hundred Years War.

TIP: Do not worry if you didn't think that the cause in the statement was more important. That won't mean you won't be able to answer the question – remember that the question asks you whether you think one cause was *more important* than the others – if you don't think it was, that's OK, as long as you can explain why you think this.

2 **Judge:** Once you have thought about the different causes, you need to decide: Which do you think was the most important cause? List in bullet points the reason for your choice.

TIP: Can you explain why you have put them in this order?

3 **Answer:** Remember – this question type is focused on your response to a statement. So, after steps 1 and 2, do you agree with the statement you have been given? Do you *strongly* agree that French threats to English-controlled land were the main reason why the war started? Or don't you agree with the statement at all? Or do you only *slightly agree*? There is no right answer for this, it is down to what you think!

TIP: You could begin your answer by saying 'I strongly agree with this statement…' or 'No, I don't agree with the statement very much…' or 'I agree with the statement to a certain extent…'

4 **Explain:** You now need to add details/reasons to support your decision and explain why you are taking this view. Use your plan to help you add detail and so on. Try to refer to other reasons when answering the question.

TIP: Write why your choice is the *most* important – and why you don't think the others are as important.

TIP: Don't simply write about your choice only. Include other reasons and back them up with factual detail.

5 **Conclude:** Remember to include a concluding sentence stating your overall point of view.

Now, considering all these points, look at the next page and try putting this into practice!

Assessment: Causation

Your challenge is to answer this statement question about causation:

> 'The main reason why the Hundred Years War started was because the French threatened English controlled land in France.' How far do you agree with this statement? Explain your answer.
> (20)

The steps below will help you structure your answer. Use the example sentence starters to help you begin each point.

1   **Plan:** Study the statement. In this case the judgement is that French threats to English-controlled land in France were the main reason why the Hundred Years War began. This assumes that the French threats to English land did play a role. So, do you agree with that? What do you *know* about this?

There may be several reasons why the war started. In fact, the statement itself hints at this when it says that the French threats to English-controlled land in France were the '*main*' reason. This implies that there were *other* reasons why the war started. So, what other reasons were there? Create a mind-map to help you.

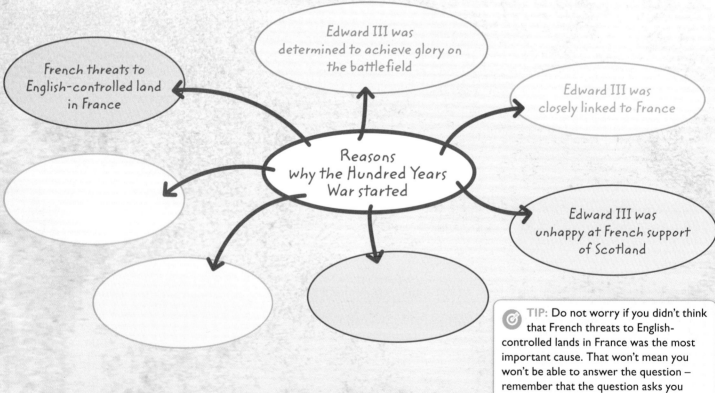

French threats to English-controlled land in France

Edward III was determined to achieve glory on the battlefield

Edward III was closely linked to France

Reasons why the Hundred Years War started

Edward III was unhappy at French support of Scotland

2   **Judge:** Look at your mind-map. Which of the causes do you think was the *most* important? Try to explain why you think one reason was more important than the others.

TIP: Do not worry if you didn't think that French threats to English-controlled lands in France was the most important cause. That won't mean you won't be able to answer the question – remember that the question asks you whether you think one cause was *more important* than the others – if you don't think it was, that's OK, as long as you can explain why you think this.

3   **Answer:** Now you've made your judgement, respond to the statement so you are **directly answering the question**. Remember that the question asks you *how far* you agree with the statement. It is asking you the extent (or how much) you agree with the statement. Do you *strongly* agree that French threats to English-controlled land were the main reason why the war started? Or don't you agree with the statement at all? Or do you *slightly agree* with the statement? There is no right answer for this, it is down to what *you* think!

> **TIP:** Pick one of the phrases below that you think fits best with your judgement:
>
> strongly agree…
>
> don't agree very much…
>
> agree to a certain extent…

> I … with the statement that 'the main reason why the Hundred Years War started was because the French threatened English-controlled land in France'. The Hundred Years War was a series of wars that started because…

> **TIP:** It's OK to disagree with a statement, or only agree with a statement a little, as long as you back up your argument with facts and reasons.

4   **Explain and conclude:** Sometimes, causes can be linked together. For example, the French threats to English-controlled land in France gave Edward III the chance to try to achieve military glory. If the French did not threaten the land, perhaps Edward III would not have tried to achieve military glory!

Finally, add some **details and reasons** to support *why* you think *what* you think. Try to refer to other reasons when answering the question.

> The Hundred Years War was a period in history when…   (5)

> **TIP:** It is useful to set up your answer by introducing the topic you are writing about.

> The Hundred Years War had several causes. In my opinion, the main reason why the war started was…
>
> This was important because…   (5)

> Another important cause was that…
>
> There were other causes, too. For example…
>
> However, these were less important because…   (5)

> Overall, I (strongly agree/agree to a certain extent/disagree) with the statement because…   (5)

> **TIP:** Remember to conclude your answer. Explain *how far* you agree with the statement.

Was King Henry VII a gangster?

Have you ever heard of a 'gangster'? Some of you will have. Take a moment to think and talk about what a gangster is and what the word means. Could the word ever be used to describe an English king?

Objectives

- Investigate the life of Henry VII.
- Assess the tactics Henry VII used to become more powerful.

A gangster is usually someone who is powerful. And they are often involved in unfair or criminal activities. They get money from people (sometimes unfairly) and make deals to increase their power. They often live lavish lifestyles and enjoy showing off their wealth and power. They sometimes use weapons to bully people.

Henry VII was not a criminal: he was King of England and Wales. In 1485, when he was simply Henry Tudor, he had beaten King Richard III in the Battle of Bosworth Field, near Leicester. Richard was killed and Henry Tudor became the new king – Henry VII.

Henry VII, who had become king by fighting, was desperate to remain king. So, he had to do things to keep his position safe. Now that you know what a gangster is, see if you think Henry VII acted like one.

He made sure he had the best weapons

Cannons first appeared in Britain in the 1300s. They were the most destructive and feared weapons by the time Henry became king, so he made sure he had the finest cannons in the land.

He married a rival

Henry was a member of the Lancaster family. The Lancasters' bitter rivals were the members of the York family, who were also keen to rule the country. In 1486, Henry married a member of the rival family – Elizabeth of York. She was the daughter of Edward IV and the older sister of Edward V – the king who had disappeared in the Tower of London in 1483. With Elizabeth of York as the new queen, it meant that the king was a Lancaster and the queen was a York.

He banned private armies

Some powerful men in England had their own private armies. Henry knew these armies could be used against him… so he made a law that banned them. One rich lord who failed to get rid of his private army was fined £10,000!

NO PRIVATE ARMIES ALLOWED

He forced people to give him money

Henry made the rich people in his kingdom pay him heavy taxes. He sent ministers around the country looking for large, expensive houses. If they found one, Henry said they could afford to pay a large tax and forced them to pay. In addition, if the officials found nobles who were not living a lavish lifestyle and were being careful with their money, Henry assumed they must be saving money… so he forced them to hand over some of their savings in tax!

He made deals with other countries

Henry once got Parliament to give him money to fight the French – then got the French king to pay him not to fight! He also made his eldest son, Arthur, marry a Spanish princess called Catherine of Aragon in order to become friendlier with Spain. And when Arthur died, he said his youngest son, Henry, should marry her as well. He even encouraged his 18-year-old daughter Mary to marry the 52-year-old King of France, and his other daughter, Margaret, to marry the King of Scotland.

He made sure everyone knew he was king

Henry was very careful with money but liked to enjoy himself. He spent huge amounts of money on lavish parties and entertainment. The Tudor rose symbol appeared all over the country – in churches, paintings, palaces and cathedrals.

Meanwhile... 1486

In 1486, the same year Henry VII married Elizabeth of York, the word 'football' was first used to describe a game where a ball is kicked (see pages 92–93).

Henry dies

When Henry VII died in 1509, the throne was safe, and England was at peace. His son and heir, Henry VIII, became king without any opposition. He also left Henry VIII a fortune! But what do you think? Was Henry VII a bit of a gangster?

▶ **SOURCE A**
A painting of Henry VII dating from 1505. He sent his picture to a possible new wife after his first wife, Elizabeth of York, died in 1503. Notice that he is clutching a rose in his right hand, one of the many Tudor symbols.

Over to You

1 In your own words, explain what is meant by the word 'gangster'.

2 ✏️ Imagine you are Henry VII and have been on the throne for several years. A new king in another country has written you a letter asking how you have become so powerful, raised so much money, and made yourself safe and secure. Write him a letter back in reply.

3 Look again at your answer to question **1**. Do you think Henry VII acted like a gangster? Explain your opinion.

Consequence

1 Make a brief list of the actions taken by Henry VII to secure his kingdom.

2 Explain two of the following:
• The importance of banning private armies in making Henry VII a secure king
• The importance of marrying Elizabeth of York
• The importance of making lots of money in order to be a secure king.

What was young Henry VIII like?

Everybody has heard of Henry VIII. Most people think they know a few things about him too. They usually say:

- He was a big fat bloke.
- He had six wives… or was it eight?
- He beheaded most of his wives.

Some of these statements are true. Henry did have six wives, but he didn't chop the heads off most of them (although he did behead two!). As for him being a big fat bloke – well, yes, he was – but only for the last few years of his life. In fact, on his forty-fifth birthday, Henry was the same size as when he became king just days before his eighteenth birthday!

Objectives

- Examine how young Henry VIII spent his time and money.
- Judge how religious he was as a young man.

A new Tudor king

Henry's father, Henry VII, was unpopular towards the end of his reign because he taxed people heavily. When he died, and Henry VIII became king in 1509, there were wild celebrations. The new king was tall, handsome and full of youthful energy. The diagram on this page shows why many people thought he was ideally suited to be king.

Fact ✓

Henry VIII employed someone to wipe his bottom! He was officially called the Groom of the Stool. It was a much-prized job because the employee got to spend so much time with the king!

Henry loved entertaining.

He enjoyed hunting.

Bonjour! Buenos días!
He spoke four languages.

▼ **SOURCE A** A portrait of King Henry VIII, showing him in his late twenties in 1520.

Henry was a keen sportsman.

He loved jousting.

He was a keen poet.

He wrote music.

Henry the Great?

Henry was desperate to become known as a 'super king' and even liked to call himself 'Henry the Great'. However, he didn't achieve this aim. Instead he is perhaps best known for the number of wives he had and the significant religious changes he made. These changes affected religion not only in Henry's time; they changed religion in England and Wales for good.

▼ **SOURCE B** Adapted from a poem written by Thomas More in 1509 to celebrate the coronation of Henry VIII. More wrote this at a time when he was one of Henry's most trusted advisers. However, in 1532 he was convicted of treason and beheaded on Henry's orders.

'The King stands out the tallest, and his strength fits his majestic body... There is fiery power in his eyes, beauty in his face... He has immediately arrested and imprisoned anyone who had harmed the country.'

Henry the good Catholic

Henry was a very religious man and, like most people in the country at the time, he was a Christian, and followed the Roman Catholic religion. He visited church at least three times a day and even wrote a book supporting the Pope, who was the Head of the Catholic Church. Henry was such a good Catholic that in 1521, the Pope rewarded him with the title Fidei Defensor, which means Defender of the Faith. Henry loved this title and was very proud of it – and so were many other kings and queens. You can still see the letters FD or 'Fid. Def.' on British coins today.

Later on...

Can you see 'FD' on this British £1 coin? And the Tudor rose?

It all goes wrong

However, by 1533, Henry had fallen out with the Pope, who excommunicated him, meaning he was expelled from the Catholic Church. This was a very serious punishment at the time because it meant you could not talk to a priest about your sins. If a priest did not forgive you for your sins, you wouldn't get to heaven. Also, monarchs from other countries might believe it was right to attack Britain because they would be pleasing the Pope – and God. So why did Henry VIII and the Pope fall out with each other? What had Henry done that was so terrible that he received the worst kind of religious punishment? The next few pages chart an amazing story.

Fact

Henry loved to bet on anything – cards, dice, tennis, wrestling or jousting. He would sometimes win (and lose) the equivalent of thousands of pounds in one day. Henry also loved to dress in the smartest, most expensive clothes. His fine shirts, gold buttons and jewel-encrusted jackets would have cost a fortune. So, too, would his legendary parties, held at any of Henry's 55 palaces.

Over to You

1 Write a profile of the young King Henry VIII. Search through the text to find out details about the young king, using the following subheadings to guide your writing:
   - The athlete
   - The good Catholic
   - The big spender.

2 Write your own opinion in answer to the following question: 'Should the young King Henry have been called Henry the Great?'

Source Analysis

1 Study **Source B**. Choose three words that summarise More's opinion of Henry VIII.

2 Explain how this source is useful to a historian studying Henry VIII at the time of his coronation.

Henry VIII, his first wife and his big problem

Henry's problems with religion started with his love life. His first wife was a Spanish princess called Catherine of Aragon. He first met her in 1501 when she came to England to marry his older brother, Arthur! So how did Henry end up marrying her? What problems did this cause? And what did his relationship with Catherine mean for the future of religion in England?

Objectives

- Recall how and why Henry VIII fell out with the Pope.
- Examine how this affected the life of Henry and religion in England.

Henry marries his dead brother's wife!

The marriage between Prince Arthur and Princess Catherine meant friendship between England and Spain. However, Arthur died only a year after the marriage. Henry VII then arranged for his second son, Henry, to marry her. This meant that the friendship between England and Spain was kept. The wedding took place in 1509, the same year that King Henry VII died. Seventeen-year-old Henry became King Henry VIII, and Catherine of Aragon was his first queen.

Henry in love

Henry and Catherine were a popular and loving couple. Catherine also showed herself to be a skilled leader. In 1513, while Henry was in France, she ran the country for him. She sent an army to beat a Scottish army at the Battle of Flodden. Catherine brought Henry a present home from the battle… the dead King of Scotland's coat, still stained with his blood.

Henry and Catherine were happily married for nearly 20 years. Henry once said, 'If I were still free, I would choose her for a wife above all others.' But the marriage didn't last. As we all know, he had five more wives after Catherine, so what went wrong? Read the story carefully to discover why their marriage ended.

Henry changes a nation

Henry's desire for a son began a series of events that altered religion in England forever. In one move, he got his divorce and made himself more powerful.

1 Henry desperately wanted a son. This was a time when a male heir was crucial to continue the royal line and secure the kingdom. In England there had never been a ruling queen, and a female ruler would be challenged.

Catherine gave birth to six children, but only one, a girl called Mary (born in 1516), survived.

2 By 1527, Henry thought Catherine was too old to have any more children. Henry wanted to divorce her. He'd fallen in love with another woman too – Anne Boleyn.

3 Henry got his lawyers to look secretly into whether his marriage to Catherine was legal or not.

The marriage was found to be legal – but Henry still wanted his divorce.

4 The Pope was the only man who could give Henry the divorce he wanted, but he refused

Henry hated the fact that the Pope had this power over him… but he had a plan.

5 Henry ignored the Pope. In 1531, he created a new title for himself: Head of the Church of England. He said the Pope was no longer in charge of the Church.

The Pope was furious, but Henry could do as he pleased.

6 In April 1533, Henry gave himself the divorce he desired.

Henry had already married Anne Boleyn in secret in January that year!

7 Anne Boleyn was already pregnant when Henry married her.

Anne gave birth to a girl, Elizabeth. Henry was very disappointed. Why?

8 Some of the monks in England didn't support Henry's new Church of England. They supported the Pope.

So, Henry closed down all the monasteries and their land was sold.

9 The monasteries' treasures were seized and sold, and the king made a good profit.

This made the Pope furious again. Not only had Henry ignored him and closed all of the Catholic monasteries in England, but he had now taken all their treasures. In 1538, Henry VIII was officially excommunicated by the Catholic Church.

The Pope no longer controlled the English Church – Henry did, and all its wealth too! To this day, the Head of the Church of England is the king or queen.

Yet despite this change of Church leader and the closing of the monasteries, Henry only really made one other major religious change. From 1538, he ordered that every church must have an English copy of the Bible. At last, ordinary English people could understand what their religion was teaching them.

Key Words   Dissolution   Reformation

Fact ✓

Historians like to give titles to major historical changes! Henry's changes to the Church are known as the English **Reformation** because Henry was reforming (another word for changing) the English Church. When he closed down the monasteries, it was known as the **Dissolution** of the monasteries. Dissolution is another word for breaking up.

Over to You

1 The following are all important dates from Henry's marriage to his first wife:
   - 1533
   - 1527
   - 1513
   - 1509
   - 1516
   - 1501

   Write each date, in chronological order, on a separate line. Beside each date, write what happened in that year. Be careful – several things happen in one of the years!

2 Explain why Henry married Catherine of Aragon.

3 Why did Henry close down the monasteries? Give more than one reason.

4 a Why did Henry want a son?
   b What do you think about his reason?

5 Write a sentence or two to explain the following words:
   - Reformation
   - Dissolution

Cause

1 Which of the following statements do you think was most important in making Henry want to divorce Catherine of Aragon? You might want to put them in order – from 'most important reason' down to 'least'.
   a Henry was bored with Catherine.
   b Henry wanted to have a son.
   c Henry loved Anne Boleyn.
   d Henry disagreed with the Pope over religion.

2 Explain why Henry VIII divorced Catherine of Aragon.

What did Protestants protest about?

Henry wanted to break away from the Roman Catholic Church mainly because he wanted a divorce… but he wasn't the first person to criticise the Pope and want changes to happen. In the early 1500s, some people in Europe started to question the Catholic Church and its ways of worship. Why were people unhappy? Was it a big issue at the time?

Objectives

- Explain why some people criticised the Catholic Church.
- Examine how Protestants got their name and what they believed.

For some people today, it is difficult to imagine the importance of the Church in everyone's lives centuries ago. Today, lots of people visit a church only for weddings or funerals. It was very different in Tudor times. There were no televisions or cinemas to entertain people. Houses weren't full of carpets and comfy sofas. However, there was the local church – a welcoming meeting place, and a place to enjoy summer fairs, have a chat with friends and, of course, worship God.

The importance of religion

During the Middle Ages and Tudor times, the vast majority of people in Western Europe believed in the Christian God. They used religion to explain things they didn't understand. For example, nasty illnesses or infections were seen as punishment from God. And if the harvest was bad, it was because God wished it so. They also believed that heaven and hell were real places. If you led a good life on earth and prayed regularly, you would probably go to heaven when you died. However, if you were a bad person who committed crimes and didn't attend church regularly, you would definitely go to hell.

Spreading the word

By 1500, the increase in printing in Europe meant that many books on different topics were available to read. There were several books on religion, for example, and soon copies of the Bible were available in local languages, like German (in 1525) and English (in 1537), rather than just Latin. For the first time, ordinary educated men and women were able to read the Bible for themselves instead of having to go to church and listen to what the priest told them. Some people started to think very deeply about the Catholic Church and wonder whether everything they had always been told was entirely correct.

Some people began to criticise the Church. They still believed in God; they just felt that there might be different ways of worshipping. Look at the following four main criticisms of the Catholic Church at this time across Europe.

Criticism No. 1 – the Church was too rich!

The Church owned about one-third of all the land in England. Also, an ordinary peasant had to give 10 per cent of their harvest (a tithe) to the priest every year. Some felt that the bishops, priests and monks lived in luxury while the poor suffered.

Criticism No. 2 – the priests and other religious leaders didn't lead a very 'holy' life.

Some priests had several different jobs and neglected their work. Ordinary people thought some priests were not setting a very good example to the people in the village or town.

Criticism No. 3 – ordinary people couldn't understand the church services.

Church services were held in Latin. People said they found it difficult to feel close to God if they couldn't understand what was being said in church.

Criticism No. 4 – poor people couldn't afford indulgences.

When a person died, it was believed that they went to heaven or hell. It was thought people passed through a place called purgatory on the way to heaven. In purgatory, people believed you were punished for any sins you committed while you were alive. It wasn't meant to be a nice place to stay for very long. So when you were alive, you could buy 'indulgences' from a bishop. This meant that you travelled through purgatory quicker. Rich people could buy lots of indulgences. Poor people didn't think it was fair. They thought that they were being punished for being poor.

A protest in Germany

Remember: when we talk about religion at this time, there was only one type of Christianity in Western Europe – the Roman Catholic religion. This was the official religion of countries in Western Europe. But some people wanted change.

In 1517, a German monk called Martin Luther wrote out a long list of criticisms of the Catholic Church and had it nailed to his local church door. His list was quickly reprinted, translated into different languages, and distributed throughout Germany and Europe.

Luther wanted the Church to change – and soon his ideas and beliefs attracted many followers. By 1529, the followers were known as **Protestants** because they protested against the Catholic Church. Now there were mainly two Christian groups in Europe – the Catholics and the Protestants – but both wanted to worship God in slightly different ways:

The Protestant way:

- A country's monarch should be the Head of the Church.

- The Bible and prayer books should be in a language that the worshippers understand – not in Latin.

- A church should be a plain and simple place to worship God. Money shouldn't be wasted on decorations or robes for the priest.

- People should not pay indulgences for their sins.

The Catholic way:

- The Pope in Rome is Head of the Catholic Church and is chosen by God.

- The Bible and prayer books are written in Latin.

- A church should be an inspiring place to worship God, with pictures on the walls, stained-glass windows, a large stone altar, silver cups and crosses, and priests in magnificent robes.

▼ **INTERPRETATION A** An image, from 1830, of Martin Luther directing the nailing of his protests against the Catholic Church to a church door in Wittenberg, Germany, in 1517.

Fact ✓

Although Henry VIII made himself the head of the Church of England, he still regarded himself as Catholic. However, he started to do a few things you would expect a Protestant to want. For example, traditionally Catholic bibles were written in Latin and could only be read by those who understood Latin, such as priests. But in 1536, Henry made it legal to translate the Bible into English. This change gave ordinary people direct access to the Word of God.

Over to You ‧ıll

1 Explain why religion and the Church played such an important part in people's lives at this time.

2 Explain the origin of the word 'Protestant'.

3 In your own words, summarise the four main criticisms of the Catholic Church. Aim to summarise each criticism in no more than 15 words.

4 The printing press was quite a new invention at this time. How do you think this helped Martin Luther and other people who agreed with his views?

Who'd want to marry King Henry VIII?

Henry VIII had more wives than any other British king. Being his wife must have been a very tricky business. They may have enjoyed a luxurious lifestyle, but there were huge risks involved. Who did he accuse of being a witch? Who did he divorce for being too ugly? And who did he execute for having a boyfriend before she met him?

Objectives

- Explain and analyse the marriages of Henry VIII and his wives.
- Construct advice for his sixth wife on how to survive being married to Henry.

Your task is to look through the tangled love life of Henry. Imagine that you are a friend of Katherine Parr. She is a sensible, intelligent and kind 31-year-old widow who 52-year-old King Henry wants to marry. She would be Henry's sixth wife. Despite her family's pleasure that the king has chosen her, she is a little bit worried, perhaps frightened. The marriage date has been set for 12 July 1543. Your job is to give her advice. Read about each of Henry's previous wives and what went wrong for them. How might Katherine be able to keep the king happy? What should (and shouldn't) she do?

Let's start by looking at the ageing king:

- 52 years old
- Cruel, bad tempered and paranoid. He was convinced that people were trying to assassinate him.
- So fat that he needed a special machine to get him on (and off) his horse!
- Often complained about headaches and stomach aches – and suffered from fever, smallpox and malaria. His legs were covered with ulcers, which later turned to gangrene. One visitor wrote that Henry 'had the worst legs in the world'.

Now read about his five former wives.

Catherine of Aragon:

Wife No. 1: 1509–1533

- She was Catholic.
- A Spanish princess, once married to Henry's older brother, she brought friendship with Spain.
- She was clever and popular.
- All her sons died, which frustrated Henry, who wanted a male heir; she had a daughter called Mary who survived.
- Henry thought Catherine was old and boring when she reached her forties. He divorced her.

Anne Boleyn:

Wife No. 2: 1533–1536

- She was Protestant.
- She was young, attractive and very fashionable.
- She made Henry wait until it was clear they were going to marry before consummating their relationship.
- She had a daughter, Elizabeth. Henry sulked for weeks because he wanted a boy.
- She miscarried a baby boy in 1536.
- Henry accused Anne of being unfaithful with several other men. Despite having no proof, Henry had her beheaded in 1536.

Fact ✓

Henry had a party to celebrate Catherine's death in 1536 (there were rumours at the time that she'd been poisoned). He even wore yellow clothes, the traditional colour of celebration!

Fact ✓

When Anne found out the name of the person who was going to execute her she bravely said 'I have heard that the executioner is very good, and I have a little neck'.

Jane Seymour:

Wife No. 3: 1536–1537

- She was Protestant.

- She was calm, gentle and caring. She tried hard to be friends with Henry's daughters.

- She would not consummate their relationship until they were married.

- She had a son, Edward. Henry was delighted – a boy at last!

- Jane died of an infection a few days after the birth.

Fact ✓

When Henry died, he was buried with Jane in St George's Chapel in Windsor Castle.

Anne of Cleves:

Wife No. 4: 1540

- She was Protestant.

- Cleves was an area of what is now Germany, close to Flanders and France. Henry married Anne because it brought friendship between England and this powerful European region.

- She was serious and unfashionable. Friends tried to teach her some of Henry's favourite card games, but she didn't understand them.

- Henry had seen a painting of her and liked what he saw. However, when he saw her in person, he described her as a fat 'Flanders mare' [horse].

- Henry divorced her.

Fact ✓

Henry's six-month marriage to Anne was never consummated. After the divorce, Anne was given land, money and the rather strange official title of the 'King's sister'.

Key Words   consummate   gangrene
miscarry

Catherine Howard:

Wife No. 5: 1540–1542

- She was Catholic.

- She was young (aged 16 or 17), lively and very pretty.

- She flirted with lots of men… and Henry found out.

- She once finished off a letter to another man with the words, 'Yours as long as life endures'. Henry was furious.

- Henry also found out that she had several serious boyfriends before she met him. A queen should not have a past like this!

- She was executed.

Fact ✓

When Catherine Howard found out she was going to be beheaded, she ran shouting and screaming towards Henry to beg his forgiveness. He locked the door and ignored her. Her crying ghost is said to haunt the same corridor at Hampton Court Palace.

Over to You

1   You learned a little about Katherine Parr at the start of these pages. Now write her a letter, giving her advice about her forthcoming marriage. In your letter include:

a   details of Henry's previous five marriages.
  - What attracted Henry to each of his wives?
  - What went wrong with each marriage?
  - What happened to each of his wives?

b   top tips on how to keep Henry happy and interested in her. Remember how old he is and what sort of wife he might want.

2   Find out what happened to Katherine Parr. Find out about her life with Henry… and after. Use the Internet or carry out some research using books in the library.

Despite six marriages, Henry VIII left only three children behind when he died on 28 January 1547. Edward was nine, Elizabeth was 13 and Mary was a woman of 30. Henry had absolutely no doubt as to who he would leave in control of the country: the nine-year-old, of course! The young prince may have been the same age as a Year 5 student – but he was male! Henry believed this made him a much better choice as ruler than his older sisters. So what kind of king was young Edward? Which faith did he follow? And what did this mean for the way people worshipped God?

Objectives

- Explain how and why Henry's son changed religion in England.
- Describe what kind of boy Edward VI was.

Changes in religion

As you have learned, Henry VIII had made some important changes to religion. He had closed all the monasteries (and taken their money), and allowed the Bible to be printed in English (rather than Latin). Most importantly, he had made himself, and future kings and queens, Head of the Church of England (instead of the Pope). Henry didn't make any more major changes to religion and many, many people, including the king, still thought of themselves as Catholic – they simply thought of the Church of England as *part* of the Catholic Church.

However, Henry's son (now King Edward VI) believed deeply in the Protestant faith. As a Protestant, he thought that the Catholic Church did not worship God in the correct way. Edward felt that God should be worshipped in a plain and simple manner. And as he was Head of the Church, he could alter it in any way he wished. Look at the two illustrations. The first shows what a Catholic church would have looked like. The other shows how it would have changed when Edward ordered people to worship as Protestants.

▼ **A** Inside a Catholic church.

- Stained glass
- Rood screen (to separate priest from worshippers)
- Lamps kept permanently lit to show the continued presence of God
- Paintings to explain Bible stories
- Gold crosses, candlesticks and chalices
- Expensive stone altar
- Statue of the Virgin Mary
- Catholic priests could not marry
- Expensive robes
- Bible in Latin – people relied on priests to read and interpret it because most ordinary people couldn't read Latin

▼ **B** Protestant churches and ways of worshipping were much simpler.

Stained glass destroyed and replaced with plain glass

Plain clothes

Rood screen removed

Wall plaques with the Lord's Prayer and parts of the Bible in English

Royal coat of arms

Prayer book in English, not Latin

Protestant priests could marry

Pulpit for preaching the new English services

Simple wooden table

▼ **SOURCE C** A painting of Edward VI at Windsor Castle (c1546), made around the time Edward became the King of England.

Religious turmoil

Edward became king when he was just nine, and his father had asked that he was helped by a close group of advisers. However, they often argued among themselves – and sometimes carried out changes without properly consulting the new king. Many people, especially in the countryside, didn't like some of the changes to the way they worshipped. They loved the old services and churches, and in some areas there were rebellions. A group of rebels in Devon saw just how ruthless young King Edward could be. He sent his soldiers to capture them and around 900 rebel prisoners were killed in just ten minutes by having their throats slit.

What was Edward like?

- A sickly child, he constantly needed a doctor.
- Small for his age; short-sighted.
- Despite his illnesses, he was lively and polite.
- Good-looking, with light red hair and grey eyes.
- Loved sports and hunting.
- By the age of 15, he was dying of a lung disease called tuberculosis.

Edward died on 6 July 1553. He had no children, so he named his Protestant cousin Lady Jane Grey as the new queen. She only ruled for nine days, then Edward's older half-sister Mary became the new queen. Mary was a deeply religious Catholic. Protestant England was about to change!

Over to You

1 Why did Edward become king after his father's death, and not Mary or Elizabeth?

2 Design and write an obituary for King Edward VI. An obituary briefly tells of some of the most important events and achievements of the person who recently died, as well as details about their personality. Begin with Edward's birth in 1537 and end with his death in 1553 at the age of just 15.

3 Lady Jane Grey became known as the 'Nine days queen'. Look up who she was, why Edward chose her, and what happened to her.

Similarity and Difference

1 a Describe what you would have seen if you had entered a Catholic church before 1547.

 b Now imagine you visited the same church after Edward had made his Protestant changes. Describe what you see.

2 Explain two ways in which the Catholic ways of worshipping God and the Protestant ways of worshipping God were different.

How bloody was Bloody Mary?

Nicknames are sometimes used between friends who know each other very well. Other times, they are used by people to be nasty. Queen Mary had a very nasty nickname: Bloody Mary. But why? What could she have done to be remembered in such a horrible way? And did she deserve it?

Objectives

- Examine how and why Bloody Mary got her nickname.
- Analyse whether she deserved her nasty nickname.

A new queen

Mary was Henry VIII's eldest child. When she became queen in 1553, Mary was unmarried, 37 years old and a strict Catholic. Some people were delighted to have Mary as queen. They didn't like all the religious changes that had taken place in Edward's reign. They looked forward to a time when Mary would bring back the old Catholic ways.

Soon after becoming queen, Mary married the Catholic King Philip of Spain. This was an unpopular move – many people were angry at the thought of her marrying a foreign king. They thought it might mean that England could come under Spanish control if Philip began interfering in the running of the country. In 1554, a group of rich nobles led by Thomas Wyatt organised a rebellion. Their plan was to make Elizabeth, Mary's younger sister, the queen. However, the Wyatt Rebellion failed and Wyatt (and the other leaders) were executed.

Religious changes... again!

As soon as she was crowned, Mary started to undo all the changes her father and brother had made:

> England was officially made a Catholic country once more.

> The Pope controlled religion again.

> The churches were redecorated with stone altars, brightly painted walls, statues and gold crosses.

> Married priests were made to leave their wives (because Catholics believe priests should be unmarried).

> Church services and prayer books were in Latin once more.

Mary's changes didn't please the Protestants. Her message to them was simple – change religion or be punished! You might now see how Mary acquired her nickname.

▼ **SOURCE A** A painting of Queen Mary. This was painted in 1554, soon after she became queen, and is known as one of the best likenesses of her.

▼ **B** A table showing the number of people executed for **heresy** in England and Wales under different monarchs. Heresy is a belief that is against the official religious belief in the country at the time.

Monarch (dates of reign)	Executed
Henry VII, 1485–1509	24
Henry VIII, 1509–1547	81
Edward VI, 1547–1553	2
Mary, 1553–1558	283
Elizabeth I, 1558–1603	4

Fact ✓

Remember – the figures in **B** are for heresy only. In Henry VIII's reign up to 70,000 people were executed for other crimes.

▼ **SOURCE C** From the diary of Henry Machyn, an English cloth merchant who wrote a diary at the time of these executions in Mary's reign.

'Three men were burned for heresy in Canterbury on 12 July... On 22 January, five men and two women were burned in Smithfield in London. They were burned at 9 o'clock at three posts.'

▼ **SOURCE D** Drawing of the execution of Latimer and Ridley, two Protestant bishops who refused to become Catholics, in Oxford in 1555. A year later, Thomas Cranmer (the first Protestant Archbishop of Canterbury) was executed in this way too. These executions were deeply unpopular.

Bloody Mary?

During Mary's reign, people who wouldn't declare they were Catholics or accept the Pope as God's leader on earth were sent to prison and often tortured. If they still refused, they might be burned alive.

As a result of her harsh measures, Mary became more and more unpopular – the Protestants hated her for trying to turn England back into a Catholic country, many Catholics disliked her for being too harsh, and everyone disliked her Spanish husband!

Queen Mary died in November 1558, aged 42, possibly of cancer. She didn't have any children. With no child to inherit her throne, she was succeeded by her half-sister, Elizabeth.

▼ **SOURCE E** This is another extract from the diary of Henry Machyn.

'... when Mary died, all the churches of London did ring, and at night did make bonfires and set tables in the street and did eat and drink and be merry'.

Over to You ..ıl

1 What actions did Mary take to reverse the changes made by her brother, the Protestant King Edward VI?

2 The celebrations mentioned in **Source E** took place when Mary died in 1558. The same author wrote in 1553 that 'the people of London rejoiced and made many great fires. They set out tables and feasted' when Mary became queen.

   a In what ways are the two diary extracts different?

   b Why do you think public opinion had changed so much during Mary's time as queen?

3 a Why do you think Mary was given the nickname 'Bloody Mary'?

   b Do you think she deserves such a nasty nickname? Give reasons for your answer.

Quick Knowledge Quiz

Choose the correct answer from the three options:

1 Who did Henry VII marry in 1486?

   a Elizabeth of York
   b Anne Boleyn
   c Elizabeth Woodville

2 How many wives did Henry VIII have?

   a eight
   b six
   c none

3 Who was Henry VIII's eldest child?

   a Elizabeth
   b Edward
   c Mary

4 Which role did Henry VIII create for himself?

   a Head of the Roman Catholic Church
   b King of Scotland
   c Head of the Church of England

5 Who started a protest against the Catholic Church in Germany in 1517?

   a Catherine of Aragon
   b Martin Luther
   c Thomas Wyatt

6 Which religion did Anne Boleyn, Jane Seymour and Anne of Cleeves follow?

   a the Protestant religion
   b the Roman Catholic religion
   c neither religion

7 Which of the following was one of the changes Henry VIII made to religion in England?

   a The Bible was available in English, not just Latin
   b Gold and silver decoration were to be added to all altars
   c Priests were not allowed to get married

8 How old was Edward VI when he became king?

   a 9 years old
   b 15 years old
   c 37 years old

9 What nickname was given to Queen Mary, sister of Edward and Elizabeth?

   a Mary the Murderer
   b Heresy Mary
   c Bloody Mary

10 Who became the monarch after Queen Mary died?

   a Edward VII
   b Elizabeth I
   c Elizabeth II

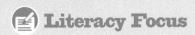 **Literacy Focus**

Writing in detail

1   Look at the paragraph below. It is a very basic answer to the question: **What methods did Henry VII use to control England and secure his kingdom?**

However, the answer does not contain many specific, factual details. Rewrite the paragraph to include more detail – adding names, dates, examples, facts where possible.

> Could you add some detail here? Perhaps mention when he became king. For example, *Henry VII, who became King of England in 1485…*

> Try to give an example of a deal with another country (for example, *he made his eldest son, Arthur, marry a Spanish princess called Catherine of Aragon in order to become friendlier with Spain*) – and explain why it was important to have foreign allies.

Henry VII wanted to remain king so he had to do things to keep his position safe, such as making deals with other countries and banning barons from having private armies.

> What other methods did Henry VII use? Check pages 184–185 to help you.

> You might mention why it was so important for Henry to quickly control his kingdom. Remember, he had won his throne by fighting and beating King Richard III of the rival York family. He knew he would have to act swiftly to keep the crown.

> Can you explain *why* he did this?

Homophones

2   A homophone is a word that sounds the same as another, but has a different spelling and meaning. For example, think about a 'sale' in a shop and a 'sail' on a ship. Although both 'sale' and 'sail' sound the same, they are not spelled the same, and mean something different.

Copy out the sentences below, writing the correct choices in brackets.

a   (Our/hour) word 'holiday' comes from the term '(holy/wholly) day'. On (one/won) of these days, after going (to/two) a church service, people would usually make (their/there) own fun, creating home-made equipment with whatever they had.

b   (For/Four) (nights/knights) murdered Thomas Becket (in/inn) Canterbury Cathedral.

c   To avoid catching the Black Death, (sum/some) people (would/wood) kill a toad, dry it in the (son/sun), and hold it on the boils.

d   If you caught the Black Death, (ewe/you) (would/wood) usually (dye/die) within a (weak/week).

e   During the (reign/rain) of King Edward I, many wars (were, whir) (fought/fort) in (Whales/Wales) and Scotland.

f   Henry VIII, (sun/son) of Henry VII, was desperate (for/four) a (male/mail) heir to take over the (throne/thrown) after his death.

Historians use sources to help them piece together what has happened in the past. Sources help them find out about the past and make sense of it. It is important that you know two of the most important ways that historians use sources:

- **Comprehension:** Historians try to understand (or 'comprehend') what information the source contains and analyse the source to find this information.

- **Inference:** Historians also try to work out something from the source that isn't actually written or shown. They read 'between the lines' of a source and work out what a source is *suggesting*, rather than what it actually says.

So, what's the difference between 'comprehension' and 'inference'? Imagine you have been asked an inference question:

> Give two things you can infer from **Source A** about how Mary I wished to be portrayed.

Look at this portrait of Queen Mary I. On the left-hand side are one student's examples of comprehension, which do *not* answer the question. On the right-hand side are another student's examples of inferences, which correctly infer from the source and address the question.

TIP: Remember, comprehension is about describing what can be seen in the source. Student 1 describes what they can see in the source.

TIP: Inference is about suggesting what something might mean. Student 2 infers that Mary is rich (because of her expensive jewellery) and proud to be part of the Tudor family (because she has insisted that she is painted holding a rose). The student also explains why they think what they think.

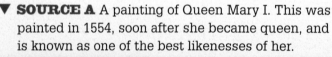

▼ **SOURCE A** A painting of Queen Mary I. This was painted in 1554, soon after she became queen, and is known as one of the best likenesses of her.

Student 1

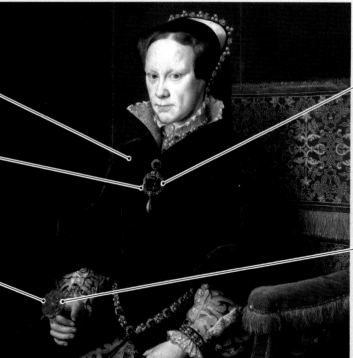

Comprehension: Mary I is seated on a chair.

Comprehension: She is wearing a lot of jewellery.

Comprehension: In her right hand she is holding a rose.

Student 2

Inference: I think that Mary is trying to show that she is very rich. **I can infer** that Mary is trying to show that she is very rich. **Details in the source that tell me this include** the jewellery, which is gold and full of precious stones. Only the very rich could afford such luxuries.

Inference: I can infer that Mary is proud she belongs to the Tudor family. **The detail in the source that tells me this is** the rose, which was a symbol of the Tudor family.

The same methods can be used with written sources. Imagine you have been asked this inference question:

Key Words ambassador

 Give two things you can infer from **Source B** about the executions that took place during Mary's reign.

Read the following source carefully.

▼ **SOURCE B** A letter written by Simon Renard – he was a Catholic, and was also the Spanish **ambassador** in London. He wrote to King Philip of Spain in 1555 after watching the first Protestant being burned at the stake during the reign of Queen Mary I.

> 'A certain [person named] Rogers was burned publicly yesterday. Some of the onlookers wept, others prayed to God to give him strength to bear the pain, others gathered the ashes and the bones and wrapped them in paper to preserve them. Others threatened the bishops. I think it would be wise not to be too firm against Protestants, otherwise I foresee that the people may cause a revolt. The lady Elizabeth has her supporters, and there are Englishmen who do not love foreigners.'

TIP: Remember – King Philip of Spain was married to Mary I! The 'lady Elizabeth' mentioned in the letter is Princess Elizabeth, the Protestant younger sister of the Catholic Mary I.

Student 1

Comprehension: A man named Rogers was burned alive in front of people. This made a big impression on the people who saw it – some wept and others prayed for him, for example.

Comprehension: The writer thinks that people in England may start a revolt if the firm treatment of Protestants continues.

TIP: Comprehending sources is about understanding what information the source actually contains. Here, Student 1 outlines the key things that the source covers.

Student 2

Inference: People in the crowd were unhappy about the execution of Rogers because they were so upset that they cried or even prayed to God to give him strength to help him bear the pain. They would not be like this if they were glad to see Rogers die – they would be cheering instead, perhaps.

Inference: The writer also thinks that, if this treatment of Protestants continues, then it might lead to a revolt by people who support Mary's Protestant sister, Elizabeth. The writer might be warning King Philip of Spain to step in and do something about this. After all, Philip is married to Mary and perhaps thinks that people do not like this anyway – because he is a 'foreigner' – and Mary's treatment of Protestants might be the final straw and spark a revolt.

TIP: Student 2 'reads between the lines' and goes beyond the surface detail of what the source actually says to try to interpret what it might suggest. This is a valuable skill for historians – sources don't always tell us everything, so it is up to the skilled historian to try to work out what they mean.

Now turn to the next page to have a go at answering this type of question.

Your challenge is to answer the source inference question below. The questions on the next page will help you structure your answers. Use the tips and sentence starters to help you get started.

1   Give two things you can infer from **Source C** about how Henry VIII wanted to be portrayed.

2   Give two things you can infer from **Source D** about the character of Henry VIII.   (20)

▶ **SOURCE C** A copy of a portrait of Henry VIII by the workshop of Hans Holbein the Younger, painted around 1536. Holbein, originally from Germany, had been appointed the 'King's Painter' in 1536.

He is wearing lots of jewellery including large rings and a pair of necklaces.

He is shown with a very large codpiece (a pouch to cover and protect the male genitals). Interestingly, the painting may have been commissioned to celebrate the coming birth of Henry's son, Edward, born in October 1537.

His legs are spread apart and his arms held away from his side in the pose of a warrior or a wrestler.

His hand is next to a dagger.

Comparisons to surviving sets of Henry's armour show that his legs were really much shorter than in the painting.

▼ **SOURCE D** Adapted from a letter written by an Italian ambassador to England in 1515 who was describing a conversation he had with King Henry VIII.

'His Majesty said, "Talk with me a while. The King of France, is he as tall as I am?" I told him there was little difference. He continued, "Is his chest as broad as mine?" I said it was not. He then enquired, "What sort of legs has he?" I replied, "long and strong". Whereupon he opened his jacket, placed his hand on his thigh and said, "Look here; I also have good legs too."'

TIP: Remember, **comprehension** is about trying to understand (or comprehend) what information the source actually contains. **Inference** is something you learn from the source that goes beyond what you read. What does this source make you think about Henry? Read between the lines – what does it *suggest* about him?

1 Give two things you can infer from **Source C** about how Henry VIII wanted to be portrayed. (10)

Complete the table below to explain your answer.

What I can infer (2)
Details in the source that tell me this (3)
What I can infer (2)
Details in the source that tell me this (3)

> **TIP:** It is important to write down what made you think what you think! In other words, if you think that Henry is trying to show that he is strong and powerful, write down and describe the details of the source that made you think this.

2 Give two things you can infer from **Source D** about the character of Henry VIII. (10)

Complete the table below to explain your answer.

What I can infer (2)
Details in the source that tell me this (3)
What I can infer (2)
Details in the source that tell me this (3)

As the Tudor age began, Europeans were beginning to make some amazing discoveries about the world. By this time, most educated people realised that the Earth is a **sphere**, but didn't really know its true size or how much land there was. So how did this change? Why were people so keen to explore and find out more about the world? And who were the important individuals in this age of exploration?

Objectives

- Identify why explorers were keen to discover new routes to foreign lands.
- Examine the achievements of some key explorers from this time.

Who knows what?

By the early 1400s, Europeans obviously knew about European lands such as England, Spain, Scotland, Portugal, France and Italy. They also knew of the Holy Land (the area around Jerusalem), much of Africa, Russia and lands in the east such as China and India. Other than that, they weren't really sure (see **A**).

Money, money, money

One of the main reasons Europeans were so keen to travel to foreign places was to make lots of money. For centuries, European traders (or merchants) had travelled *by land* to places like India and China, where they bought wonderful silk cloth, spices, perfumes, jewels and porcelain (see **B**). When these exotic and very fashionable goods arrived back in Europe, they were sold at very high prices and the traders made huge profits.

▼ **SOURCE A** This map, by Henricus Martellus from around 1489, shows what Europeans thought the world was like at that time.

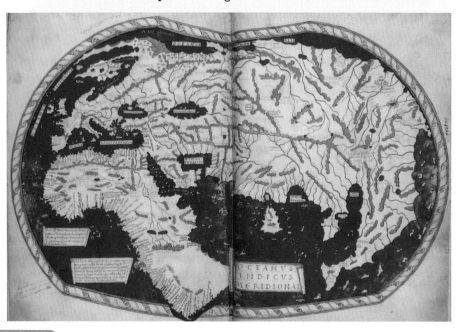

▼ **SOURCE B** A porcelain bowl imported to Britain from China, created c1580–1600.

Travel problems

However, the journey by land from Europe to India and China (and back) was very dangerous and could take over three years. In some places, local tribes and rulers charged traders a fortune to pass through their lands. As a result, some traders wanted to find an alternative route to these faraway lands... perhaps by sea?

New technology

Fortunately for the traders, a number of improvements in shipbuilding and **navigation** were taking place at this time. For example, better sails made ships easier to steer, and an Ancient Greek invention (developed further in the medieval Islamic world) called an **astrolabe** was developed to help sailors work out how far north or south they were while at sea (see **C**). These improvements meant that sailing to China and India might be possible for traders, rather than going by land.

A new theory

By the 1490s, there was a growing belief that it was possible to reach lands in the east – such as China and India – by sailing west from Europe, across the Atlantic Ocean. In other words, traders could sail all around the Earth by sea, instead of having to go overland. Remember, people had absolutely no idea that the continents of North and South America existed, so they did not realise they would reach these areas first. One man, Christopher Columbus, decided to test the theory in 1492, and set off for the eastern lands by sailing west.

Who was Christopher Columbus?

Christopher Columbus was born in Italy in 1451. He later moved to Portugal where he worked as a trader. He also learned how to read maps and navigate ships. In 1485, he began looking for money to fund a journey across the Atlantic Ocean in the hope of reaching India. He approached the kings of Portugal, France and England, but they all refused. Eventually, tempted by the promise of gold and spices, Queen Isabella of Spain funded his voyage.

Columbus then bought three ships, the *Pinta*, the *Niña* and the *Santa María*, and hired around 100 men as his crew. They set off on 3 August 1492.

Key Words astrolabe navigation sphere voyage

▶ **SOURCE C** This astrolabe was made in England around 1480.

▼ **MAP D** Columbus thought he could sail to China like this. He had no idea that North and South America were in the way!

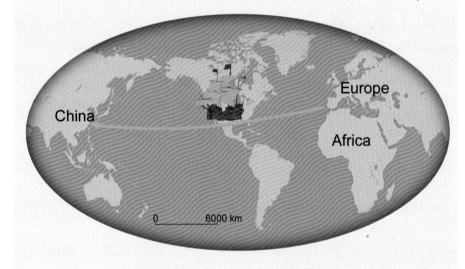

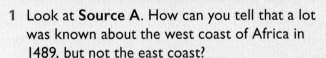

Over to You

1 Explain why some European traders were so keen to find a new route to the eastern lands of China and India.

2 a What is an astrolabe?
   b How might an astrolabe have helped Christopher Columbus?

3 In your own words, describe Columbus' plan to reach China and India.

Source Analysis

1 Look at **Source A**. How can you tell that a lot was known about the west coast of Africa in 1489, but not the east coast?

2 Make a list of some of the places in the world that we know exist today that Europeans had not discovered in 1489. You might need to look at a modern atlas.

3 How useful is **Source A** to a historian studying exploration in the 1400s?

All at sea

Columbus' voyage went well for about six weeks. However, by early October the crew were becoming unhappy. Water and food supplies were getting low and there was no sign of India. Was Columbus wrong? Had he made a mistake with his calculations? Perhaps the world wasn't a sphere after all – and they were about to fall off the edge of the world!

Land, land!

On 12 October, Columbus' luck changed when a lookout named Rodrigo (who was on the *Pinta*) spotted land. Columbus sailed ashore and named the island San Salvador, meaning 'Holy Saviour'. He spent the next few months sailing around the Caribbean islands and Cuba. He found the local people of these islands and kidnapped six of them to take back to Queen Isabella. He also took some gold, several fish and some parrots.

A new hero

Columbus returned home to a hero's welcome. He made three more trips to these new islands and also landed on the South American mainland. Until his death in 1506, Columbus still thought he'd found a new route to India. He called the local people 'Indians', and the term 'Native American' has been used until recently. Now, the terms 'American Indian' (in the USA) and 'First Nations' (in Canada) are more widely accepted. The islands Columbus visited are still known as the 'West Indies'. Columbus had no idea that he had found the new continents of North and South America, which Europeans did not know existed. Only in later years, after explorers had found vast areas of other land in this region, did people realise that Columbus had discovered a 'new world' for Europeans.

Fact ✓

It is important to remember that Columbus **did not** discover the Americas. It is estimated that around 100 million people were living there already – about the same number of people who were living in Europe at that time!

▼ **SOURCE E** Adapted from the logbook (a diary kept on a ship) of Columbus' first voyage in 1492.

10 October 1492: 'He navigated west-south-west. They went ten miles an hour and at times twelve and sometimes seven… The men could now bear no more. They complained of the long voyage. But Admiral Columbus cheered them as best he could, holding out bright hopes of the gains they could make. He said God would keep them safe.'

Columbus – the first of many

Columbus' success inspired other European explorers. Better maps, compasses and sails, as well as the promise of wealth, made many more people eager to explore the world.

Vasco da Gama (from Portugal) – In 1498, he proved it was possible to reach India by sailing around the bottom of Africa and up its eastern coast.

Amerigo Vespucci (from Italy) – From 1499 to 1504, he continued exploring the area where Columbus had sailed and went further down the South American coast. Many people think America was named after him.

Ferdinand Magellan (from Portugal) – In September 1519, five ships and 270 men set off on a journey around the world. Magellan, the leader, died on the voyage but his crew sailed on. One ship and 18 of his original crew made it home in 1522.

John Cabot (from Italy, but working for King Henry VII of England) – In 1497, he tried to reach Asia by sailing north-west. He sailed to Canada.

Earlier on...

Columbus wasn't the first European to reach the Americas – an Icelandic explorer named Leif Ericson landed in Newfoundland (North America) around 1000. However, Columbus was the first European to land on the South American mainland – and his voyage started the exploration of this area of the world by Europeans.

Later on...

Explorers brought back interesting new goods from their voyages. These items had never been seen in Europe before, and were a huge success. They included tomatoes, pineapples, tobacco, potatoes, turkeys and cocoa.

▼ **INTERPRETATION F** A painting from 1839 by French painter Eugène Delacroix called 'The Return of Columbus'. Columbus is shown presenting treasures from his explorations to Queen Isabella of Spain.

▼ **MAP G** This map shows the routes of five famous explorers' voyages.

Over to You

1 Write out sentences **a–d**. Label each one 'true' or 'false'. If you believe a sentence is false, write the correct sentence underneath.

 a Vasco da Gama reached India by sailing around the bottom of Italy.

 b It is thought that America is named after the British explorer Amerigo Vespucci.

 c Ferdinand Magellan did not survive the first full journey around the world.

 d John Cabot, from Scotland, tried to reach Asia, but landed in Africa.

2 Read **Source E** carefully.

 a What examples can you give to show that Columbus was a strong leader?

 b Write your own logbook entry for 12 October. Remember to mention Rodrigo.

3 a Where did Columbus think he had discovered in 1492?

 b Was he correct?

4 Look at **Interpretation F**.

 a Describe what is happening in the picture.

 b According to the person who created this image, for what reasons might Columbus' voyage have taken place?

5 Explorers were treated as heroes at this time – why do you think this was?

Key

→ Columbus – first to America in 1492

⇨ Cabot – first to Canada in 1497

→ Da Gama – first to India in 1498

→ Vespucci – explores further down the South American coast from 1499–1504

→ Magellan – first trip around the world in 1522

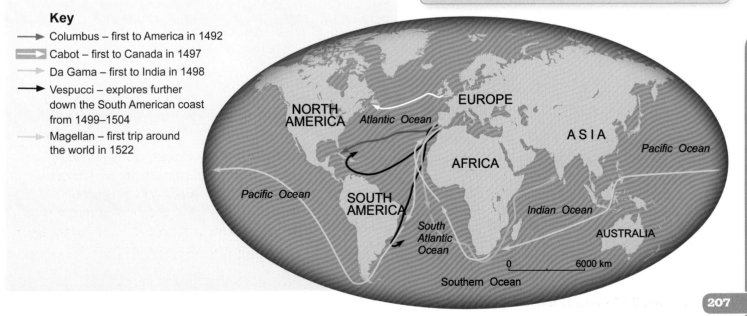

NORTH AMERICA

Atlantic Ocean

EUROPE

ASIA

Pacific Ocean

AFRICA

Pacific Ocean

SOUTH AMERICA

Indian Ocean

AUSTRALIA

South Atlantic Ocean

0   6000 km

Southern Ocean

What was Britain like by 1558?

Often a single discovery, invention or idea can have a huge impact on people and their way of life. For example, think how the invention of the Internet or the aeroplane has changed the way we live. But sometimes things don't change a great deal. For example, in today's world, the way some people worship God has remained unchanged for hundreds of years. But what about changes in the Middle Ages? If someone in early Tudor times, when exploration was at its peak, could look back a few hundred years to around 1100, would they think life had changed much?

Objectives

- Examine some of the key discoveries, theories, ideas and inventions of the Middle Ages.

- Assess how new ideas, theories, discoveries and inventions changed Britain.

Meet Edwin, a man who lived around the time of the Norman Conquest, which started in 1066. Look below at what he thinks and believes about the world he lives in.

Exploration
People in Europe, like me, know that Africa and Asia exist, but don't know much about them. There are rumours of faraway lands in the south and west... Explorers and traders go east on long journeys over land or by sea. But travelling by sea can be dangerous because ships are so difficult to steer.

The Earth
A long time ago, some people thought the Earth was flat... but not any more. We know the Earth is a globe, but aren't sure how big it is. We think the Earth is the centre of the universe, and that all the planets, the Sun and the stars move around us.

Religion
Religion is a vital part of everyday life. Everyone goes to church and knows that God controls everything — bad harvests, good weather, births, deaths... it's all God's work (or the Devil's!).

Warfare
War is very brutal and armies fight up close with swords and axes, or charge at each other on horses. Some soldiers are trained to use bows that can fire arrows a long way. Huge, stone, heavily fortified castles are dotted all over the country too — barons and knights live in them.

Health
Poor people make their own medicines from plants and herbs, or ask the local wise woman to make a special potion. There aren't many doctors — and they get their medical knowledge from books written by the Ancient Greeks or Romans.

Medicine
Most doctors will treat an ill patient by trying to get their body 'back in balance' again. They might attach leeches to you to suck out the 'bad blood'. Sometimes holes are drilled into a patient's head to get rid of a headache... but the patient often dies.

Literacy
Most people can't read or write. Some rich children are taught by priests or monks, but books are still rare and expensive. They are usually written out by hand, in Latin, by monks — and it sometimes takes them a whole year to copy out a Bible.

Who rules?
The king rules over everyone. His loyal friends help him rule the land and control different areas. Most people are peasants and live in the countryside and farm the land. There aren't many large towns — only eight have a population of over 3000.

Now you've met Edwin and got to know him a little, take a journey through some of the big ideas, new advances and major discoveries of the next 400 or so years.

1150
Paper-making introduced in Europe

1167
University of Oxford begins to grow – where men learn how to become doctors, priests and lawyers

1180
Rudders used on ships so they can be steered better

1182
Simple compasses first used in Europe, making it easier for sailors to sail in the right direction

1185
Windmills first used to grind grain into flour in Britain

1231
University of Cambridge founded

1265
First Parliament meets; after this, more people begin to have a bigger say in how the country is run

1279
Glass mirrors brought back by Crusader knights who had been fighting in the Holy Land

1280
Spinning wheel invented, which speeds up cloth-making

1280
Mechanical clocks invented; they begin to appear on big buildings so people don't have to listen to church bells to find out the time

1282
Spectacles first used

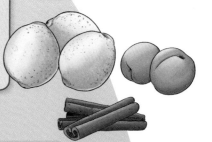

Knowledge and Understanding

1 Review some of the key concepts, terms and events you have learned in this textbook. Complete the sentences below with an accurate term.

a The system of controlling land introduced by William the Conqueror was called the _____.

b The earliest types of castles built after the Norman Conquest were called _____ and _____ castles.

c In medieval towns, a group of traders and craftsmen that made rules for its members to follow was called a _____.

d In June 1215, King John agreed to follow a list of rules and freedoms known as _____.

e For 116 years, the English and French fought a long war in France known as the _____.

f The Yorks and the Lancasters fought for the throne of England during the _____.

1300
Foods like sugar, lemons, apricots and spices such as ginger are brought back by Crusaders from the Holy Land and become more common in Britain

c1300
Gunpowder (invented in China) first used in English cannons

1326
Handguns first used; cannons and handguns change the way battles are fought. Swords, axes, and bows and arrows are no match for them

1543
Polish astronomer Nicolaus Copernicus publishes his calculations showing that the Sun – and not the Earth – is the centre of the universe. He proposes that the Earth and all the other planets move around the Sun

1543
In Italy, a doctor called Andreas Vesalius publishes some of the first accurate drawings of the human body. He carries out experiments which prove that some of the ancient medieval theories are wrong

1534
A new English law (the Act of Supremacy) makes the English king head of the English Church, rather than the Catholic Pope in Rome. Soon, England becomes a Protestant country (under Henry VIII's son, Edward) – and decades of religious upheaval begin

1500
London's population reaches around 50,000. By this time, there are about 30 towns with a population of more than 5000, but most people still live in the countryside

1492
Christopher Columbus, an Italian explorer, sets sail for China but reaches the 'new world' of the Americas instead. In the years to follow, lots of explorers go to the Americas and beyond. These voyages of discovery begin to change people's view of the world and bring new goods and knowledge to Europe

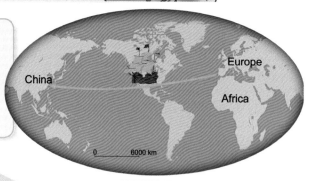

1477
William Caxton begins printing books in Britain. Many of his books are printed in English, rather than Latin, so more people read them. By the late 1500s, around a third of the population can read

1464
Bamburgh Castle in Northumberland is the first castle in Britain to have its walls knocked down by cannon fire. Soon, lords and barons begin to build smaller castles (made from brick and with larger windows) for comfort rather than defence

1450
A German, Johannes Gutenberg, invents his printing press; books in Europe can be printed onto paper rather than copied out by monks. Books become cheaper and cover all sorts of subjects, so people begin to read more and gain more knowledge. This helps spread the new ideas of the Renaissance

1450
Numbers 1 to 9 used in Britain; copied from the Arabic system used in Muslim countries

1400
The Renaissance begins and lasts about 250 years. Starting in Italy and spreading around Europe, there is a renewed interest in learning – people become fascinated with new discoveries, works of art, exploration and ways of thinking. It is the time of William Shakespeare, Christopher Columbus and Leonardo da Vinci

Earlier on...

Around 1040, the Chinese developed 'movable type' – a method of printing that allowed individual letters to be moved around easily and printed onto paper. The most widely used movable type (using metal letters) was first created in Korea in 1377.

Now it's time to meet Lady Alice, who lived in the 1500s, around the time Henry VIII, Edward VI and Mary I were England's monarchs. Based on the new ideas, inventions and discoveries that are featured in the timeline and the rest of this book, discuss with a partner the answers to the questions on this page.

Key Words   Renaissance

Literacy

Are books still as expensive as they were?

Who rules?

Is the king still in complete control of the country?

The Earth

Have there been any developments in knowledge about the position of the Earth in relation to the Sun and other planets?

Technology

What new technology or inventions would Alice know about? How might these things have changed people's lives?

Health and medicine

Have there been any major medical advances? What could this mean about the development of health and medicine?

Knowledge

How has Alice's knowledge of the world changed (especially after 1492)?

Exploration

How has travelling by ship changed?

Warfare

How has warfare changed... and what has caused this change?

Over to You

1 a Write down five things that a medieval person like Edwin might think about Britain, the world, science and medicine.

   b For each thing you've written down in part **a**, write whether you think someone living 400–500 years later (like Alice from the Tudor period) would still think the same thing – or would they think differently? Write in full sentences and explain yourself clearly.

2 Inventions change things. For example, the invention of the passenger aeroplane meant that we could travel further and faster than ever before. Think about the following inventions:
   • spinning wheel for quickly winding wool into threads
   • gunpowder
   • compasses and rudders for ships
   • printed books.
   Write a few sentences saying how each of these inventions might have helped changed things.

3 Do you think *we* know all there is to know? Or are there lots of things we still don't know or understand about the world, science or medicine? Explain your answer.

Diet

What new foods might Alice know about? And how would she know of them?

Change and Continuity

During the period you have studied in this book, you will have noticed there were things that changed and things that continued (stayed the same).

1 Make two lists: one of the similarities and one of the differences between Britain around 1100, and Britain around 1558. You may use pages 208–211 and the rest of the book to help you.

2 Explain two ways in which the world John lived in and the world Alice lived in were similar.

⟳ Quick Knowledge Quiz

Choose the correct answer from the three options:

1 At the start of the Middle Ages, which of these continents did Europeans know about?

   a   Africa
   b   Antarctica
   c   South America

2 Why did many people travel east to China and India?

   a   To trade, and bring exotic goods back to England
   b   England's population was booming and towns were overcrowded
   c   They wanted to find a new route to the Americas

3 What is an astrolabe?

   a   a place where experiments were carried out
   b   a type of spice that traders brought back to England
   c   a piece of navigation equipment used by sailors

4 Which monarch funded Christopher Columbus' voyage?

   a   Elizabeth I
   b   Queen Isabella of Spain
   c   Ferdinand II

5 When did Christopher Columbus reach the Americas?

   a   1392
   b   1450
   c   1492

6 How many early medieval towns had a population over 3000?

   a   218
   b   78
   c   8

7 When was paper-making introduced in Europe?

   a   1150
   b   1280
   c   1500

8 How long did the Renaissance last?

   a   around 37 years
   b   over 500 years
   c   around 250 years

9 When did Johannes Gutenberg invent his version of the printing press?

   a   1450
   b   1492
   c   1543

10 What was London's population by around 1500?

   a   5000
   b   50,000
   c   500,000

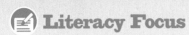 **Literacy Focus**

Note-taking

Note-taking is a vital skill. To do it successfully, you must pick out all the important (key) words and phrases in a sentence. The important words and phrases are those that are vital to the meaning (and your understanding) of the sentence. For example, in the sentence:

> Christopher Columbus was born in Italy in 1451. He later moved to Portugal where he worked as a trader. He also learned how to read maps and navigate ships. In 1485 he began looking for money to fund a journey across the Atlantic Ocean in the hope of reaching India. He approached the kings of Portugal, France and England, but they all refused. Eventually, tempted by the promise of gold and spices, Queen Isabella of Spain funded his voyage.
>
> Columbus then bought three ships, the *Pinta*, the *Niña* and the *Santa María*, and hired around 100 men as his crew. They set off on 3 August 1492.

….the important words are: Christopher Columbus; born Genoa, Italy, 1451; moved to Lisbon (Portugal); trader; read maps, navigate ships; money, journey across Atlantic 1485, India; approached kings Portugal, France, England, refused; Queen Isabella Spain funded voyage, promise gold, spices; bought three ships, *Pinta*, *Niña*, *Santa María*, 100 crew men, sailed 3 August 1492.

The original sentence was 107 words long – but the shortened version is fewer than 50. Being able to take notes will help you with revision.

1 Now try to reduce the following information into note form:

   a Vasco da Gama was an explorer from Portugal. In 1498, he proved it was possible to reach India by sailing around the bottom of Africa and up its eastern coast.

   b Amerigo Vespucci was an explorer from Italy. From 1499 to 1504, he continued exploring the area where Columbus had sailed and even went further down the South American coast. Many people think America was named after him.

   c Like Vasco da Gama, Ferdinand Magellan was from Portugal. On 20 September 1519, five ships and 270 men set off on a journey around the world. Magellan, the leader, died on the voyage but his crew sailed on. One ship and eighteen of his original crew made it home in 1522.

   d John Cabot was originally from Italy, but worked for King Henry VII of England. In 1497, he tried to reach Asia by sailing north-west, but sailed to Canada.

History skill: Change and continuity

Historical **change** can be quite complicated! Sometimes there can be changes in one area of life, but very little change in another. When something stays the same, historians call this **continuity**. In short, it's the opposite of change!

Historians have to study change and continuity not just over a short period of time, but also over many years or even centuries. Change and continuity can happen at the same time – but in different areas of society.

Change can also happen at different speeds.

Analysing change and continuity

There are many ways to analyse change and continuity. One way to approach this might be to think deeply about the changes that have (or haven't) taken place in the period you are studying.

1 **Think about change:** What do you know about the period you are asked to assess? Identify examples of some changes.

2 **Think about continuity:** Then identify some examples of continuity.

3 **Judge:** How much change was there? How much did things stay the same? Were the changes quick – or slow? Was there a particular turning point?

4 **Answer and explain:** Now, write your answer. Be sure to include strong and clear reasons and examples for your answer.

TIP: An example of continuity in the Middle Ages might be the belief that disease and illness was a punishment from God for sin. This belief stayed the same for many, many hundreds of years.

TIP: For example, after the Norman invasion of 1066, most of the rich, landowning Anglo-Saxons lost their land, their status and, sometimes, their lives. This was a huge *change* for them. However, for many ordinary peasants, life *continued* as before – they still farmed the land, paid their taxes, lived in the same place and worshipped the same God.

TIP: At some points in history (such as the Bronze Age), change happened very slowly over many hundreds of years. However, in the twenty-first century, for example, change has happened very quickly. The world you are growing up in is very different from the one your grandparents lived in (just ask them about mobile phones!).

TIP: A turning point is a time of great change, leaving things different from how they were before. Turning points can be triggered by inventions, revolutions, new laws, the work of key individuals or developments, for example.

TIP: To explain your judgement and your reasons, you can use phrases like:

This was a change because...

A turning point was...

This stayed the same because...

This is similar to...

This had not been seen before...

This can be seen in both periods through...

TIP: You will need to use examples in your answer. Don't simply say 'The population grew' – why not say 'the population of Britain changed greatly, it doubled from around 3 million in the early 1100s to between 6 and 7 million in the mid-1500s'.

Now that you have reached the end of this book, you can consider the change and continuity in the period you have been studying from the late eleventh century (Middle Ages) to the mid-sixteenth century (early Tudor period). The diagram below shows some of the key areas to consider.

How many people?

c1100s England = c1.5 million. Wales = 0.2 million. Scotland = 0.5 million. Ireland = 0.75 million. Total = c3 million

1558 England = 4–5 million. Ireland, Scotland and Wales made up a further 2 million of Britain's overall population. Total = 6–7 million

Society

c1100s King and his barons at top of society – peasants at the bottom

1558 Monarch and the ruling classes such as landowners still very powerful. Peasants still very poor, but feudal system had disappeared, and all Englishmen were free and benefited from rights in Magna Carta

How many large towns and cities?

c1100s Towns with a population of over 2000

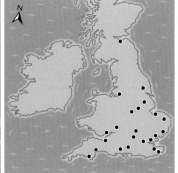

1558 Towns with a population of over 2000

How united was the United Kingdom?

c1100s Two monarchs, one for England, one for Scotland. The English monarch controlled Wales and large parts of Ireland too

1558 Two monarchs, one for England, one for Scotland. The English monarch controlled Wales and large parts of Ireland too

What about religion?

c1100s Everyone Roman Catholic, Church very powerful

1558 During Queen Mary I's reign, Roman Catholicism had once again become the official religion of England. This followed many years of religious upheaval under the Tudor monarchs – and more was to follow! Church still a major feature of life

How did people get around?

c1100s The rich travelled by horse, the poor walked

1558 Richer men and women still travelled by horse and carriage – and the poor still walked

Popular entertainment

c1100s Hunting, jousting, falconry (for the rich), fighting games and blood sports. The poor liked a good drink at the local inn or tavern (pub) too

1558 Hunting still very popular for the rich. Blood sports and mob football were popular for the poor – and so was drinking at the local inn or tavern

The relationship between the monarch and Parliament

c1100s Monarch in complete control

1558 Monarch in control, but takes more advice from Parliament, which gets taxes for the monarch

Eating and drinking

c1100s Beer, wine, cheese, meat, bread, vegetables, knives and spoons

1558 Beer, wine, cheese, meat, bread, more vegetables, salad, tobacco, knives and spoons. New foods brought back from the Crusades and by explorers were becoming more common – lemons, melons, apricots, sugar, syrup and spices like nutmeg and cinnamon, for example

The main types of communication

c1100s Mainly word of mouth

1558 Printed books available, but still quite expensive

What places did Europeans know about?

c1100s Areas of the world known to Europeans

1558 Areas of the world known to Europeans

Science and medicine

The earth is the centre of the universe, and God holds the answer to everything.

c1100s Very little is known about science or the human body

1558 More understanding of earth's place in the universe. Better knowledge of the human body due to more accurate drawings. Treatment of war wounds improved

Law and order

c1100s Trial by ordeal common. Stocks, pillory, whipping and execution are common types of punishment – but fines remain the most popular type of punishment. No police force

1558 Trial by ordeal dies out, trial by jury introduced. Older forms of punishment still used. Torture is commonly used to get confessions. No police force

Assessment: Change and continuity

Your challenge is to answer this question about change:

⭐ | How far did England change between 1066 and 1558? | (20)

The steps below will help you structure your answer. Use the tips and sentence starters to help you get started.

1 **Think about change: review what you know:** What do you already know about England between 1066 and 1558? Identify examples of **change**. Choose at least five examples of change between 1066 and 1558.

1 _____

2 _____

3 _____

2 **Think about continuity:** Identify some examples of **continuity** between 1066 and 1558.

1 _____

2 _____

3 _____

3 **Judge:** Look at your list for the bullets in step 1 and decide: how much did things stay the same and how far did things change?

4 **Answer and explain:** Now write your answer and be sure to include strong and clear reasons and examples. The sentence starters below can help you.

I believe that England changed (a lot/a little/to some extent) between 1066 and 1558. For example...	
One of the key areas of change was...	(5)
Another one of the key areas of change was...	(5)
There were also areas of continuity. For example...	(5)
In conclusion...	(5)

TIP: The question doesn't simply ask you to write about what has changed. It also asks you to think about the amount (or extent) of the change and reach a judgement. Think of it like a scale:

| No change | | Major change |
| Everything stays the same | | Nothing is the same |

TIP: Don't just look at the diagram on pages 215–216 – look through Chapter 9 and the rest of the book.

TIP: Despite the fact that it says 'change' in the question, a well-rounded answer will also write about continuity. After all, the question asks you about the *extent* of the change.

TIP: Start with your judgement. Your opening statement will be determined by the amount of change you think there has been. When working through steps 1 and 2 above, do you think there were major changes, some changes, few changes or no changes?

TIP: Make sure you don't simply say what changes had happened – describe what the situation was like in 1066, and then explain what changed. Try to explain the impact of this. For example, if you write that very little was known about science or the human body in 1066, but then write that by 1558 there was a greater understanding of the human body due to more accurate drawings, you should explain what impact this might have had on health and medicine.

Glossary

abbot the head of an abbey or monastery of monks (an abbess was head of an abbey or convent of nuns)

ale a watery type of beer

almonry the place where food, clothing and money (known as 'alms') were distributed to the poor

ambassador government official based in another country

Anglo-Saxon collective name for the tribes who settled in Britain after the Roman army left in the fifth century AD

apothecary a person who prepared and sold medicines

archaeologist a person who studies things that people made, used and left behind; their aim is to understand what people of the past were like and how they lived

artefact the material remains of past human life and activities

astrolabe a piece of navigation equipment that helped sailors work out how far north or south they were while at sea

barber-surgeon a man who performed surgery and dentistry as well as cutting hair

barbican the outer defensive tower of a castle, found above the drawbridge

baron a Norman landowner

battering ram a heavy beam swung or rammed against a door to break it down

battlements the top of a castle wall with openings for archers to shoot through

bloodletting the practice of making someone bleed to help cure an illness

boil tender, red, painful lump; a symptom of the Black Death

bubonic one of the two types of plague during the Black Death; carried by fleas

burgess wealthy townsperson

cause the reason why something happens

century a period of 100 years

ceorl an ordinary Anglo-Saxon villager

cesspit a pit for the disposal of liquid waste and sewage

Chancellor the most important position in England after the king; it involved sending out royal letters and charters

chapter house a place where meetings are held

charter a statement of a group of people's rights and freedoms, written by the king or a lord

chivalry the moral and social code followed by medieval knights

Christian a person who follows Christianity, a religion based on the life and teachings of Jesus Christ

chronicle a written account of important historical events, usually written by monks

chronology the arrangement of dates or events in the order they happened, starting with the earliest

civilian a non-military person

cloisters a covered walkway

coat of arms a distinctive design belonging to a knight or family, often used on shields, flags and clothing

concentric castle a castle built with several walls of decreasing heights, so soldiers could shoot attackers more effectively

consequence the impact or results of something that has happened

constable a man in charge of a group of watchmen

consummate to make a marriage legally recognised by having sex

contagion the spreading of a disease or illness from one person to another

council a group of people elected to manage a town or city

crossbow a mini wooden catapult used to fire bolts through armour at a range of over 100 metres

Crusades a series of journeys made by Christian Europeans to take the Holy Land back from Muslims in the Middle Ages; also known as the 'Wars of the Cross'

curtain wall a strong wall around a castle that linked towers together

democracy a system where people are able to decide how their country or community should be run, usually by voting for leaders

Dissolution the act of officially breaking up an organisation; used to describe the time when Henry VIII closed all the monasteries in England and Wales

doom painting a painting in a church designed to show people images of heaven and hell

dormitory a large bedroom for a number of people to sleep in

dowry money that a bride's family give to her husband when she marries, or to a nunnery when she becomes a nun

dubbed when a squire is touched on the shoulder with a sword and becomes a knight

earl a ruler of an earldom

earldom a large area of land, ruled by an earl on behalf of the king

empire a set of different countries, regions or states – made up of many different cultures – controlled by one 'mother country' or ruled by one person (usually an emperor/empress); famous empires include the Roman Empire, the Byzantine Empire and the Islamic Empire

enquiry an investigation

evidence facts or information about a particular event, person or place that historians use to help them understand the past; this could be written evidence

excommunicated when someone has been officially excluded from the Christian Church

export a product that is sold to another country

famine an extreme shortage of food

feudal system a system developed by King William where each group of people owed loyalty to the group above, starting with villeins, knights, barons and ending with the king

flagellant people who whip themselves or someone else for religious reasons

freemen men who were freed from most (or all) of their feudal duties to a lord

fyrd warriors who fought for Harold at the Battle of Hastings; they were numerous, but not very well trained

gangrene the death of tissues in the body caused by an infection or obstruction of blood flow

garderobe a medieval toilet

gong farmer a person who cleared away sewage

Great Council a group, including the king, his barons and leading churchmen, that met to discuss how the country should be run

guild a group of a certain type of craftspeople, with their own rules

herald a person who supervised tournaments, made announcements and carried messages

heresy a belief that is against the official religious belief in the country at the time

housecarl a well-trained warrior who used battleaxes and fought for Harold at the Battle of Hastings

hue and cry a loud cry calling for people to pursue and capture a criminal

humour one of the four humours (blood, black bile, yellow bile, phlegm)

hunter-gatherer a person who lived mainly by hunting, fishing and harvesting wild plants

illuminated a manuscript that is decorated with gold, silver and coloured designs

immigrant a person who has travelled from another place to settle

indulgence people could buy one of these from a bishop; they helped a person pass through Purgatory more quickly

infidel a person who has no religion or whose religion is not the same as that of another group of people

infirmary a place where ill people are looked after

inhabit to live in a place

inherit to receive money, land or property as an heir at the death of the previous holder

interpretation historical evidence created much later than the period studied, produced by people with a particular opinion about an event in the past

invasion when an army or country uses force to enter and take control of another country

jury a group of people who decide whether someone is innocent or guilty of a crime

keep a type of strong, fortified tower built within a castle

lance a long weapon with a pointed steel tip, usually used by warriors on horseback; knights also used blunt versions when jousting in tournaments

leech a blood-sucking creature used in medieval medicine

longbow a long bow that could fire an arrow over 200 metres

loyalty staying true to someone, and being honest and helpful to them

mace a heavy metal club covered in spikes that could pierce armour

Magna Carta a document setting out people's rights; the barons made King John sign it in 1215

mangonel a device used in sieges that could throw stones and other objects

Marcher Lord a baron given land along the Welsh border by William the Conqueror

marshal a man responsible for supervising tournaments and making sure competitors didn't cheat

mayor the head of a town, often elected by members of the council

merchant a person who is involved in the buying and selling of goods

miscarry when a baby dies while it is still in the womb

monarch a person who rules a country, for example a king or a queen

monk a member of a religious community of men

motte and bailey an early castle that featured a fort on a hill surrounded by a fence or wall

Murdrum Fine a heavy fine payable to a king by the entire area where the criminal lived if a Norman was killed

narrative a written account of connected events: a story

navigation the process of working out where you are and where you need to go

noble a rich landowner, such as barons, earls, lords, etc.

nun a member of a religious community of women

order a group of monks or nuns living under the same rules

oubliette a tiny, secret dungeon with access only through a trapdoor in the ceiling

page a boy (aged 7 to 14), in service to a knight, who is training to become a knight himself

Parliament controls the country and is made up of the monarch, the House of Lords and the House of Commons

paying homage when a man publicly shows respect and loyalty to his lord

peasant a poor person of low social status who works on the land

pilgrim a person who travels to a holy place for religious reasons

pilgrimage a journey of religious importance

plague a very infectious disease that spreads quickly and kills large numbers of people

pneumonic one of the two types of plague during the Black Death; spread by germs in the air

Pope the head of the Catholic Church

portcullis a heavy, strong barrier that can be lowered to block a castle gateway

pottage a thick vegetable soup, usually without meat

privy a toilet in a small shed outside a house or building

protest an action that shows that someone is unhappy or angry about something

Protestant Christians who protested against the Catholic Church and wanted reforms made to the religion; they still believed in the teachings of the Bible but didn't recognise the Pope as their religious leader on Earth

provenance details about the place of origin or earliest known history of something

public health the general state of health and cleanliness of the whole population

purgatory the place between heaven and hell; a person is believed to be punished in purgatory for any sins they have committed while alive

purging making someone sick or go to the toilet in the belief that this would cure their illness

quack person pretending to have medical knowledge or cures

rebellion a violent protest, often with the aim of removing and replacing a country's leaders

refectory a room used for meals

Reformation the name used to describe the changes made to the Roman Catholic Church in the sixteenth century, mainly in Europe by Martin Luther, and in England by Henry VIII and his son, King Edward VI; the reforms led to the creation of the Protestant Church

Renaissance a rebirth in learning that began around 1400

revolt another word for a rebellion or uprising

Roman Catholic a follower of Roman Catholicism, which is now a group within the wider Christian Church. It was the only religion recognised in medieval Europe and specifically in Western Europe; Roman Catholics accept the Pope as their leader on Earth

Saracen the name for a Muslim used at the time of the Crusades

schiltron a large circle or rectangle of soldiers from which soldiers pointed out their spears or pikes like a giant lethal hedgehog

scriptorium a room in a monastery in which manuscripts were copied

siege a method of attack where an army surrounds a castle, cutting off essential supplies, until the enemy is forced to surrender

source historical evidence from the period studied, usually created by someone who was directly involved with an event or an eyewitness to an event; sources provide information historians need to create interpretations.

sphere ball-shaped

squire a young man (aged 14 to 21), in service to a knight, who was training to become a knight himself

supernatural above or beyond what is natural and explained by natural laws

symptom the ill feeling and bodily change caused by sickness

tax sum of money paid to the government or king; in medieval times this was used to pay for the monarch's lifestyle, as well as armies, weapons, etc.

thegn a local landowner in Anglo-Saxon England

thrall sea slave in Anglo-Saxon society

tilt the barrier between jousting knights that prevented a fallen knight being trampled by the horses

tithe a tenth of the food peasants grew had to be given to the Church

tithing a group of ten people who were responsible for each other's behaviour

tournament a medieval event in which knights mounted on horseback jousted with blunted weapons

treason a crime against the king or country, punishable by death in the Middle Ages

trebuchet a machine used in siege warfare that could throw large stones or other objects

trencher a thick slice of bread used as a plate

trepanning drilling a hole in a patient's head in the belief that this would cure their headache

trial by ordeal a way of letting God decide whether someone is innocent or guilty; common trials were fire, water and combat

UK an abbreviation for 'United Kingdom'; the UK is made up of England, Scotland, Wales and Northern Ireland

undermine to dig beneath a castle's walls in order to make them collapse

vellum writing material made from animal skin

Viking invaders from Denmark, Norway and Sweden who fought with the Anglo-Saxons; by the mid-1000s, they had settled in Britain and lived in peace

villein a peasant who worked for a lord in return for land

voyage a journey, usually by sea

watch a group of people who patrolled the streets at night

wattle and daub a medieval building material made of interwoven sticks covered with mud or clay

wise woman local woman who had knowledge of traditional medicines

Witan an Anglo-Saxon king's council of advisers

Index